WAR SERVICES

OF THE

9TH JAT
REGIMENT

1803 – 1937

BY
LIEUT.-COLONEL W. L. HAILES, M.C.

The Naval & Military Press Ltd

❖

Published by

The Naval & Military Press Ltd

Unit 10, Ridgewood Industrial Park,

Uckfield, East Sussex,

TN22 5QE England

Tel: +44 (0) 1825 749494

Fax: +44 (0) 1825 765701

www.naval–military–press.com

© The Naval & Military Press Ltd 2004

AUTHOR'S NOTE

CERTAIN paragraphs in this account of the War Services of the Jat Regiment have been copied, with little or no alteration, from original sources. No attempt has been made to write a complete history. Changes of organization and armament are only referred to when these have a direct bearing on the course of events. Only such intermediate history between campaigns has been included as is necessary to constitute a background for the ensuing operations. When events of minor importance are recounted this background has been omitted, which may have resulted in certain passages appearing disconnected.

Some of the books named in the bibliography at the head of each chapter are " for official use only." These are included, not as the source from which information has been derived—nothing has been quoted from them which has not been made available to the public elsewhere—but as the most readily accessible authority to serving officers, copies being available in all battalion and brigade libraries.

My thanks for assistance are due, among others, to the Librarian of the Imperial Library at Calcutta, who gave me access to many books which, but for his courtesy, would have remained unknown to me ; to the Historical Section of the Committee of Imperial Defence, who gave me facilities to consult war diaries ; to the India Office, who permitted me to examine their records. I owe a debt of gratitude to those individuals whose private papers have proved a mine of information. The publishers, Messrs. Gale & Polden, Limited, have given me the benefit of their unrivalled experience.

W. L. HAILES,
Lieut.-Colonel.

MERSHAM,
　BITTERNE,
　　HAMPSHIRE.
1st *June*, 1938.

v

CONTENTS

PLATES

MAPS

BATTLE HONOURS

THE KING'S COLOUR

" La Bassee, 1914 "

" Festubert, 1914, '15 "

" Shaiba "

" Ctesiphon "

" Khan Baghdadi "

" Neuve Chapelle "

" France and Flanders, 1914–15 "

" Defence of Kut-al-Amara "

" Tigris, 1916 "

" Mesopotamia, 1914–18 "

REGIMENTAL COLOUR

" Nagpur "

" Ghuznee, 1839 "

" Ghuznee, 1842 "

" Maharajpore "

" Mooltan "

" Punjaub "

" China, 1858–59 "

" Afghanistan, 1878–80 "

" China, 1900 "

" Afghanistan, 1839 "

" Candahar, 1842 "

" Cabool, 1842 "

" Sobraon "

" Goojerat "

" Ali Masjid "

" Kandahar, 1880 "

" Burma, 1885–87 "

" Afghanistan, 1919 "

PAST AND PRESENT TITLES

1st ROYAL BATTALION

1803	1st Battalion, 22nd Regiment of Bengal Native Infantry.
1824	43rd Regiment of Bengal Native Infantry.
1842	43rd Regiment of Bengal Native (Light) Infantry.
1861	6th Regiment of Bengal Native (Light) Infantry.
1885	6th Regiment of Bengal (Light) Infantry.
1897	6th (Jat) Regiment of Bengal (Light) Infantry.
1901	6th Jat Light Infantry.
1921	6th Royal Jat Light Infantry.
1922	1st Royal Battalion, 9th Jat Regiment (L.I.).

2nd (MOOLTAN) BATTALION

1817	1st Battalion, 10th Regiment of Bombay Native Infantry.
1824	19th Regiment of Bombay Native Infantry.
1885	19th Regiment of Bombay Infantry.
1901	19th Bombay Infantry.
1903	119th Infantry (The Mooltan Regiment).
1922	2nd Battalion (The Mooltan Battalion), 9th Jat Regiment.

3rd BATTALION

1823	1st Battalion, 33rd Regiment of Bengal Native Infantry.
1824	65th Regiment of Bengal Native Infantry.
1861	10th Regiment of Bengal Native Infantry.
1885	10th Regiment of Bengal Infantry.
1897	10th (Jat) Regiment of Bengal Infantry.
1901	10th Jat Infantry.
1903	10th Jats.
1923	3rd Battalion, 9th Jat Regiment.

xi

TRAINING BATTALION

1917 2nd Battalion, 6th Jat Light Infantry.

1921 2nd Battalion, 6th Royal Jat Light Infantry.

1922 10th Battalion, 9th Jat Regiment.

In 1923 took over identity of former 18th Infantry, whose previous titles were :—

1795 Calcutta Native Militia.

1859 The Alipore Regiment.

1861 22nd Regiment of Bengal Native Infantry.

1861 18th Regiment of Bengal Native Infantry.

1864 18th (The Alipore) Regiment of Bengal Native Infantry.

1885 18th Regiment of Bengal Infantry.

1902 18th Musalman Rajput Infantry.

1903 18th Infantry.

1922 4th Battalion, 9th Jat Regiment.

Amalgamated with the training battalion of the 4th Bombay Grenadiers and became in

1930 10th Battalion, 4th/9th Regiments.

THE STORMING OF MOOLTAN.

65th NATIVE INFANTRY.

The 19th Bombay Native Infantry.

THE 19th BOMBAY NATIVE INFANTRY IN 1839.

A JAT RECRUIT.

WAR SERVICES OF THE 9th JAT REGIMENT

Chapter I

THE MAHRATTA WARS, 1803-4, AND AFTER

Bibliography.—Regimental Records ; *Life and Military Services of Viscount Lake* ; *Hindustan under Free Lances* ; *Military Memoirs of George Thomas* ; British Indian Military Repository ; East India Military Calendar ; *The Services of the Bengal Native Army* (Cardew).

In the beginning of the nineteenth century the whole of India was in a very disturbed condition. The Moghal Emperor at Delhi, though still acknowledged as Emperor, had very little real power.
1803. Delhi itself, and all the neighbouring country, was tributary to the Mahratta Maharajah Scindiah of Gwalior and was actually ruled by a Frenchman, by name Perron, who commanded Scindiah's armies in the north of India. The so-called Mahratta armies in the north were not composed of Mahrattas. The principal officers were mostly Frenchmen, and the men were natives of Oudh, Rohilkhand and the Doab, or country lying between the two great rivers, the Jumna and the Ganges.

The kingdom of Oudh, lying to the north-east of the Ganges, though nominally independent, was entirely under British influence, and British troops were stationed there in accordance with a treaty signed with the Nawab Wazir.

That war was inevitable between the British and the Mahratta ruler of Delhi was obvious to all, and the cold weather of 1802 was spent in preparing for it. The majority of the Bengal troops were concentrated at Cawnpore and Kanauj for training, and in 1803 orders were issued for the raising of two more regiments of infantry, each composed of two battalions.

The 22nd Bengal Native Infantry was ordered to be raised at Fatehgarh, a military station near the great city of Farrucknagar, and nearer to the Mahratta frontier than Cawnpore. The names associated with the raising of the 1st Battalion, 22nd Bengal Native Infantry, now the 1st Royal Battalion, 9th Jat Regiment (L.I.), and which will be referred to in future as the 1st Royal Battalion, were those of Major J. Malcolm and Lieutenant W. Ball. The former appears never to have joined. The recruits were not enlisted by officers of the battalion, but were drafted in from what was known as a "Gulhake Paltan," a formation

B   1

which appears to have enlisted recruits but not undertaken their training. They were all young, scarcely more than boys, and consisted of about three Hindus to one Mohammedan, the former being largely Brahmins and Rajputs. The minimum height accepted was five feet six inches, though many were considerably more. Ten havildars, 50 naiks and 50 trained sepoys were also drafted in from other units. The battalion was organized in ten companies, each 70 strong, of which two were grenadiers.

When the Commander-in-Chief, General Lake, advanced from Cawnpore in August, he was joined by the brigade from Fatehgarh, and at the same time appointed Lieutenant-Colonel Kyan as commandant of the whole of the 22nd Bengal Native Infantry being raised at that station. From this circumstance the 1st Royal Battalion became known as " Kyne ki dahini paltan," or the right-hand battalion of Colonel Kyan.

General Lake had a rapid series of brilliant victories, the first of which was the capture of Aligarh Fort and the town of Koil, followed by victories at Delhi, Agra and Laswari. After the battle of Laswari, Captain Samuel Wood, who had escorted the guns captured at that action to the fort of Agra, was instructed by the Commander-in-Chief to take over command of the 1st Royal Battalion at Fatehgarh and to discipline and prepare it for active service as quickly as possible. He joined the battalion in December, 1803, and within six months of the time the men had first had a musket in their hands reported the battalion fit for any service.

In August, 1804, the battalion, under the command of Captain Wood, was ordered to Aligarh to garrison that fort. When the battalion **1804.** first arrived there were no provisions of any sort available, and it had been the custom to bring these from the town of Koil. At this time the Maharajah Holkar of Indore, who had now declared war against the British, invaded the district, the whole of which was in a state of rebellion. The inhabitants of Koil welcomed the arrival of the Mahrattas, and the town was taken over by the Maharajah. The battalion was now in a dangerous situation. Four companies had been detached on another service, and there were only 400 rank and file available in the fort, and these were entirely without rations, surrounded by a rebellious population and in the immediate neighbourhood of a greatly stronger hostile force. Captain Wood decided to attack the town, and with his small force of under 400 young recruits, assisted by a small detachment of artillery, stormed and captured Koil on September 22nd, 1804, though opposed by 2,000 horse and foot of Holkar's as well as the rebellious inhabitants of the town. Koil was now declared subject to military law and, as well as the fort, placed under Captain Wood's jurisdiction.

The battalion remained at Aligarh for over a year after this, during which the district was again invaded, this time by a military freebooter known as Ameer Khan. Parties of the battalion saw constant service maintaining order in the district until relieved towards the end of 1805, by which time all apprehension for the safety of the district had passed.

1805.

During this period a detachment of the battalion was employed in accompanying the collector to enforce the payment of revenue by refractory landowners. In the course of an action in which this detachment was engaged, Lieutenant Higgins of the battalion was severely wounded in the right elbow, which rendered the arm useless.

In the year 1805 General Lake set out to deal once and for all with the Maharajah Holkar, and that prince marched northwards, hoping to obtain the support of the southern Sikh chiefs. He left his infantry, numbering about 3,000, with 1,000 cavalry and 30 guns, in the neighbourhood of Dadri and Jhajjar to harry the British territory. General Lake himself marched north in pursuit of the Maharajah, and left a large containing force under the command of General Dowdeswell to keep the Mahrattas from crossing the Jumna river into the Doab. Major Wood, who had been promoted to that rank on June 5th, was ordered with the battalion to join this force. The Mahrattas made no serious attempt to enter the Doab, and the Maharajah was brought to book at Jullundur and forced to sign a treaty.

When General Dowdeswell's force was broken up the battalion was ordered to Saharanpur, a frontier station which had recently been destroyed and burnt by Sikhs. Here the battalion was brigaded with the 1st Regiment of Native Cavalry and two battalions of the Begum Sumroo's with their artillery, the whole being under the command of Major Wood. The Begum Sumroo was an independent princess who ruled at Sardhana, a few miles from Meerut. She had acquired her name and state from Walter Reinhardt, known as Le Sombre or Sumroo on account of his dark complexion. He had arrived in India as a soldier of the French army ; after a career chiefly notable for repeated desertions and remarkable cruelty, he succeeded in commanding a force manned largely by low Europeans whom he attracted from among the tramps of the time. Under fire a sort of stolid discipline prevailed ; in camp drunkenness and disobedience ruled supreme. When the side he was fighting for was defeated, he took his brigade bodily into the service of the victors. As the result of this policy, his brigade was eventually taken into the Imperial service and a considerable fief assigned for its support. Sumroo died at Agra in 1778, leaving an insane wife and a son still in early childhood, and his fief was assumed by a favourite slave girl whom he had purchased at Delhi. She settled with her brigade at Sardhana. Taking an active and very prominent

1806.

part in suppressing the rebellion of the Musalman Rajput, Najaf Kuli, in Gurgaon, she was raised to great honour. Later a mutiny among her troops caused the death of her French husband while she had to lie in the courtyard, wounded and tied to a gun ; the remnant of her disreputable European followers celebrating the occasion with one of their drunken orgies. Her restoration to power was caused by George Thomas, the Irish rajah of Hansi, who, with his own money, bought back the allegiance of her followers, backing his generosity with threats of the action likely to be taken by the Maharajah Scindiah.

The battalion remained at Saharanpur until the end of September, 1806, when it appears to have moved to Meerut. Before leaving, Major Wood received the following letter signed by all the officers of the detachment, a remarkable tribute in view of the history and character of the Begum Sumroo's battalions :—

" SIR,—About to leave Saharunpore, you are not permitted to depart without a recorded testimony of our extreme satisfaction with your public conduct whilst in command of the detachment, and of our deep regret at the loss of your society. The expression of sentiments we all so sensibly feel, it would be unjust to withhold ; to yourself the conveyance of them, we hope, will be a source of some little gratification. We offer you our ardent wishes for honour and happiness, in compliance with the dictates of sincerity ; and remain, Sir,

" Your most obliged and faithful servants,
(*Signed by every officer of the detachment*).

" SAHARUNPORE,
"*September* 29th, 1806."

While at Meerut the battalion lost Lieutenant James Merryck, who died on September 19th, 1808, and who is buried in the middle of the present race-course, where a tombstone was erected to his **1808.** memory by his brother officers. During the year 1808 one of the battalion companies was converted into a light company, and early in 1809 this was grouped with the light companies of other battalions and formed part of a force under Major-General St. Leger which was assembled near Ludhiana to prevent inroads by the Sikhs. At this time Ranjit Singh, the Sikh ruler of Lahore, was beginning to consolidate his power in the Punjab, and he met a British representative and agreed to prevent any further inroads. This led to the breaking up of the force and the company rejoined the battalion in May.

Among the territory which had fallen into the hands of the East India Company as a result of the recent Mahratta Wars was the country of Hariana, including the modern districts of Rohtak and Hissar, later to become the principal recruiting area of the regiment. For a very long time this country had acknowledged no master, but became in turn the prey of each succeeding invader until 1798. In this year a native of Tipperary, George Thomas, who, although a deserter from the British Navy, was of an upright, straightforward and loyal character, built up for himself an independent state with his capital at Hansi. He was engaged in constant wars, but his great power caused Scindiah to ask him to act in conjunction with Perron against their common enemies. Thomas replied that, as he and Perron belonged to different nations which were in a state of actual hostility, it was impossible they could ever act in concert. He could never serve under the command of a Frenchman. Eventually a meeting was arranged between Thomas and Perron at Bahadurgarh, which only resulted in the opening of hostilities. Perron immediately seized Jhajjar, which was unfortified, and sent a force to attack Georgegarh or, as it is now sometimes called, Jahazgarh, a small fort built by George Thomas when he first took possession of the country.

Thomas marched from Hansi to its relief, defeated the hostile force, which had retreated towards Jhajjar, and returned towards Georgegarh. Here he learnt that Perron's main army, under Bourquin, a Frenchman of very dubious character, had arrived at Beri. A battle was fought the following day and Thomas, although left master of the field, suffered severely and was quickly surrounded by enemies. Scindiah's allies and tributaries, including Bhartpur and the Begum Sumroo, were joined by several Sikh chieftains who saw a chance of revenging themselves against the Irishman, who had always previously succeeded in defeating them. Treachery and desertion on the part of his Mohammedan soldiers, whose homes were in Scindiah's territory, were added to his troubles, which, according to James Skinner, who was in the opposing camp, he made worse by indulging in a prolonged drinking bout. Eventually he escaped to Hansi with only one Hindu regiment which had remained loyal and joined his garrison there. Here, again, his Mohammedans made offers to Bourquin, who, believing Thomas might still defend the place with his faithful Hindus, in which case he might lose many of his own men unnecessarily, made Thomas acquainted with the treachery in the garrison. Thomas then agreed to evacuate the fort, but stipulated for a battalion of sepoys to escort him to the English frontier, where he arrived in the middle of January, 1802.

The whole country then came under Mahratta rule until the following year, when it fell into General Lake's hands. It was not yet to enjoy tranquillity. In 1805, when General Lake pursued Holkar into the Punjab, that chief left a large force near Jhajjar to harry the British territory; this was prevented from entering the Doab by General Dowdeswell's army, but had a free hand in Hariana until the following year, when peace was declared.

In view of the vicissitudes through which their country had lately passed, it was not to be expected that the Jats would readily settle down to ordered government, and they refused to attend at Delhi or enter into any engagements for future good conduct and submission to the authority of government. In 1809 it became necessary to send an expedition into their country, and the 1st Royal Battalion, under Major Wood, formed part of this. The Jats retreated to Bhiwani, which was strongly fortified, in front of which the British took up a position, and after battering the walls for a few hours advanced to the assault at noon on August 29th. The enemy met them in the breach and defended their houses and strongholds for some time, but at length yielded to superior prowess and discipline, with considerable loss on both sides, having themselves suffered nearly 3,000 casualties. The only British officer killed in this action was Lieutenant Stephen O'Brien of the 1st Royal Battalion, which also lost 7 men killed and 18 non-commissioned officers and men wounded. All these casualties occurred in the grenadier and light companies, which alone were engaged in the assault. Lieutenant Nicholetts, the adjutant, was thanked in orders for his behaviour.

A letter from the Vice-President in Council referring to this action stated that " His Lordship considers the success of this assault, rendered doubly arduous by the strength of the place and the desperate resistance of the enemy, as worthy of being ranked among the number of those brilliant exploits which have added lustre to the British arms and security to the British interests in this quarter of the globe."

No sooner had the operations in Hariana come to an end than the battalion was ordered to Bundelkhand, the country lying across the Jumna river immediately south of Cawnpore, for operations against Ameer Khan. This military freebooter, after his invasion of the Aligarh district in February, 1805, had moved south-east and south and, after suffering several defeats from British forces, had entered Bundelkhand and Malwa, the hilly country which lies to the west of Bundelkhand and north of the Narbada river. Here he continued to cause considerable embarrassment to the British authorities, and in 1809 a force was assembled under the command of Colonel Martindell to act against him in co-operation with a Madras army under Colonel Sir Barry Close.

The 1st Royal Battalion joined this force in January, 1810, and advanced into Malwa, but was not engaged in any action, and Colonel **1810.** Martindell's detachment was broken up in May, the whole of the troops receiving the thanks of Sir George Hewett, then Commander-in-Chief in India.

Major Wood was now in a poor state of health and suffered from a lameness which made him incapable of mounting a horse. The battalion was joined by Major Goddard Richards from the 2nd Battalion, 22nd Native Infantry, who assumed command. Major Wood continued to serve with the army in the field, and in March, 1811, was promoted to Lieutenant-Colonel, but never again commanded the battalion in action.　Eventually he retired from the service in September, 1816, and was appointed a Companion of the Bath.

During the absence of Colonel Martindell's force in Malwa, Gopal Singh, an able, bold and popular chief who had been dispossessed of some districts a short time before by the British Government, invaded the Bundelkhand, from which nearly the whole of the troops had been withdrawn.　Descending into the level province at the head of a large body of horse, he easily eluded the pursuit of infantry by the length and rapidity of his marches ; and proceeded coolly to collect the revenues and to burn wherever payment was refused.　In consequence of this Lieutenant-Colonel Thomas Brown was detached into Bundel-khand with the 1st Regiment of cavalry, and succeeded in driving Gopal Singh into the hills.　In October, 1810, permission had been obtained to pursue Gopal Singh through the jungles and destroy his strongholds instead of merely repelling his incursions, and Lieutenant-Colonel Brown was ordered into the hills and instructed to take command of all the detachments he found.　The 1st Royal Battalion thus came under his command, and Major Richards commanded the whole of the infantry of the force.

The fort of Logassi surrendered to a detachment under Major Richards without opposition, and the year 1811 was spent in pursuing

1811.　　and harassing the marauding chief, whose force, whenever he attempted to draw it together, was dispersed.　At last Gopal Singh was so wearied out by this incessant pursuit that he came in and surrendered himself, and quiet was restored to the province. This service had led the 1st Royal Battalion into parts of the country which were, till then, almost entirely unknown and were considered as impracticable, and had involved very rapid marches through extremely difficult country.

In January, 1812, the battalion was part of a force under the com-mand of Colonel Martindell which operated against the fortress of

1812.　　Kalinjar, twenty miles south-east of Banda in Bundelkhand, the owner of which had refused to acknowledge British suzerainty.　An attempt was made to storm the place on February 2nd ; the assault was repulsed, but was so nearly successful that the fortress surrendered the following day.

CHAPTER II

THE PINDARI AND MAHRATTA WARS, 1817-18, AND AFTER

Bibliography.—Regimental Records ; Prinsep's *Political and Military Transactions in India* ; *The Mahratta and Pindari Wars* (official) ; McNaghten's *Memoir of the Military Operations of the Nagpore Subsidiary Force* ; East India Military Calendar ; Nolan's *History of the British Empire in India and the East* ; The British Indian Military Repository.

THE great extent of territory which had come under British rule as a result of the Mahratta Wars of 1803 and 1804 was not desired by the directors of the East India Company ; consequently in the treaties which followed the conquered chieftains were regarded as equals and were left in possession of large states in which the British adopted a policy of non-interference. The most important of the Mahratta chieftains were the Peshwa, nominal head of them all, with his government at Poona ; the Bhonsla, Rajah of Nagpur ; Holkar of Indore ; and Scindiah of Gwalior.

1817.

Conditions were ideal for the gangs of dacoits which always spring up readily when the country is not well policed, and there were large numbers of men everywhere who had been discharged from the services of various governments. During the years following the conquest of Delhi these gangs swelled enormously and terrorized the whole country even as far south as Madras. They were known as Pindaris, and consisted of men of all castes and both religions. These Pindaris were animated by one object only—the rapid collection of wealth. Mounted on horses, they would travel immense distances in a single day, seize everything movable and destroy that which they could not carry away. They indulged in every variety of torture which their minds could conceive in order to make their unfortunate victims disclose the whereabouts of hidden wealth. In numbers they sometimes amounted to 30,000 men.

The principal gang of these Pindaris, under a chief called Chitu, had its headquarters in Malwa, between the northern bank of the Narbada river and the Vindhya mountains.

In the Mahratta states these Pindaris were in many cases openly encouraged by officials who shared their profits. When the British Government asked for the assistance of these states in suppressing the activities of the Pindaris, the chieftains agreed but took no action.

In the year 1816 one of three parties of Pindaris entered British territory, and in twelve days killed and wounded nearly seven thousand persons and carried off or destroyed property worth £100,000.

As a result of this and in accordance with a treaty made with the Regent of Nagpur, shortly to become rajah, a force of five battalions of Madras Infantry with a regiment of cavalry was sent to the valley of the Narbada to check the inroads of the Pindaris. As this force was divided up into posts extended over a front of one hundred and forty-seven miles on the south bank of the river, it had little chance of success. The Pindaris, who when they went on a raid were usually all mounted, had immense mobility and were not tied down to any definite lines of communication. They had no intention of fighting against armed troops, and they terrorized the villagers so much that it was impossible to get information of their movements. Several parties succeeded in getting through the posts on the Narbada.

Meanwhile a force of Bengal troops, known as the Nagpur Subsidiary Force, had been collected under the command of Lieutenant-Colonel Adams, with orders to hold itself in readiness to proceed to the Narbada at the close of the rains in order to relieve the Madras troops. The 1st Royal Battalion was part of this force. It was commanded at the time by Captain Charles Thomas Higgins, the officer who had lost the use of his right arm as the result of a wound received at Toorkaponah in June, 1805, when a lieutenant in the regiment. He had been away for some years in civil employ in Java.

The battalion was now composed of eight companies only, and on January 15th, 1817, when the force had arrived at Bisram Ganj Ghat, the light company and one of the two grenadier companies were removed and formed temporarily into a light battalion, together with the light and grenadier companies of other units. Within a few hours of its formation this light battalion was sent off with the 5th Regiment of Native Cavalry, and by means of very rapid marching succeeded in intercepting several large parties of Pindaris who were returning from a plundering expedition, and in inflicting a large number of casualties upon them. Throughout the operations which followed this light battalion was used in conjunction with cavalry as a striking force and was constantly engaged in very rapid marches and in engagements with the Pindaris.

On arrival in the Narbada valley, the six companies of the 1st Royal Battalion under Captain Higgins relieved an equal number of Madras Infantry at Sohagpur on February 22nd, and on the following day a detachment of three companies was dispatched as a movable column. These three companies were ordered to be constantly on the move along a line parallel to the Narbada river and, as far as the country would admit, six miles distant from it. The total distance to be covered was forty miles, which was generally to be done in three marches.   As other battalions had similar columns constantly on the move, the whole line of the Narbada was patrolled by bodies of troops who were sufficiently distant from it to intercept any parties of the enemy who succeeded in crossing.   This activity resulted in the Pindaris being confined to the hilly country north of the river, where they were compelled to carry on their trade of plunder for mere subsistence only.

Towards the middle of June the rains set in and the rivers became impassable.   There was no longer any need for constant activity, and the battalion was withdrawn to temporary cantonments at Hoshangabad.

Sanction was now obtained from England for a large force to be assembled in order to enter the Pindari country and destroy and disperse their gangs entirely.   The Mahratta chiefs, despite verbal assurances, not only would take no action to help in their destruction, but could not be trusted to allow the British to carry it out without interference. Consequently steps had to be taken to safeguard the forces in the field from attack by these princes.   At first the Peshwa at Poona and the Rajah of Nagpur were not expected to take hostile action.   The greatest British armies ever assembled in India were collected together, one in Northern India and the other in the Deccan, with the intention of closing in on the Pindaris at their headquarters, and they were moved in such a manner as to render it impossible for Scindiah of Gwalior to act against them.   The troops at Hoshangabad, including the 1st Royal Battalion, formed part of the 2nd Division of the Army of the Deccan.   The battalion was now commanded by Major Thomas Garner, an officer who had been absent for some time on active service with Sir David Ochterlony in Nepal.

Though the majority of the Nagpur Subsidiary Force was to remain guarding the line of the river, a mobile portion of it was to advance northwards into the Pindari country, and this was to include the two companies of the 1st Royal Battalion which were already with the light battalion as well as the remaining grenadier company.   These arrangements were largely upset by events which occurred at Nagpur.   The Resident there had an escort of two companies of Bengal Infantry. A small force of four 6-pounder guns, three troops of the 6th Bengal Cavalry and two weak battalions of Madras Infantry, under the command of Lieutenant-Colonel Hopetoun Scott, had also been sent to Nagpur.   The Peshwa at Poona then took hostile action, and it became evident that the Rajah of Nagpur intended to follow his example. The small force was attacked in overwhelming numbers on November 26th, on Sitabuldi Hill and it was only after extremely severe fighting that the Rajah's troops were driven off.   A second determined attack in similar strength would have resulted in the complete extermination of the troops at Nagpur, and reinforcements were extremely urgently needed.

The six companies of the 1st Royal Battalion had been away from Hoshangabad and only marched back into that place on the morning of the 27th, having already covered a distance of twenty-five miles. Nevertheless, that night, at four hours' notice, they again marched for Nagpur, together with three troops of Bengal Cavalry and two 6-pounder guns.

In view of the extreme urgency it was decided that every available combatant should accompany the battalion on its march, and there was no escort with the baggage, which was left to follow as best it could— the numerous camp followers as well as the women and children, amongst whom were the wife and four children of Captain Higgins, struggling along with the transport. The battalion accomplished the march of nearly sixty-seven miles to Nagpur in thirty hours with only one halt of two hours, thus covering nearly one hundred miles in sixty hours. It was bitterly cold weather, and the anxiety lest the baggage with the women and children should fall into the hands of the enemy or be attacked by villagers added to the sufferings of the battalion.

The arrival of this force on the early morning of November 29th inspired complete confidence in the garrison of Nagpur and prevented a second attack being made on the Residency. Larger reinforcements under the command of Brigadier Doveton arrived on December 12th. The Bhonsla, or Rajah of Nagpur, now agreed to make terms ; he agreed to appear in person on the 15th, to surrender his guns and order his troops to disperse. These terms he did not carry out, and early on the 16th the British troops moved and took up a position near the Residency and facing the enemy at a distance of a mile and a half. The Rajah arrived at the Residency at 9 a.m. and promised that all his guns would be surrendered to the British troops at noon. The force moved forward to take possession of them, the 1st Royal Battalion forming part of a brigade commanded by Lieutenant-Colonel McLeod which was on the right of the infantry line.

The first battery was taken possession of without opposition, but, on entering a plantation and passing between two villages, heavy musketry fire was opened upon Colonel McLeod's brigade. The advance was not checked and the second battery was captured by cavalry ; but, as the latter continued to move forward, the enemy again took possession of the battery and were preparing to open fire with the guns when the infantry charged. The enemy immediately fled. By half-past one the Mahrattas had been driven from all their positions, leaving their camp standing, 40 elephants and 64 guns. In this action the 1st Royal Battalion lost 8 killed and 17 wounded.

The majority of the Nagpur army was now scattered about the country, but a force of 5,000 Arabs and Hindustani troops had retired into the city and these refused to surrender. Accordingly it was decided

to make a systematic attack upon the city itself.   The city of Nagpur
is surrounded by an irregular wall some three miles in extent with round
towers at intervals, and outside this wall there are extensive suburbs
with narrow streets, extremely difficult for troops to advance through
in the face of an enemy.   The advance was necessarily cautious, and
obstacles were cleared away as far as possible by artillery fire.

It was not until the 23rd that a breach, believed to be practicable,
was made in the walls of the city, and on the morning of the 24th an
attack was launched.   The task of seizing the breach
and entering the city first was allotted to the 1st Royal
Battalion, to which were attached two companies of The
Royal Scots, one of which was to assist in the assault, and a few sappers
and miners.   At 8.30 a.m. the storming party dashed forward from the
trenches which they were occupying and succeeded in gaining the top
of the breach.   Here they were crowded together in a narrow space
and under very heavy fire from the numerous adjacent houses.   The
heaped rubble from the fallen wall was a difficult obstacle to negotiate,
and only a few men succeeded in getting to the bottom of the rubbish
inside the city walls.   The remainder were driven to take cover and
eventually were called off by Brigadier Doveton.   Although the assault
had failed in its immediate object, the Arabs next day began negotiations
which were finally successful, and the battalion was highly complimented
on its behaviour.   Major Garner was most favourably mentioned in the
despatches of the Commander-in-Chief.   The casualties in the battalion
during the advance through the city and in the assault amounted to
7 killed and 36 wounded, so that altogether at Nagpur the battalion
lost 15 killed and 53 wounded.   After the capture of Nagpur the
battalion remained to garrison the place.

It is unnecessary to follow the very complicated operations against
the Pindaris.   These were always anxious to avoid battle.   Several
columns having advanced into their strongholds from different
directions, they were unable to assemble anywhere in numbers without
being at once pursued by British troops.   When in small numbers they
were liable to be attacked and their horses taken by the villagers,
whom they had formerly plundered with impunity.   The majority were
forced to surrender.   Chitu himself succeeded in remaining at large,
though with a very small following, until May, 1819, when he was
killed by a tiger, over a year after the other Pindari chiefs had either
surrendered or been killed. The two companies of the regiment serving
with the light battalion took a very prominent part in these operations.

Towards the middle of March, 1818, the Peshwa approached the
Nagpur frontier, and it was discovered that the Rajah of Nagpur was
in communication with him with a view to joining him
with all his forces.   Accordingly, on March 15th, the

1817.
1st Battalion.

1818.
1st Battalion.

Rajah was arrested under the orders of the Resident by Captain Browne of the battalion with the help of a few unarmed sepoys. Captain Edward Cave Browne, who received great credit for his tact, which enabled the arrest to be carried out without resistance, had served with the battalion since 1804.

In view of the state of affairs at Nagpur and the fact that hostile preparations were being carried out at Chanda, a fortress in Nagpur territory which it was believed to be the intention of the Peshwa to enter, a force was dispatched with the object of cutting him off from any communication with that fortress and to hold him in check until the arrival of Colonel Adams with a strong force. This expedition, which was under the command of Lieutenant-Colonel Scott, comprised a battery of European horse artillery, some cavalry, two Madras battalions and two companies of the 1st Royal Battalion.

Lieutenant-Colonel Scott reach Wardha, about fifteen miles from Chanda, on April 3rd, and here fell in with the van of the Mahrattas and drove it back across the River Wardha, though with the trifling loss of ten or twelve only as, the encounter being quite unexpected by the enemy, they fled on the first appearance of a British force. Lieutenant-Colonel Scott then moved towards Chanda, hoping to succeed in investing the place, or at least in cutting off all communication with outside, but he found the fortifications so extensive that with his small force it was impossible to cover it entirely.

On April 11th Lieutenant-Colonel Scott was ordered to Hinganghat, where he joined Colonel Adams on the 14th. Colonel Adams had with him, besides a strong force of cavalry, the now famous light infantry battalion, one other battalion and two grenadier companies of another unit ; so that the force contained four companies of the 1st Royal Battalion, or half its total strength. The following day the combined force marched to Alanda, when Colonel Adams's agents reported the presence of the ex-Peshwa at Seoni. Marching all night, the combined force reached Pipalkot before daylight the following morning, where a short halt was made to refresh the troops and to form daylight dispositions, with the light infantry battalion leading and the cavalry and horse artillery immediately behind them. When the march had continued another five miles, and the slow-moving portion of the troops had been left far in rear, the advanced guards of the opposing forces suddenly met within 150 yards of each other in the thick forest.

The light infantry battalion immediately formed square, but the resultant battle was fought mainly by the cavalry and horse artillery as the ex-Peshwa with his personal guard fled at the beginning of the action. He escaped, as the cavalry, who had already marched thirty-one miles from Alanda, were too fatigued to carry the pursuit beyond the Seoni valley. Five 6-pounder brass cannons as well as the enemy's elephants, camels and treasure were captured, and a great part of the ex-Peshwa's followers dispersed to their homes. This was the last action fought by the ex-Peshwa in person ; he became a fugitive with an ever-lessening band of followers, while the other Mahratta chiefs had already been reduced to submission. He eventually surrendered and was granted a pension by the Government and settled at Bithur, near Cawnpore.

After the battle of Seoni, Colonel Adams, having been joined by a siege train and another Madras battalion, advanced to Chanda and arrived before that fortress on May 9th. The following few days were spent in reconnaissance, during which the reconnoitring troops were subjected to heavy fire from the ramparts, to which they were unable to reply effectively ; and it was not until the 18th that the batteries opened fire. They succeeded in making a breach and the assault was delivered on the 20th. The storming parties were directed, on ascending the breach, to strike off right and left along the ramparts, but on no account to enter the body of the town till all the bastions had been cleared of the enemy. These parties were composed of two strong columns of infantry ; the right, which consisted of Bengal troops, included the two companies of the 1st Royal Battalion which had accompanied Lieutenant-Colonel Scott. The left consisted of Madras troops. The light infantry battalion remained in reserve, while the cavalry guarded the camp. The advance was made in silence under a heavy fire till the leading companies reached the breach, when the enemy retreated from bastion to bastion till they found themselves between the two columns, and then they jumped off the walls and fled in all directions.

The walls of Chanda were about thirty feet high and of amazing thickness besides being in most thorough repair—a very unusual circumstance at the time ; and some of the guns taken were of immense calibre.

The force then returned to Nagpur, where the place of the 1st Royal Battalion was taken by the 1st Battalion, 23rd Bengal Native Infantry. While the column was still at Nagpur, on May 30th, cholera broke out in the camp, and by June 2nd had carried off a large number of sepoys and followers. The force therefore moved by very easy marches towards Hoshangabad, and there was an immediate diminution of the disease which, by the time Hoshangabad was reached on June 18th—just in time to avoid the rains which set in the following day—had entirely disappeared. The light infantry battalion was now broken up, and the two companies which had served throughout the campaign with that unit rejoined the 1st Royal Battalion.

Meanwhile the ex-Rajah had been sent from Nagpur towards

Allahabad under a strong escort which included the remaining wing of the 1st Royal Battalion, the whole being commanded by Captain Browne, who had effected the arrest.   On the night of June 12th-13th the prisoner succeeded in escaping.   Captain Browne was tried by court-martial and was honourably acquitted of all blame whatever.

To the east of the road leading from Nagpur to Hoshangabad there is an extensive range called the Mahadeo Hills, covered with forest and inhabited by an aboriginal people known as Gonds.   The principal place in these hills is Pachmarhi, and to this place the ex-Rajah made his way, befriended and heartily assisted by the Gond chieftains.   He was quickly joined by large numbers of those Arab and Hindustani troops who had formerly served him and who were without a leader.

During July a party of these made their way into the plains and succeeded in defeating a small party of British troops in the Betul valley, about half-way between Nagpur and Hoshangabad, and a series of operations commenced during the rains in which, at first, the 1st Royal Battalion did not take part.   All reports received at this time led to the belief that the climate in the hills was extremely unhealthy until some months after the rains had stopped, and it was determined not to enter them until January, when it was intended to send in three columns, of which the right, under Colonel Adams, was to advance straight on Pachmarhi.   This column, which included the left wing of the 1st Royal Battalion, moved out of Hoshangabad to Synkerah, about twelve miles distant, on November 23rd, 1818, where it remained in camp, while various other parties of troops endeavoured to confine the enemy, including the Gonds, to the hills.

On November 28th a party of the enemy, driven to the plains largely by hunger, succeeded in establishing themselves in a small town called Fatehpore at the foot of the hills, where they were attacked by a detachment of cavalry.   These cavalry were unable to drive the enemy out of the well-built houses in which they had taken cover, and the left wing of the 1st Royal Battalion, under Lieutenant Tulloch,* was sent from Synkerah with a couple of guns for the purpose.   The attack was made on December 4th.   The enemy were found encamped in the rear of the town and on the slope of the hills, which were thickly covered with forest and had two nullahs in front ;   the streets of the town were strongly barricaded.   While the guns opened fire from a height, the wing of the 1st Royal Battalion, supported by half the cavalry, moved on to clear the town.   When they had penetrated as far as one of the nullahs on the far side of Fatehpore, the fire of the enemy from the heights became very brisk, and the guns were again moved up to a position close enough to enable them to fire grape, soon after which the enemy commenced to retreat.   The nature of the ground forbade the

---

* Afterwards Lieutenant-General J. Tulloch, C.B.

use of cavalry in pursuit, but the casualties of the enemy were very great, while the 1st Royal Battalion lost 3 killed and 37 wounded.

In the beginning of 1819 the 1st Royal Battalion was relieved, and on January 11th it commenced its march northwards under the command of Major Garner, and went to Sikrora in Oudh, where it was stationed for two years, the commencement of a long period of garrison duty.

1819.
1st Battalion.

After the sanction of the British Government had been obtained to complete the destruction of the Pindari gangs, and it seemed likely that many of the Mahratta chiefs would again take up arms against the British, it became necessary to increase the forces available. As a result of this the 2nd Battalion (The Mooltan Battalion) was raised at Bombay by Lieutenant-Colonel Michael Kennedy on October 29th, 1817, as the 1st Battalion, 10th Regiment of Bombay Native Infantry. The men enlisted consisted of all classes—Mohammedans, Hindus, Jews and some Christians—who were mixed indiscriminately. Among the Hindus the lower tribes of Mahrattas and the Parwari, Surti and Frost sects were more numerous than Rajputs and higher castes. The majority were deserters from the Peshwa's army. The minimum height accepted was five feet three inches, and the average height about five feet five inches ; but they were robust and hardy, capable of enduring great fatigue upon very slender diet, and cheerful under difficulties.

1817.
2nd Battalion.

The battalion was not allowed long in which to organize and train. In January, 1818, while it still consisted of recruits, many of whom had only been embodied a few days, and the old soldiers intended to form the basis of its discipline had been unable to join owing to the war, Lieutenant-Colonel Kennedy was ordered to move to the Konkan, the country south of Bombay lying between the Western Ghats and the sea.

1818.
2nd Battalion.

This battalion of recruits, assisted by a detachment of 180 men of the 1st Battalion, 11th Native Infantry, and the crews of two cruisers which had succeeded in working up the Bankot river, some seventy miles south of Bombay, attacked the fort of Mundanghur on February 15th, 1818. The attack was covered by the fire of two 12-pounder guns from Prince of Wales Island, which had been brought up a steep mountain, seven miles in length, on the men's shoulders. The garrison of the fort was three times the strength of the attackers, and the fort one of the strongest hill forts in the Konkan. The enemy stockaded the whole line of approach, which consisted of a climb of over a mile, and defended every irregularity. The stockades were stormed in succession, the commander of the fort and most of the garrison killed, and the place finally carried by assault. A strong garrison was then left in Mundanghur, and Lieutenant-Colonel Kennedy took the battalion to Suvarndrug, a few miles to the south of the Bankot river and near the sea, to continue recruiting and training.

On March 2nd Lieutenant-Colonel Kennedy took a party of 250 volunteers of the battalion and marched to the attack of the hill forts of Palghur and Ramghur. He arrived before them on the evening of the 3rd, and next morning attacked and took the forts by assault without the loss of a man, though the enemy were prepared to offer a strong resistance. He succeeded in doing this by not advancing up the hill the way the enemy expected and so avoiding their stockades.

From this time on the battalion was engaged in subduing the country between the Ghats and the sea. The majority of the forts were peaceably surrendered, as the Killedars, or commanders of the forts, had orders to this effect from certain chieftains in the Deccan. The country was finally pacified by the capture of Ratnagiri on June 4th, where no effective resistance appears to have been offered.

Not long after the suppression of the Mahrattas and Pindaris, the Burmese annexed Assam and their troops entered British territory and **1823.** actually attacked a party of British sepoys, so that war **3rd Battalion.** became inevitable. The majority of troops in the Bengal army were not liable to serve overseas, and they frequently objected to crossing the *khara pani*, or salt water. Under these circumstances the 3rd Battalion was raised at Dinapore in 1823 by Lieutenant-Colonel Mossem Boyd as the 1st Battalion, 33rd Regiment of Bengal Native Infantry, and only men willing to serve overseas appear to have been enlisted. Castes were mixed throughout the regiment, but there were about three times as many Hindus as Mohammedans, and the great majority of the Hindus were Rajputs. No recruits under five feet six inches were accepted, and the majority of men in the grenadier companies were six feet and upwards.

The war with Burma actually started early in 1824, but events elsewhere prevented the battalion taking part in the expedition to Rangoon. **1824.** In the same year the Malay Peninsula came under **3rd Battalion.** British protection, having been taken over from the Dutch in exchange for the British possessions on the island of Sumatra, and in 1825 the 3rd Battalion was sent to garrison this newly-acquired territory and was stationed at Penang. During the previous May Lieutenant-Colonel Thomas Penson of the 10th Bengal Native Infantry, who had been employed in the Barrack Department, had been appointed commandant of the battalion, but he did not accompany it to Malaya as he went on furlough, and the battalion moved under the command of Lieutenant-Colonel Boyd, who was appointed permanent commandant in May, 1825. Although all the chiefs did not immediately acquiesce in British authority, no steps were taken to enforce it during the two years the battalion stayed in that mountainous

c

country, where the few principalities were little more than patches of cultivation scattered about a vast primeval forest, where the roads were but footpaths cut by the Malays with their knives as they moved along, and the bridges but felled trees.

Throughout the time of the Burmese encroachment on British territory and during the whole period of the resultant war the situation in India was very unsatisfactory. The deposed princes, especially the Peshwa, who spent his time between Bithur and Benares, were intriguing to foment disturbance and shake British power. Agents of the Peshwa circulated false intelligence and represented the Burmese as invincible, so that at last the native merchants of Calcutta could with difficulty be dissuaded from removing their property and withdrawing from Bengal. The whole of India was swarming with military adventurers, the relics of defeated armies or the mercenaries who had served the British in their various wars as irregular cavalry. There were numbers of men ready to join the British against any enemy or to join any power, foreign or native, against the British. On the whole there were more willing to serve against than for the prevailing power.

The disturbed condition of the country affected the 2nd Battalion in Bombay considerably more than it did the 1st Royal Battalion, which was now stationed in the north close to the friendly and powerful Sikh kingdom, united under the firm rule of Ranjit Singh. The 3rd Battalion, moving overseas, was not affected.

1823.

In March, 1823, there was a serious rising of the Nahol Bhils, and a detachment of the 2nd Battalion, consisting of 200 rank and file under the command of Captain Brown, marched against the insurgents and suppressed them. Again, in the autumn of the following year two detachments of 200 rank and file each, under Captains Liardet and Nixon, marched to Champaner, twenty miles north-east of Baroda, and successfully operated against insurgent Bhils. Another detachment of 200, under Captain Adamson, marched in December of the same year against insurgents at Mahi Kanta. This detachment found it necessary to capture the town of Dungarpur, fifty miles due south of Udaipur, by assault. One sepoy was killed and 22 wounded in this action, for which the detachment was complimented by His Excellency the Commander-in-Chief of Bombay.

1823.
2nd Battalion.

In February, 1826, the 2nd Battalion received orders to enter Kathiawar and occupy the town of Jetpur. On the 15th of the following month a small party of 25 rank and file, under the command of Havildar Ramjee Sinday, was attacked by about 500 Kolis under a well-known leader, Gossain, at Thasra, on the bank of the Mahi river. The party performed brilliant service and killed several of the Kolis, including their famous leader, took many prisoners and put the remainder to flight.

1826.

In September of the same year the battalion moved to Sirdarpur, where it joined a brigade commanded by Lieutenant-Colonel Pierce. It then moved to Akalkot and Bhoira against insurgent Khatees. In April, 1827, a detachment of 50 rank and file, under Lieutenant Thornton, was sent against a robber gang which had taken up a strong position in the Asserpod Hills, near Kottywana. Sixteen of the gang were killed and many wounded, and a large quantity of plunder was recovered. Three sepoys were slightly wounded.

1827.
2nd Battalion.

During the year 1827 the 3rd Battalion returned to India from the Malay Peninsula. The country now quietened down after its long series of wars, and all three battalions had a period of rest.

1827.
3rd Battalion.

Chapter III

THE FIRST AFGHAN WAR

Bibliography.—Regimental Records ; *Frontier and Overseas Expeditions from India* (official) ; Stacy's *Narrative of Services in Baluchistan and Afghanistan* ; Kennedy's *Army of the Indus* ; Hypher's *Deeds of Valour of the Indian Soldier.*

For many years the intrigues of the Russians in Persia and Afghanistan caused considerable misgiving both to the British rulers in India and to Ranjit Singh, the Sikh ruler of the Punjab. An inde-
1838. pendent Afghanistan in which British influence predominated was considered a necessity as a barrier to invasion, but Afghanistan was not a united country in 1838, and those British agents who knew most about it were convinced that, were it to be united under the rule of Dost Mahomed, then Amir of Kabul, there was little likelihood of British influence predominating. There was living in British India at that time a claimant to the throne of Afghanistan, by name Shah Shuja, who had already made several fruitless attempts to establish himself at Kabul, and it was believed that if he were once established the designs of Russia would be frustrated and all dangers of an invasion from the north would be at an end.

Accordingly a treaty was signed between the British, Shah Shuja and Ranjit Singh. Under this a force was to be raised, officered by British officers and designated Shah Shuja's army, and this was originally intended to be the chief instrument in establishing Shah Shuja in Afghanistan, entering the country by way of Quetta while the Sikhs moved up the Khyber.

At the same time a strong Bengal force, which included five brigades of infantry, one of which was eventually left behind, was assembled at
1st Battalion. Karnal and moved to Ferozepore, then the frontier, in November, 1838. The 1st Royal Battalion, which was stationed in Cawnpore, moved to Karnal in September and joined the 2nd Brigade of this army. Another force was collected in Bombay, and in this was the 2nd Mooltan Battalion.

The Bengal Division, preceded by Shah Shuja's army, commenced leaving Ferozepore on December 10th and marched in a south-westerly direction along the bank of the Sutlej to Bahawalpur, crossing the Sind frontier near Subzilkote. It then moved along the left bank of the

Indus to the fort of Rohri, just opposite the island of Bhakkar, the temporary cession of which had been demanded from the Amirs of Khairpur. Here some delay occurred, and the 1st Royal Battalion was joined by Lieutenant-Colonel L. R. Stacy, who had been appointed Commandant.

Meanwhile, the Bombay force, including the 2nd Battalion, had arrived by sea at Vikkur, near the mouth of the Indus, where it had **2nd Battalion.** disembarked without any opposition, but was unable to move upstream owing to the absence of transport. The camp was dismal and dreary in the extreme ; the horizon, nowhere a mile distant, was fringed with tamarisk bushes, and the air was always clouded with dust.

Sind was ruled at the time by no less than nine princes, known as Amirs, four of whom lived at Hyderabad, three at Khairpur and two at Mirpur, and these adopted a policy of obstruction, not amounting to hostility. It was not until December 24th that transport was obtained and the 2nd Battalion commenced its march up the right bank of the Indus. Christmas Day was a depressing one for the battalion. During the night two men were attacked by cholera and both died. A short march of ten miles was done, and five more cases occurred. Altogether there were twelve cases, of which eight died, during the period from the 25th to the 29th, after which there were no more. Little was known about cholera at the time, and the outbreak caused a certain amount of alarm, particularly as the victims, three of whom were recruits who had done no night duty at all, had not slept in the same tents, nor had they eaten together or been on duty together.

On January 25th the force reached the town of Jerruck, where it was halted to await the result of negotiations taking place at Hyderabad. **1839.** The Amirs here were taking up a hostile attitude, and very exaggerated rumours were believed regarding their military strength.

The bulk of the Bengal troops, still at Rohri, were ordered to move down the left bank of the Indus to co-operate with the Bombay force against Hyderabad, and their spirits were extremely high as the city was believed to contain a vast quantity of treasure, so that large sums of prize money were anticipated. Eventually, to the great disappointment of the troops, the Amirs consented to a treaty.

The Bengal Division then crossed the Indus at Rohri and moved to Shikarpur, where the 1st Royal Battalion was temporarily transferred **1st Battalion.** to the 4th Brigade. The scarcity of transport made it quite impossible for the whole force to move forward at once, and the lack of training in Shah Shuja's army made it advisable for the regulars of the Bengal Division to take the lead. Accordingly, Shah Shuja's army remained for the time being at Shikarpur, and the

Bengal troops, including the 1st Royal Battalion, commenced a terrible march of 146 miles to Dadur, at the mouth of the Bolan Pass—a march which took sixteen days, during which the troops crossed a practically waterless desert. Both men and animals suffered terrible agonies from thirst, and the shortage of forage caused many camels to die, further aggravating the shortage of transport and consequently the shortage of rations. Rations were reduced to a minimum, and both men and followers of the 1st Royal Battalion were unable to satisfy the cravings of hunger, a condition of affairs which lasted for three and a half months.

After a short halt at Dadur the leading column entered the Bolan Pass on the 16th, the 1st Royal Battalion entering on March 29th. The distance through the pass is sixty miles ; the road was execrable, being the bed of the Bolan river, and was crossed six times by a stream of water from thirty to forty feet broad and from one to three feet deep. The mountains on every side were abrupt, sterile and inhospitable— not a blade of vegetation anywhere, except in the bed of the stream, where there was some coarse grass. There was no organized opposition to the move of the Battalion through the pass, but hovering round the column were numerous Baluchi thieves who cut off stragglers and looted baggage animals with amazing cleverness. Many followers were lost in this way. The march lasted for six days, after which the battalion arrived at Quetta. The soldiers' rations were now only half a seer of atta a day, while followers received a quarter of a seer. Numerous and dangerous attacks were constantly being made by various Baluch tribes on the lines of communication.

Meanwhile, the Bombay force, including the 2nd Battalion under the command of Lieutenant-Colonel Stalker, as well as the Shah's **2nd Battalion.** troops, were advancing and reached Quetta early in April, when the combined forces came under the command of Sir John Keane, who had formerly commanded the Bombay troops only. The 1st Royal Battalion was part of a force which remained at Quetta under General W. Nott for temporary duty on the lines of communication, while the rest of the forces advanced into Afghanistan. The Khojak Pass was surmounted without opposition, though a few straggling parties of thieves were seen and a little desultory firing from the rear-guard was necessary to keep them at a distance ; and the 2nd Battalion arrived at Kandahar on Saturday, May 4th, 1839, where it encamped south of the city.

The 2nd Battalion, at Kandahar, was no better off than the 1st Royal Battalion at Quetta. Although the surroundings were pleasant to the eye, the city itself was disappointing. It was necessary to remain there until the ripening of the crops, as rations were very scarce. The life was extremely monotonous as it was quite unsafe to venture out of sight of the camp unless in armed parties prepared for action.

Little happened until the end of June. The 2nd Battalion remained healthy, although most of the troops at Kandahar suffered severely from fever and dysentery.

While at Kandahar the British officers of the 2nd Battalion took part in an unusual ceremony. Shah Shuja was now recognized by the British as the ruler of Afghanistan, and officers were invited to be introduced at "Court" and present "Nazaranas," the latter being provided by Government at the rate of five gold mohurs each for field officers and two for captains and subalterns, a gold mohur being at the time the equivalent of about thirty shillings. Although Shah Shuja was by no means popular with the British officers and was not regarded with very much respect, they attended partly through curiosity and partly through a sense of duty as their presence seemed to be expected. The ceremony was very simple. The Shah was seated in a neglected courtyard which had once been a garden, surrounded by ruined buildings. Very few Afghans were present, and these were chiefly his domestic servants. The officers moved in front of him in slow succession, dropping their "Nazaranas" as they passed, the Shah looking on with an abundance of satisfaction.

On June 27th the 2nd Battalion marched with the rest of the force towards Kabul. There was still no organized opposition, though not a day passed without attempts being made to carry off the camels while they were grazing, and on July 21st Ghazni was reached. The fort of Ghazni was extremely strong, and no Afghan believed that it was possible for the British to capture it. Such artillery as accompanied the force was powerless against the strong walls. There were a number of hostile Afghans in the surrounding villages and gardens, but these were soon dislodged as they had no intention of resisting seriously. The Amir Dost Mahomed believed that the British would pass the fort without attempting its capture, and that the main battle would be fought nearer to Kabul; it was then his intention that the garrison of Ghazni should emerge and attack the British army in rear.

The whole of the 22nd was spent in reconnaissance, and it was decided that it was possible to blow in the gate on the Kabul road. Under cover of darkness, before dawn on the 23rd, powder bags were laid at the gate and this was blown in. An assaulting column, composed entirely of British troops, rushed through the aperture ; severe hand-to-hand fighting followed, but the fort was quickly captured. During this action the 2nd Battalion was holding a position on the Kabul road, ready either to act as a support to the assaulting column or to resist the advance of Afghan reinforcements which were known to be approaching from Kabul.

The fall of Ghazni was decisive in its effect. The Amir's following commenced deserting and there was no further opposition to the advance of the British.   The 2nd Battalion arrived at Kabul on August 6th, when the Amir Dost Mahomed fled to Bokhara and Shah Shuja assumed the government.   The war was now regarded as over. Lieutenant-Colonel Stalker and Major Hancock, of the 2nd Battalion, both received the Order of the Durani Empire, while all ranks received permission to wear the medal issued by Shah Shuja to commemorate the capture of Ghazni, as well as the British War Medal.   The battalion left Kabul on September 18th, marched back through Ghazni, arrived at Quetta on October 31st, and returned to India.

Meanwhile, the 1st Royal Battalion had moved from Quetta on July 12th as part of a small force, the whole being under the command **1st Battalion.** of Lieutenant-Colonel Stacy, escorting treasure and stores for the army at Kandahar.   At the Khojak Pass the enemy had assembled in great force and had possession of a hill which commanded the road.   From here they were dislodged and a piquet established.   During the night, which was dark, an attack was made upon this piquet which continued until nearly dawn, when the main column again advanced and crossed the pass, reaching Chaman after midnight.   During this move there were no casualties beyond a few men slightly wounded and several camels, laden with grain, which dropped exhausted during the day.   The battalion arrived at Kandahar on August 1st, some eleven months after it had left its cantonment at Cawnpore.

Although Shah Shuja was now established on the throne at Kabul, it was not considered possible to withdraw all the British troops until he was more firmly established, and the 1st Royal Battalion remained as part of the garrison of Kandahar.   The question of housing the troops was a difficult one.   At first the battalion was encamped outside the town, but with the approach of winter it moved into the town on October 10th, 1839.

During the year 1840 the Ghilzais rose in revolt against Shah Shuja and cut the communications between Kabul and Kandahar.   The **1840.** headquarters and right wing of the 1st Royal Battalion **1st Battalion.** marched into their country early in June to assist in suppressing the disturbances, but were not engaged in any action and returned to Kandahar late in the following month.

Meanwhile, serious events had been occurring in Baluchistan, where a rebellion had occurred at Khelat.   A force, which had advanced from Quetta after defeating the rebels, had withdrawn towards Sind, leaving a political officer at Khelat who made himself very unpopular with the Brahui chiefs.   Unrest again arose and the rebels attempted to capture Quetta.   On August 14th the 1st Royal Battalion marched from Kandahar with a battery of Shah Shuja's horse artillery to assist in the defence of Quetta, but the rebels had been beaten off before the arrival of the battalion. After failing to capture Quetta the rebels had moved to Khelat and, after besieging that town for a few days, succeeded in capturing it, allowing the Khan to depart for Sind and nominating their own young leader in his place. The 1st Royal Battalion was now joined by another Bengal battalion with two guns; the whole, under the command of General W. Nott, moved to Khelat and arrived there on November 3rd, but found the place deserted.

While these events were occurring, on October 28th the rebels made a vigorous attack on the post of Dadur, the repulse of which was due mainly to a splendid charge of 120 of Skinner's Horse, led by Lieutenant A. F. Macpherson of the 1st Royal Battalion, who penetrated right through the masses of the enemy and returned victorious. Lieutenant Macpherson, who was promoted Brevet Captain, was wounded in this charge. The battalion then returned to its old quarters in Kandahar. The return march over the Khojak was very fatiguing. The weather was miserably cold with drifts of snow, and the two guns which accompanied the battalion, as well as all the wagons, had to be hauled along by drag-ropes; the tackle was rotten, but, by dint of hard and constant labour, the journey was accomplished without a halt.

In December, Lieutenant-Colonel Stacy, Commandant of the battalion, was appointed specially to go to Khelat to open up negotiations with the young Khan and endeavour to induce him to disband his army. Colonel Stacy immediately went to the Brahui chiefs, accompanied by a few attendants, but without escort of any kind. Thus from the start he gained their confidence, and the chiefs made themselves responsible for his safety. His courteous treatment of the Khan and his chiefs gained for him a great personal influence over them, and to this was largely due the complete success of his mission.

The Ghilzais continued hostile throughout the year 1841, and the 1st Royal Battalion, together with another battalion and part of the 5th Light Cavalry and some irregular horse, under Colonel Chambers, moved against them early in August. The enemy were met on the 5th and were immediately charged by the cavalry, who scattered them in disastrous flight. After this action the battalion returned to Kandahar in September, and on November 4th, with two other battalions, commenced to march to India as the country appeared tranquil and it was desired to reduce the army of occupation. It had only moved one day's march when it was halted and ordered back, as information had just arrived that a party of 130 men marching from Kandahar to Kabul had been attacked near Ghazni and annihilated.

1841.

Soon after this information was received of the outbreak which had occurred at Kabul on the morning of November 2nd, and reports started coming in which showed that the insurrection was spreading.

The 1st Royal Battalion, together with the other two battalions which had started their movement towards India and a troop of Horse Artillery, were then ordered to Kabul, the whole force being under the command of Colonel Maclaren.   When this detachment had moved half-way to Ghazni it encountered very severe weather, and Colonel Maclaren, who was not yet in a position to realize the seriousness of the situation in the capital and who knew that General Nott had never wished him to leave Kandahar, decided to return.   The battalion then marched back, dropping three companies under Captain Webster and Lieutenant Trotter at Kelat-i-Ghilzai to reinforce the garrison there.

On January 10th, 1842, a party of 40 men of the 1st Royal Battalion, under the command of Subedar Basti Singh, which was sent out of the town of Kandahar with all the battalion camels to secure forage, was attacked by a body of Durani horse, some three hundred in number, and about one hundred foot.   The party distinguished itself greatly by driving off the enemy and bringing all its camels back safely.   Subedar Basti Singh received the Order of Merit for his conduct on this occasion.

1842.
1st Battalion.

Meanwhile, the British army had withdrawn from Kabul and had been annihilated (except for one individual, Doctor Brydon) on its march to Jalalabad, and the fort of Ghazni had also fallen to the Afghans, who had a number of British prisoners in their hands.   Kelat-i-Ghilzai, the only British garrison between Ghazni and Kandahar, was still holding out in the presence of large numbers of the enemy, and an Afghan army was in the neighbourhood of Kandahar.

On March 7th the 1st Royal Battalion, less its three companies at Kelat-i-Ghilzai, formed part of a column which moved out of Kandahar under the personal command of Major-General Nott.   The enemy were met at Kunji Kuk, where they put up slight resistance ; they then crossed the Tarnak river, and on the 8th again put up a weak resistance, at Pangwaie.   On the 9th at Shilu Khan they seemed inclined to make a stand and opened fire from a range of hills on which their infantry were posted ; but this was in reality a stratagem to cover a serious attack upon the greatly reduced garrison of Kandahar.   This attack, fortunately, failed and the whole column re-entered the town on March 12th without having taken part in any serious engagement.

During this period the three companies of the battalion at Kelat-i-Ghilzai were bravely holding out.   This fortress stands upon a barren eminence some eighty miles from Kandahar, and is one of the most dreary and exposed spots in Afghanistan.   The garrison consisted of the Shah's 3rd Infantry Regiment (later the 2nd Kelat-i-Ghilzai Battalion Bombay Pioneers), 40 European artillerymen, some sappers and miners, and the 250 men of the 1st Royal Battalion, the whole commanded by Captain Craigie of the Shah's service.   For months the cold was a worse foe than the enemy. The barracks were unfinished and had neither doors nor windows, and fuel was scarce. During the winter the enemy were inactive, but with the spring came the renewal of hostilities. The garrison employed themselves in strengthening the defences while the enemy, ever growing more numerous, drew the cordon closer. By degrees they made trenches, to the fire from which the defenders could not give an effective reply.

It was not until May 19th that a force started from Kandahar to relieve the garrison. The enemy, hearing of its coming, decided to make a desperate assault upon the place. They therefore prepared ladders and practised escalading. In the early morning of May 21st they advanced in two columns of 2,000 each. Placing their ladders, they gallantly mounted to the assault. Three times they were repulsed ; the heavy showers of shot and grape did not, however, turn them from their purpose, and they advanced again and again to be bayoneted on the walls. The struggle had lasted upwards of an hour before the enemy abandoned the assault with a loss of nearly five hundred, while there were no casualties among the garrison. During this attack Sepoy Bhowani Sing displayed distinguished gallantry. The enemy were within the ditch constructed round the neck of the fort and pressed so hard that the artillery were unable to fire, and they had almost effected an entrance. Bhowani Sing, on seeing this, leaped over the sandbags, which had previously been thrown up for the protection of the gunners, and bayoneted unaided five or six of the enemy in the presence of the European artillerymen, cleared the gun and enabled it to open fire with great effect. The European artillerymen attributed their ability to work the gun throughout the attack to the extraordinary gallantry of Bhowani Sing, who was rewarded with the Order of Merit. Kelat-i-Ghilzai was then relieved and the detachment returned to Kandahar and rejoined the battalion. In an official notification regarding the defence of the post the Governor-General wrote : " The late Shah Shuja's 3rd Regiment of Infantry and the detachment of the Bengal 43rd Regiment of Native Infantry displayed that decided superiority over their enemies which has been uniformly manifested by the several corps comprising Major-General Nott's force."

Before this detachment had rejoined, the 1st Royal Battalion was again in action. On May 12th it had been sent out across the Arghandab river with two other battalions to protect the crops and property of the people generally from enemy who were gathering in the neighbourhood, but as these immediately withdrew the force returned to Kandahar on the 17th. Ten days later parties of the enemy again gathered in the neighbourhood, and on the 26th the battalion was sent to join a small force encamped outside the town. On the morning of the 29th the battalion, with another Bengal battalion, two guns and a squadron of cavalry, was ordered to occupy the old cantonment, which at the time was not held. The whole force was commanded by Lieutenant-Colonel Stacy and the battalion by Major Nash. As, in addition to the three companies at Kelat-i-Ghilzai, there were two complete companies on grazing guard duty and others occupied in various duties outside the city, the battalion went into action only 322 strong, and the other battalion was not much stronger. As soon as they had cleared the house and gardens nearly facing the northern gate of Kandahar, the enemy were seen in strong parties occupying the country extending between two hills close to the cantonment and the Babawali Pass. As the force approached the open country near the cantonment the enemy were observed to be in great strength ; they were assembling on the plain between the main watercourse and the Babawali, with the Babawali and Kotal-i-Moolieh Passes in their rear and the main road on their right. The force was halted while information was sent back to Kandahar, and during this halt the 1st Royal Battalion had three or four men wounded by long-range fire from some men who had got behind the wall of an old house, but these were quickly dislodged.

Considerable reinforcements then arrived and General Nott himself took over command. The enemy were in considerable strength on the hills on the left, and the light companies of the two battalions, under the command of Brevet Captain Macpherson of the 1st Royal Battalion, were ordered to drive the enemy off these hills, supported by the remainder of the 1st Royal Battalion. These companies were soon formed up, and on the word " Forward ! " were off at the double with a cheer that prognosticated success. Major Nash, with the remainder of the battalion, moved on, inclining to the left towards a road at the foot of the hill beyond the cantonment. No sooner had the light companies driven the enemy down the hill than the cavalry was upon them. Many of the enemy, finding it impossible to escape, put up a strong resistance, but the light companies, with Major Nash in support, soon came up and scattered the enemy in every direction. After this there was a certain amount of desultory fighting, but no serious opposition was encountered. During the battle the battalion lost 19 men and 1 follower. Two thermometers had, according to Colonel Stacy, shown the temperature as 150° F. at eleven o'clock in the morning. In a letter written the following day to General Pollock, General Nott wrote : " Our troops carried the enemy's position in gallant style. These 8,000 Afghans, led on by Prince Suftur and many chiefs, would not stand our 1,200 men for one hour, and yet the cry of the press is that our sepoys cannot cope with the Afghans. I would at any time lead 1,000 Bengal sepoys against 5,000 Afghans. My beautiful regiments are in high health and spirits."

The following day the battalion again went out as part of a brigade commanded by Lieutenant-Colonel Stacy, but the enemy were disinclined for more fighting ; and Prince Sufdar Jung, referred to by General Nott as Prince Suftur, surrendered on June 19th without any further action being fought.

By this time Shah Shuja, whom the British had established on the throne at Kabul and to back up whose authority was the whole reason for the army of occupation, was dead, having been assassinated on April 4th, and orders came for the evacuation of Afghanistan. Part of the Kandahar force returned to India via Quetta and Sukkur, but General Nott decided himself to withdraw via Kabul and the Khyber Pass, and the 1st Royal Battalion was part of the army which accompanied him. The object of this movement was to co-operate with a force moving up the Khyber route to Kabul to avenge the massacre of the original Kabul army and to rescue the prisoners in Afghan hands.

On August 7th the British force quietly evacuated Kandahar without any demonstration of ill-will on the part of the inhabitants, Sufdar Jung being left in possession. On the 9th the 1st Royal Battalion commenced its march with the rest of the force towards Kabul. The march as far as Mukkur, one hundred and sixty miles from Kandahar, was uneventful and was completed by August 27th. During the following two days the cavalry were in action, and on the 30th, when the force arrived at Ghoyen, the enemy were found to be in possession of a fort near the camping ground, which General Nott determined to attack. The fire of the artillery on the fort was not immediately effective, and the main body of the enemy, seeing this from the hills, made a counter-attack ; an action was fought in which the enemy were completely defeated and the tribes dispersed to their homes. The 1st Royal Battalion, though present at this action, took no prominent part in it.

After the battle of Ghoyen the comfort of the Battalion was considerably added to by large numbers of Hazaras, who belong to the Shiah sect of Mohammedans. These attached themselves to the army and burnt and destroyed everything as it moved along in order to revenge themselves for the tyranny and oppression which they had suffered from the Afghans of the Sunni sect. These Hazaras brought bullocks, sheep, goats and fowls, which they carried off from the enemy's deserted forts and villages, to the camp and sold them at very low prices.

The force encamped near Ghazni on September 4th, and on the 5th moved off early and in silence. As it approached the great fortress the road became extremely bad and was intersected with ravines and deep watercourses. All the light companies, including that of the 1st Royal Battalion, moved together at the head of the column, a formation which was thereafter usually adopted. As Ghazni was approached numerous enemy were seen, who seemed prepared to overwhelm the comparatively small force advancing against them, but they fled whenever our troops approached. At one point only was a considerable resistance encountered from a party of matchlock-men behind a long line of old wall; these did considerable execution until driven from their post at the point of the bayonet by the light companies. The hills also swarmed with men, but there seemed to be no order amongst them; they appeared to act independently of each other and were in constant movement.

The column passed to the east of Ghazni and then turned to the left back to the road. A party of enemy were now seen on the left at a turn in the road; a company of the 1st Royal Battalion, under Captain Webster, was sent against them and they were soon driven back. Captain Webster pushed forward a party of his men and took possession of an old water-course, from which he completely commanded any advance in this direction. This party remained in position until picked up by the rear-guard.

The light companies leading the advance were now driving the enemy before them, and these ascended the hills north of the city, followed by the light companies, with the remainder of the troops in support. The company of the 1st Royal Battalion went up in splendid style, with a loss of four men wounded; the enemy were given no time to rally and every high point was gained. The heights were piqueted by other units, and the 1st Royal Battalion went into camp. This was found to be within range of the famous Ghazni gun "Zabbar Jang,"* and after fourteen shots had fallen into it, the second of which fell into the lines of the 1st Royal Battalion, the camp was moved to the village of Roza, two miles off. The only casualties which resulted from the fourteen shots which fell into the crowded camp were a camel and a bullock.

The defeat of the enemy on the heights caused those in the fort and town to lose heart, and during the night they quietly took to the hills; when the fort was occupied next day it was found to contain only a few Hindus and sepoys who had been prisoners in the hands of the Afghans. The city was found to be a mass of ruins, and the day was spent in destroying what was left. The guns were burst and the town and citadel fired; throughout the night the flames lit up the sky. The gates from the tomb of Sultan Mahmud, said to be those of the temple of Somnath, taken from there by Mahmud of Ghazni in A.D. 1024 and regarded as sacred, were removed and brought back to India.

The march to Kabul was then continued in the face of a certain amount of opposition. The 1st Royal Battalion was next in action

* When this gun fell into the hands of the British it was destroyed, and two cigarette lighters made out of its metal are now in possession of the officers of the 1st Royal Battalion.

at Shaikabad on the evening of September 13th, when it was moved out of camp hurriedly to drive the enemy off a hill dangerously close. It was dark by the time the battalion reached the foot of the hill, but the enemy fled and took up a position on a hill farther back. In silence the battalion advanced to the next range, which was particularly steep ; the summit was gained, but the enemy had again retreated. The battalion then returned to camp, which it reached at about 9 p.m.

The following day the force advanced to Bani Badam, being preceded as usual by the light companies. Throughout the day the rear-guard was harassed, but it was not until the camping ground was nearly reached that any opposition was made to the advance. The firing from the hills then became incessant, and once again the eight gallant light companies stormed the heights. They succeeded, but there was one high peak isolated from the rest which remained in the possession of the enemy. Unfortunately, a cavalry wagon upset under this hill, and the enemy kept up a constant dropping fire upon the party employed in setting it to rights ; and when they saw the troops moving into camp they became bold and came some way down the hill. The grenadier company of the 1st Royal Battalion was sent out and drove them up again.

On September 15th the force advanced from Bani Badam to Maidan, and on this day the 1st Royal Battalion (less its light company, which was, as usual, preceding the column) with two guns and a detachment of cavalry formed the rear-guard, the whole being commanded by Major Nash, Lieutenant-Colonel Stacy having been placed in command of the brigade by General Nott. The enemy were on the alert on all sides ; their greatest strength was on the right in advance of the camp, and they were also strong on the hills to the rear of the camp ; but Major Nash placed a company, under Lieutenant Holroyd, in a nullah which skirted the road so that they could not come down.

Long before the bulk of the baggage had left camp, the enemy commenced their attack by some men attempting to gain a position on the left rear, and it became necessary to drive them back. Lieutenant Trotter with a company of the battalion succeeded in doing this, but not without sustaining some casualties. The strong party of the enemy on the right front then left their hill and collected on the plain, the white standard of a well-known leader being present and moving rapidly in every direction. These were caused to fall back by a few shots from the guns.

As soon as the last of the baggage had left camp the two flanking companies were called in and the rear-guard moved off, the cavalry leading, followed by the 1st Royal Battalion and then the guns, with three companies on the right under Captain Webster and two on the left under Lieutenants Trotter and Holroyd, and one company in rear of the guns. About a quarter of a mile from the old camp the enemy made their first attack on both flanks. This was carried out with great bravery, and they came steadily on until they were within close range of the muskets. At this time Lieutenants Trotter and Holroyd charged the enemy on their flank, who turned and fled ; the two companies, which had suffered considerably, Lieutenant Holroyd being wounded and a subedar killed, then opened fire and kept this up as long as the enemy were within range. The companies on the right flank also not only held their own, but drove back their assailants with much loss.

Baffled in this attempt, the enemy then prepared for a charge upon the column. As soon as they were formed up the guns were got ready, screened by the rear company. When the enemy were considered within the right distance, the company filed right and left and the guns opened, doing dreadful havoc among the enemy. Unfortunately, however, the discharge of the second shot broke the axle of the gun carriage. Without any stir the sound gun was advanced a few paces and a company of the battalion was placed in front of the broken one to conceal the misfortune as long as possible from the enemy. This did not give a long respite, and it soon became evident that the enemy suspected something was wrong as they commenced preparations for a renewed attack.

Captain Matthews of the 1st Royal Battalion now volunteered to carry a message to General Nott. He was ordered to report that the enemy were strong and bold ; that it was utterly impossible to stop the baggage ; that a gun had broken down and not a man could be spared ; and that Major Nash, therefore, begged that the broken gun might be replaced and some reinforcement sent to protect the baggage.

Meanwhile the disabled gun was taken off its carriage and slung under a wagon, the wheels and carriage were packed on camels, and in two hours all moved on, followed by parties of jezailchis on three sides, who occasionally sent in a long shot.

Upon the report of Captain Matthews, reinforcements were sent which met and joined the main body of the rear-guard. When the rear-guard was advancing up the hill which overlooks the beautiful valley of Maidan, the enemy's force united and attempted to obstruct the ascent, but were driven off by a few shots from the guns and the rear-guard was not again molested. During the fighting on this day one subedar was killed and Lieutenant Holroyd, one havildar and fifteen sepoys wounded. Great credit was given to Major Nash and the battalion for this day's work. No special order was issued, but General Nott said he would take care to bring it to the favourable notice of Government.

The force arrived at Kabul on the 19th and found the place already in possession of the British, as General Pollock had arrived from the Khyber. The battalion remained at Kabul until September 25th, 1842, and during this period the British prisoners succeeded in getting away from their captors and reaching the British camp.

A force of the enemy was now collecting in Kohistan, the mountainous country north of Kabul which had supplied the bulk of the insurgents, and the 1st Royal Battalion formed part of a column which advanced under General McCaskill to break up this force and to punish that part of the country. A rapid march was made and the enemy was surprised at the town of Istalif. This town is built in terraces on the two ridges of the spurs of the Hindu Kush range which bound the Kohistan valley on the west. The town was attacked early on September 29th, and the 1st Royal Battalion, together with two other battalions, first attacked the village of Emillah. The light companies of the three battalions, that of the 1st Royal Battalion commanded by Captain Macpherson and Lieutenant Trotter being in the centre, led the advance at the double, supported by two other companies of each battalion. The remaining part of the column had to move considerably to the left as the ground straight ahead was not passable for the guns ; also there was a very strong body of hostile cavalry about a quarter of a mile to the flank. The village was taken without a check, but a delay of about half an hour occurred during which it was destroyed. This delay allowed time for a man to carry information of its capture to the town of Istalif, which resulted in a curious and picturesque scene being witnessed by the battalion when it continued to advance. The footpath leading from the back of Istalif winding over the range of hills towards Turkistan was thronged with women wending their way along the zig-zag tracks which ran up the scarped sides of the hill, their snow-white dresses, in which they were shrouded from head to foot, giving them the appearance of a vast cavalcade of nuns.

The guns, which could not advance any farther, were now ordered to operate against the body of cavalry on the left flank, and two companies of the 1st Royal Battalion were sent with them as escort. They were entirely successful in dispersing the enemy, and the two companies remained with them while the rest of the column advanced against Istalif. Once again the light companies led, and by the time the town was reached firing had almost ceased. The company of the 1st Royal Battalion had a race with that of a British battalion belonging to another brigade to charge a gun which was still in action, and so equal was the race that both battalions claimed the credit of its capture. After the action the 1st Royal Battalion was placed on a hill which commanded the road between the town and camp for the night ; the men had had nothing to eat all day (except for the excellent fruit which

D

was growing there in abundance) until nine o'clock at night, and as they had no greatcoats the night was an uncomfortable one. Considerable booty was taken, and the town was set on fire the following day and continued burning the whole of the next night.

The force was now able to advance into the hills without any further opposition ; several fortified places were destroyed and on October 7th the battalion was back in Kabul, having accomplished its object.

Four days later the battalion commenced its return march to India. The Khurd Kabul Pass was turned and so passed without molestation. On October 15th the battalion commenced its march from Khurd Kabul over the Haft Kotal Pass to Tazin, which was fourteen miles of most difficult ground. The rear-guard made very slow progress, being constantly attacked, and it was twilight when the 1st Royal Battalion was ordered to send back one hundred men to reinforce it. Soon after these arrived the rear-guard was again attacked in great strength from both flanks as well as from the rear. The attack was driven off with difficulty, but many of the camel drivers deserted their camels ; other camels had been wounded, and those carrying the ammunition of the rear-guard managed to get away. A halt became necessary in order to ensure the safety of the baggage, and it was essential to send forward to camp for ammunition as well as for more stretchers to carry in the many wounded. Lieutenant Holroyd, who had recovered from his wound received at Bani Badam, volunteered to carry a message to General Nott, and was instructed by the rear-guard commander simply to give a statement of their present position, their total ignorance of the distance they still had to cover or the nature of the ground, and to request that ammunition and stretchers might be sent immediately. Lieutenant Holroyd had to take his message through hostile and unguarded country in the dark, but reached General Nott in safety, who immediately sent strong reinforcements. Before these arrived firing had ceased, and by ten o'clock the rear-guard had moved into camp without further molestation.

On the 19th the battalion moved through the Jagdallak Pass to Soorkhab, and on this day again was involved in serious action. The 2nd Brigade, commanded by Lieutenant-Colonel Stacy, was delayed in its march from camp, and when it arrived at the pass it was found that none of the heights were piqueted, the 1st Brigade having, through some error, withdrawn its piquets. The 1st Royal Battalion, less its light company, was therefore ordered to crown the heights, but to move on ahead of the rear-guard, which was responsible for its own protection. When the battalion was thus used up in small detachments, an important hill came in sight on which the brigade commander considered it essential to leave a strong piquet. This was furnished by another battalion, but the officer commanding it was badly wounded, and Captain Matthews volunteered to take his place. For about two hours the enemy contented themselves with taking long shots at this piquet, and then several men came running towards it calling out that the Afghans were carrying off the gun bullocks. Finding that this was not far from his post, Captain Matthews, having given orders to his subedar to hold the hill, headed a party of thirty men and moved off at the double in the direction pointed out to him. He had gone along the road about a quarter of a mile when he was shown a pathway to the right along which it was stated the Afghans had driven some of the cattle. Entering this with the few men who had been able to keep up with him, he soon came upon four of the enemy driving four of the bullocks. Still pushing on, although only a havildar, two sepoys and two Europeans were still with him, he passed over about a quarter of a mile of undulating country covered with stunted shrubs to a long, narrow valley, where nine more bullocks and two camels were recovered under a smart fire from parties hidden amongst the bushes and rocks on the hills. Captain Matthews was shot through the leg, the ball grazing the bone. Fortunately two cavalry sowars had now come up, and Captain Matthews was put upon one of their horses, while the cattle were driven back.

The battalion reached Gandamak on October 20th and encamped at Jalalabad on the 25th, where it remained until the 29th, during which time the fortifications were destroyed. On November 3rd it arrived at Landi Khana at the entrance to the Khyber Pass without opposition. The following day the brigade in which was the 1st Royal Battalion climbed the pass and moved to Ali Masjid, a considerable distance in rear of the other brigade of General Nott's column, and had a great deal of opposition. There was a field force order that the famous sandal-wood gates of Somnath should always have a complete battalion as their escort, and on this march the duty fell to the 1st Royal Battalion, less its light company, which was preceding the column, and a party with the quartermaster accompanying the baggage. The climb from Landi Khana to Landi Kotal at the top of the pass was an extremely trying one, as the men had to give constant assistance to the tired bullocks dragging the gates, and the road was execrable, but the necessary assistance was always readily and good-humouredly given. At Landi Kotal an open valley begins which extends to the mouth of the long defile ending at Ali Masjid, but near the beginning of this valley, on the left of the road, the hills were crowded with enemy, and the result was that all troops detailed for piqueting had been used up before the defile was reached. Consequently it was found necessary to send out two companies from the battalion to piquet the heights, one on a conical hill near the entrance to the defile and the other about a mile beyond this on a hill which commanded a view of the road on both sides.* Although the whole of the available troops had been used up in piqueting the road along the valley, these proved insufficient, and several camels with their loads were carried off here as well as some men killed. Captain Webster of the 1st Royal Battalion lost the whole of his kit.

During the night the 1st Royal Battalion furnished some of the piquets round the camp at Ali Masjid, and at dawn next morning a few of the men left their post to pick up dry sticks to make a fire. They were a considerable distance from their guard when they were fired on by a small party of Afghans who had been concealed behind rocks at the foot of the hill. The sepoys, of course, retreated on their post and the jemadar commanding the guard, not content with simply firing on the enemy, advanced to meet the sepoys, checked the Afghans and returned to his post.

The rear-guard this day was composed of a British battalion, but its commander, Major Browne, asked Colonel Stacy for assistance, with the result that Major Nash was ordered to place himself and the battalion under Major Browne's orders. At about noon the historic fort of Ali Masjid was blown up and the withdrawal of the rear-guard commenced ; considerable fighting took place, in which the 1st Royal Battalion had two men wounded, but no baggage was lost and the battalion reached Jamrud on the Punjab side of the pass, at about four in the afternoon. The battalion continued its march through Peshawar to Ferozepore, then the frontier of British India, where it arrived on December 23rd, 1842, and took part in a grand review of the troops held by Lord Ellenborough, the Governor-General. It finally arrived at the cantonment of Fatehgarh on February 24th, 1843, nearly four and a half years after it had left Cawnpore. On October 4th, 1842, it had been created a light infantry unit in perpetual commemoration of its distinguished services during the campaign. Lieutenant-Colonel Stacy was created a Companion of the Order of the Bath.

---

* Probably Kata Kushtia.

Chapter IV

ARAKAN, THE GWALIOR CAMPAIGN, THE SIKH WARS AND BURMA

Bibliography.—Regimental Records ; *Frontier and Overseas Expeditions from India* (official) ; Rait's *The Life and Campaigns of Hugh, 1st Viscount Gough* ; Lee-Warner's *Life of the Marquis of Dalhousie* ; Bosworth Smith's *Life of Lord Lawrence* ; Anderson's *Ubique* ; L. J. Trotter's *History of the British Empire in India, 1844-62* ; Hypher's *Deeds of Valour of the Indian Soldier.*

Lying along the north-west coast of Burma and separated from Burma proper by a range of mountains difficult for regular troops to cross, is a narrow strip of territory known as Arakan. It was from here that, in the year 1823, a Burmese force had invaded the countries between Burma and Bengal, conquered Assam and Manipur, threatened Cachar and finally, invading British territory, captured a party of British sepoys and so precipitated the First Burmese War. In the treaties following this war the country of Arakan had been annexed in order to prevent a repetition of the events which had led almost to a panic in the city of Calcutta itself* but a country once annexed has to be garrisoned, and Arakan had the reputation of being extremely unhealthy. The fact that the country had been annexed in order to ensure the safety of the province of Bengal made the measures for its security the responsibility of the Bengal Government, and there were few Bengal regiments which were liable for service overseas, so that their turn came round quickly. In the year 1839, when both the 1st Royal and 2nd Battalions were on active service in Afghanistan, the 3rd Battalion, which had been in peace stations in India for twelve years, was ordered to garrison Arakan, where it remained until 1841.

(margin: 1839. 3rd Battalion.)

The disasters which had occurred in Afghanistan were not without their effect in India, and the great review of the troops which had been held by Lord Ellenborough at Ferozepore† was held chiefly to impress the princes of India with the power of the British army, which they had begun to doubt. The great Ranjit Singh, ruler of the Sikhs, had died early during the war, and the Punjab could no longer be regarded as a strong friendly state ; in fact, the Sikhs were showing definite signs

* See pp. 17-18. † See opposite.

of hostility to the British, which must sooner or later have broken out in open war.

During the Mahratta campaigns of 1817-18 all the chief Mahratta states had been reduced with the exception of Gwalior, which had been prevented from taking part in the war by the skilful movements of the British troops,* and the army of this state now consisted of some 20,000 infantry, 15,000 cavalry and 250 guns. In the year 1843 the rajah died, leaving a widow only twelve years of age, and she, following the custom of her race, adopted a boy nearly related to her husband and four years younger than herself, who then became rajah. The result was a long series of intrigues in which the army actually obtained the chief power and a considerable amount of bloodshed occurred in Gwalior, where a decided anti-British feeling predominated.

The existence of this large army within striking distance of Agra at a time when the outbreak of war with the Sikhs was more than a possibility involved the great danger of a combination of Sikh and Mahratta, and it became essential to the British that the army of Gwalior should be reduced to a size more compatible with the requirements of the state and its revenues. It was believed that many of the Gwalior chiefs would welcome a reduction in its size, but were powerless to carry it out without active aid from the British or, at any rate, the support of a British force within their territory. Accordingly an army was assembled under Sir Hugh Gough in two parties, one at Agra and the other in the Bundelkhand. As no war had been declared and it was hoped that all conflict would be avoided, this army was not called a field force, but an "army of exercise," and ladies were present with it. The 1st Royal Battalion marched from Fatehgarh to join the army of exercise at Agra on November 13th, 1843, where it joined a brigade of which Colonel Stacy took command as brigadier, the battalion being commanded by Major Nash.

1843.
1st Battalion.

On Christmas Day it became known that the reduction of the Gwalior army would not be carried out peacefully and that a large force had marched out to Dhunela, a small town about eleven miles from Gwalior. The following day this again advanced and took up a strong position at Chonda, on the River Asun. Meanwhile, the whole of the army at Agra had advanced on Christmas Day to Hingonah, on the River Kohari, only six miles from Chonda, the country in both places being very rough and intersected by deep ravines.

On the morning of December 29th the force advanced in three columns, the 1st Royal Battalion being in the left column, which moved half an hour before daybreak. The ground passed over at first was extremely difficult, but all three columns were well led, and

---

* See p. 10.

when they arrived about a mile in front of the village of Maharajpore, about a mile and a half nearer than Chonda, they were halted. Here the soil was richly cultivated, in places covered with standing corn, in others the corn had been cut and gathered into stacks, and in some places the crop had been removed and the ground was soft with recent ploughing.

It had been expected that Maharajpore would be occupied by an outpost sent forward from the strong position among the ravines at Chonda, but it was now found that the village was held by a large part of the whole hostile force, and this caused a complete change of plans. Originally the 1st Royal Battalion was to have been part of a force carrying out a frontal attack on the position at Chonda, but now that so large a portion of the hostile army had advanced into the open plain it was intended to destroy this and so divert the fight as far as possible from Chonda. In the shuffle round of forces necessitated by this change of plan the division in which was the 1st Royal Battalion came into support.

Very severe fighting ensued, during which the battalion was not at first engaged. A portion of the enemy escaped and were pursued to Chonda, where the 1st Royal Battalion came into action ; but the enemy was already defeated and made no real attempt to defend the strong position afforded by the ravines. During the advance a number of men were killed by shots from enemy soldiers concealed by the stacks of corn, so that it became necessary to leave no stack in the rear without putting a bayonet in first. The battalion lost three non-commissioned officers and three sepoys killed during the action, and there is no record of the wounded.

On the day on which the battle of Maharajpore was fought the force which had advanced from Bundelkhand also won a complete victory at Punniar, and the double victory put an end to all resistance, so that the whole campaign only lasted forty-eight hours.

After the action at Maharajpore the battalion remained at Gwalior for some little time, and returned to Fatehgarh on March 17th, 1844.

1844. A monument, bearing the names of all who were killed both at Maharajpore and Punniar, was made out of the captured ordnance and erected outside the Water Gate of the fort at Calcutta.* Major Nash was promoted Brevet Lieutenant-Colonel for his services in the campaign.

The long-expected Sikh War broke out with an invasion of British India in the latter half of 1845, and by the end of that year the Sikhs had been driven back across the Sutlej, though their main army was far from beaten. The main British army was at

1845.

---

* The names of the men of the 1st Royal Battalion on this memorial are Naik Maun Singh, Naik Ram Singh, Naik Dookchore Misser, Sepoy Sunker Dooby, Sepoy Suroop Singh, Sepoy Mir Bakar Ally.

Ferozepore and Arufka, some twenty miles to the east, close to the river, while the principal Sikh army was concentrated in a large entrenched camp at Sobraon on both banks of the river, across which there was a ford and where they had built a bridge of boats.

The 1st Royal Battalion moved from Fatehgarh to Meerut and arrived there on November 3rd.   Early in December it was ordered **1st Battalion.**   to hold itself in readiness to move at the shortest notice, and on the morning of the 11th was ordered to march that afternoon with every available man, which it did, leaving only a guard of one havildar, one naik and nine sepoys for the protection of the regimental property left behind.   Karnal was reached on the 17th and here the recruits were left and a depot formed under the command of Subedar-Major Bhoondo Singh.

On January 9th the 1st Royal Battalion joined the army of the Sutlej and formed part of a brigade in the division commanded by Sir **1846.**   Robert Dick.   Lieutenant-Colonel Stacy took command of the brigade, and the battalion came under the command of Brevet Lieutenant-Colonel Nash.   As soon as the 1st Royal Battalion arrived the whole force moved to Boutawallah, immediately opposite Sobraon.   The Sikh entrenchments on the south bank of the Sutlej consisted of high lines of earthworks protected by deep ditches, bristling with cannon, and supported by batteries on the other side of the river.   They were formed in a semi-circle at a bend in the river, but the entrenchments on the Sikh right did not go down to the water, and this was the weakest point in their defences.   The men in the entrenchments were disciplined soldiers, trained by European officers, equipped with all the weapons of the day and inspired by centuries of great traditions.

On the evening of February 9th orders were received for the attack, and it was with great satisfaction that it was seen that the water of the river was rising rapidly, making the ford dangerous for the enemy. At 2 a.m. the troops began to form, and by dawn all were in position. Colonel Stacy's brigade, including the 1st Royal Battalion, was detailed to lead the main attack against the Sikh right, followed by a second brigade in support and with a third in reserve.   The remaining two divisions of the army, which were on the right, were to make feint attacks against the enemy's front.

A dense mist delayed operations, but as soon as it rose the attack began, and by 6.30 a.m. the whole of the British artillery, which consisted of only sixty guns, was playing on the enemy's entrenchments. After about two hours the artillery ammunition began to run short, and at nine o'clock the infantry advance commenced.   The point of the enemy's trenches closest to the attacking troops and first entered by them fell to the 1st Royal Battalion ; here the enemy were posted in great numbers, and their concentrated fire was most destructive. The battalion advanced in the steadiest possible manner until it was within thirty or forty paces of the trenches, when the enemy discharged both guns and musketry, cutting down in an instant six officers and about fifty non-commissioned officers and men of the battalion. This was sufficient to stagger the most undaunted, and caused a momentary wavering in the battalion which was speedily overcome. Subedar Ram Singh, sword in hand, gallantly rushed to the front and cheered the men on to advance. In the successful charge that followed Ram Singh led the way into the trenches and was attacked by a Sikh soldier, whom he quickly killed.

Meanwhile, Colonel Stacy had dismounted from his horse as soon as the brigade was deployed, and led the advance on foot from in front of Her Majesty's 10th Regiment. When the fire was hottest his two orderlies, Sepoy Matadeen Sookool and Sepoy Sengobind Singh, both of the 1st Royal Battalion, ran up and placed themselves in front of him. He asked them why they stood there, and they replied : " You are our father and mother, and we will shield you from the showers of bullets." Colonel Stacy had some difficulty in getting them to go back, and they did not move away until the brigade commander told them that they would take his honour from him if they remained in front of him. The sepoys then went slowly to the rear, but remained close to their officer—one on each side of him—talking as calmly as if nothing was going on. Sengobind Singh died shortly afterwards; Matadeen Sookool was admitted to the Indian Order of Merit.

The fire from a Sikh battery on the other bank of the river caused a number of casualties, but in spite of all discouragement the brigade was soon in possession of the first line of the enemy's entrenchments. The supporting brigade then came up, and the two brigades formed a continuous front along the Sikh right and began to make their way towards the Sikh centre.

The whole strength of the Sikhs was now exerted against the two brigades which had penetrated into their entrenchments, and in order to ease the strain the feint attacks of the other two divisions were converted into real ones, and these, with great difficulty, succeeded in gaining the entrenchments opposite them. While this was going on, the sappers were busy preparing openings in the entrenchments captured by Colonel Stacy's brigade, and through these openings rushed the British cavalry. Harassed by a merciless fire and pressed by horse and foot, the Sikhs, brave as they were, could stand no longer. Their fire first slackened and then nearly ceased, and the victors, pressing them on every side, precipitated them in masses over the bridge, which broke, and into the Sutlej, which a sudden rise of seven inches had rendered hardly fordable. In their efforts to reach the northern bank they suffered terribly from horse artillery fire, and hundreds were drowned.

The victory was complete and it put an end to the Sikh resistance, but it was not gained without severe loss.   The 1st Royal Battalion lost 7 rank and file killed, and Captain Lyall, Lieutenant Munro and Quartermaster-Sergeant Tale were wounded, as well as 4 native officers, 5 havildars and 85 sepoys.   Subedar Basti Singh, I.O.M., who had distinguished himself in Afghanistan four years previously* and 10 more rank and file afterwards died of their wounds.   Lieutenant-Colonel Nash's horse was wounded and Lieutenant and Adjutant Holroyd's horse killed.

Lieutenant-Colonel Stacy, who had temporarily succeeded to the command of the division owing to Sir Robert Dick having been mortally wounded, was created an Aide-de-Camp to the Queen with the rank of Colonel in the East Indies ;   Lieutenant-Colonel Nash was mentioned in despatches and created a Companion of the Order of the Bath ; Subedar Ram Singh was admitted to the 3rd Class of the Order of Merit for conspicuous gallantry ;   and the battalion received the thanks of both Houses of Parliament as well as of the Court of Directors of the East India Company.

On February 13th the battalion crossed the Sutlej and entered the Punjab, halting at the town of Kussoor ;   and on the 15th Gulab Singh, the rajah of Jummu, entered the British camp to make terms for the Sikhs.   These terms included the cession of the country lying between the Beas and Sutlej rivers and an indemnity of a million and a half sterling or, as an equivalent, the districts of Kashmir and Hazara. The indemnity could not be paid, and as Kashmir was three hundred miles from the Sutlej any garrison sent there would be out of reach of support.   An arrangement was therefore come to by which the British, while retaining the suzerainty of Kashmir, gave up that district to Gulab Singh for a payment of three-quarters of a million sterling. The British also agreed, at the request of the Durbar, to occupy Lahore for a limited time in order that the Sikh Government might be able to overawe the soldiery into accepting the treaty terms.

In accordance with this treaty the 1st Royal Battalion advanced to Lahore, where it arrived on February 20th, but did not at once enter the city.   On March 10th the distribution of the army was published, and on the 14th the battalion entered the city and was located in Tej Singh's cantonment.   The British garrison of Lahore held all the thirteen gates of the city, and did not allow a Sikh soldier inside, except those confidential ones around the person of the Maharajah, and the Sirdars composing the Government.

---

* See p. 26.

On July 30th Colonel Stacy, C.B., completed his command of the battalion, and was succeeded by Lieutenant-Colonel Nash, C.B.

It was the intention that the British troops should not remain in the Sikh kingdom beyond the end of the year at the latest, but in October events occurred which led to very important results. The Sheik Imam-ud-Din was the governor of Kashmir for the Sikhs, and he refused to give up his province to Gulab Singh. A small army, partly Sikh and partly British, was prepared and, accompanied by the commanding personality of Henry Lawrence, moved out of Lahore to force Gulab Singh upon the population of Kashmir. Lieutenant W. Q. Pogson of the 1st Royal Battalion served in this column, probably in command of a detachment of the battalion. The British portion of the force did not move beyond Jummu. No fighting occurred, and Imam-ud-Din surrendered and revealed the fact that Lal Singh, the Wazir of Lahore, had behaved treacherously. This made it clear that the withdrawal of the British troops must necessarily result in anarchy, and accordingly the Punjab was made a British protectorate for the duration of the minority of the Maharajah.

The 1st Royal Battalion moved out of Lahore city to Anarkali on January 14th, 1847, and on February 8th marched to Ferozepore, where it arrived on the 14th and remained, fully equipped for service, in readiness to move at short notice.

1847.
1st Battalion.

It was not required to take part in any operations, and during the months of August and September one wing of the battalion moved in two detachments to Kalka. On September 1st it was relieved in the army of the Punjab and moved to Shahjehanpore, where it arrived on December 13th.

Four months later, on April 20th, two British officers who had been sent to Multan to fix the land tax and to remain there as magistrates, in accordance with the decision to administer the Punjab during the minority of the Maharajah, were savagely murdered and their bodies mutilated and afterwards exposed on the walls of Multan. The Sikh forces which were sent to take part in the resultant operations joined the rebels; other Sikh forces then revolted in Hazara and Peshawar, and it became necessary to reconquer the Punjab.

1848.
2nd Battalion.

The main British army, apart from the existing garrisons in the Punjab, was collected at Ferozepore, but a force was also collected in the Bombay Presidency and was ordered to join the detachment before Multan. This force included the 2nd Battalion, which at the time was stationed in Sind. The battalion, still under the command of Lieutenant-Colonel Stalker, C.B., arrived at Rohri, opposite Sukkur, on the Indus, on November 1st. Marching up the left bank of the river along the route followed by the 1st Royal Battalion just ten years before, but in the opposite direction, the 2nd Battalion arrived on the banks of the Sutlej on December 16th. This was crossed by a bridge of boats at Philodpur, and the force arrived before Multan on the 21st.

On December 27th a combined attack in four columns was made on the suburbs which commanded three sides of the town and fortress. The right attack aimed at winning the ground which commanded the north-east corner of the citadel itself. The right centre column was led by Colonel Nash, who had been transferred from the 1st Royal Battalion, to the right of the high mound called Mundi Ava, facing the Khuni Burj, or Bloody Bastion, of the city. To the left of this mound moved the left centre column, composed of Bombay troops, including the 2nd Battalion, and commanded by Brigadier Capon. A similar mound further left formed the goal of the left attack, also composed of Bombay troops, under Colonel Dundas. On the western side of the city a fifth column, composed of irregulars, was led by Major Edwardes towards the canal bridge at Sheesh Mahal. This was meant to be wholly a feint attack, to beguile the enemy from what was at first the only real one, that on the right. Those in the centre were to become real only if circumstances favoured such a departure from the original plan. At noon Edwardes moved out his men, and in half an hour was briskly engaged with the enemy on that side of the town. A little later the remaining columns set forth on their several missions. While the left column was quietly making its way to the brick-kilns on its front, the columns of Nash, Capon and Dundas struggled forward under a heavy fire from the fort, the city and the entrenched outposts, beat back the enemy wherever they barred the way and, planting a few guns on the Mundi Ava and on another mound called Sidi-lal-ke-Beyd, swept on with unflagging fury well-nigh up to the city walls. Scared at these successes, the enemy made no serious effort to check the advance of the right column. One after another the noble tomb of Sawan Mull, father of Mulraj, Governor of Multan, the Blue Mosque, filled even then with women and priests, Mulraj's garden-house, the Am Khas, all posts of remarkable strength, were abandoned without a struggle by the bewildered foe. By four in the afternoon the British troops held the whole line of suburbs.

That evening trenches were dug, batteries were planted on the Mundi Ava, on a mound to the right and on the Sidi-lal-ke-Beyd to the left about a hundred and fifty yards from the Delhi Gate of the town, and on a fourth yet more to the left at a hundred yards from one of the city bastions. Through the whole of the next day and night a fierce fire was poured into both fort and city, Mulraj returning the compliment with more of earnestness than effect. On the 29th the whole of the British mortars were playing on the doomed town with a force which neither stone nor flesh and blood could long withstand. Hardly a shot seemed to miss its mark ; one building after another was set on fire, and the brave garrison could send back but few and feeble answers from their own guns.   A bold sally was made by two thousand of their best soldiers against the Sidi-lal-ke-Beyd, now held by Edwardes' troops, but after an hour and a half's hard fighting they were driven back within the walls.

Early next morning, the 30th, new batteries opened on the city wall at eighty yards' range.   That was a fatal day for the besieged. Four hours the heavy guns and mortars kept pouring their cruel rain upon the walls and into the town.   Four hours also did Mulraj's gunners send back shot for shot with unflinching steadiness, with an aim unusually good.   Suddenly at noon, amidst the din, the dust, the smoke of that fierce battle, there happened that which swallowed up all lesser noises in one grand far-echoing crash of its own making.   A shell from a mortar, piercing the almost bomb-proof dome of the Great Mosque in the citadel, blew up the enemy's chief magazine which lay therein. With a roar which seemed to shake the earth for miles, the huge building rose slowly, a column of smoking ruins, into the air.   At the height of a thousand feet or so the column spread and spread like a huge cloud brooding for a few moments over the hostile camps below.   As the cloud presently passed away, its heavier parts having fallen again to earth, a great shout of triumph filled the air.   The sudden explosion of four hundred thousand pounds of powder had cost the lives of five hundred men, annihilated a noble old temple and caused heavy damage to all the neighbouring defences.   Once more raged the battle of the guns, Bengal and Bombay artillerymen vying with each other in their efforts to subdue the enemy's fire, which kept thundering on as if nothing unusual had just taken place.

For two more days the dreadful argument was carried on, with the fierceness of despair on one side, on the other with the stern foreknowledge of coming victory.   About noon of the 31st a great fire broke out in the citadel in the enemy's chief storehouse, raged unappeasably all day and night, helping the British gunners to pour in their deadly salvos by the light of flames that battened on the ruin of many tons of oil and other combustibles, besides many thousand pounds' worth of good grain.   On the morning of New Year's day the fire was still blazing.   Throughout that day the British batteries kept widening the breach in the Bloody Bastion and making, as it seemed, good practice at the wall by the Delhi Gate.

The next morning was marked out for the final storming of the city. An hour after midnight Edwardes moved out his men for a feint attack on the left.   Two hours later a Bombay column, including the 2nd Battalion and commanded by Colonel Stalker, was far on its way to the breach in the Bloody Bastion, while a Bengal column was beginning an experimental attack on the breach by the Delhi Gate, a breach which was found not to exist. The Bombay column, after a short but sharp struggle, forced its way into the Bloody Bastion. The breach itself was easy to surmount, but the new works hastily run up inside checked the assailants, who were falling fast under the murderous musket fire when Havildar Kooshal Singh, of the 2nd Battalion, who was subsequently rewarded with the Order of Merit, accompanied by John Bennet, colour-sergeant of the Bombay Fusiliers, springing up the parapet with the Regimental Colour, waved it to encourage his comrades. In a moment the Colour was riddled through and through, but the sight spurred the rest to fresh efforts. With a rush that nothing could withstand they overleaped the barrier, drove the enemy before them with great slaughter and, being reinforced by the Bengal party, were soon masters of nearly the whole town.

The 2nd Battalion casualties included 1 British and 1 native officer and 47 rank and file. Lieutenant-Colonel Stalker, C.B., Major Mant and Captain Hart all received brevet promotion, and Lieutenant-Colonel Stalker was appointed Aide-de-Camp to the Queen. Besides Havildar Kooshal Singh, Sepoy Mahadeo Misser was mentioned for gallantry, having shot a standard-bearer and captured the Colour, a green silk flag with the Union Jack in one corner.* Four native officers, 5 havildars, 2 naiks and 5 sepoys also received special mention, and the battalion was granted the title of " The Mooltan Regiment."

A sad wreck the city had indeed become. Its streets were thickly strewn with dead and dying—mostly Sikhs, unearthly with their long hair. Its houses everywhere stood shattered, blackened, pierced through and through by that long-continued storm of shot and shell. Meanwhile, not a day was lost in pushing on the siege of the citadel, which Mulraj, with three thousand picked troops, was resolute to hold. On January 4th it was invested on every side. For many days yet Mulraj and his brave followers held their battered, desolated stronghold, amidst a cannonade which repeatedly drove the gunners from their guns, unroofed nearly every building, and left Mulraj himself no safer shelter than the gateway of the Sikhi Gate. On the 17th a steady fire of 8-inch shells kept tearing up as they burst the mud and brickwork of the walls into which they plunged ; while the 18-pounders and 24-pounders enhanced the havoc with their ceaseless battering at close quarters. On the 18th the counterscarp by the Gate of Dignity was blown bodily into the ditch. On the city side of the fort a like success was attained on the 21st. Over these two breaches dogs and horses were driven by the enemy with perfect ease. Inside the fortress

---

* It appears likely that this standard originally belonged to one of the Mohammedan levies raised by British political officers from amongst the frontier tribesmen, similar to the levies commanded by Herbert Edwardes at the capture of Multan.

was an utter wreck. That day all was ready for a final assault when Mulraj promised to surrender unconditionally on the morrow, which he did at 9 a.m., after a drenching storm of rain and thunder.

Meanwhile the main British army in the Punjab, under Lord Gough, had won the very dearly bought victory of Chilianwala, and the Bombay troops were ordered, after the fall of Multan, to reinforce him as early as possible. The 2nd Battalion left Multan on February 2nd and reached Ramnagar, about fourteen miles from Gujrat, on the 19th. Here it was halted as escort to supplies, but on the following morning received orders to rejoin the force, and arrived the same evening, encamping in order of battle before Gujrat.

1849. 2nd Battalion.

The Sikh army was drawn up with considerable skill in front of the town of Gujrat, where two nullahs considerably strengthened their position. They had received a large accession of strength since the battle of Chilianwala, which included bands of Afghan horsemen who were stationed on each flank. The Bombay troops, including the 2nd Battalion, and commanded by Brigadier-General Dundas, were on the extreme left of the British line, and between the two armies were cultivated fields with patches of green corn.

The morning of February 21st dawned calm and fine ; there was no dust of moving columns to cloud the purity of the air and sky, while the snowy ranges of the Himalayas made a magnificent background to Gujrat and the village-dotted plain.

At half-past seven the British advanced, and the Sikhs at once opened fire. The advance was halted just out of range of the Sikh guns, when the British artillery moved to the front and opened a terrific cannonade which lasted for two and a half hours. The British right wing then advanced, swept over the Sikh position, and by one o'clock was in possession of the town of Gujrat, the enemy's camp, artillery and baggage, while the cavalry was in full pursuit on both flanks. The 2nd Battalion on the left never had an opportunity to fire a shot.

The following day a force under Sir W. Gilbert, which included the 2nd Battalion, marched in pursuit of the defeated Sikhs and Afghans. The main body of Sikhs surrendered at Rawalpindi on March 14th, when 18,000 Sikhs laid down their arms to a British column not exceeding 8,000 men ; a very dramatic scene, the spirit of which was illustrated by one old greybeard who advanced gravely to the pile of arms, laid upon it his shield, his sword and his matchlock, then, reverently saluting the sacred steel, joined his hands together and said : " To-day, truly, Ranjit Singh is dead ! "

The Sikh resistance was over, but the Afghans, under their Amir, Dost Mahomed, were still in the field. The force hurried after them, and the 2nd Battalion reached Attock on March 18th and Peshawar on the 21st, but the Afghans had fled precipitately through the Khyber Pass.   The Punjab was then annexed, and the battalion did not remain long in Peshawar.   On December 29th Lieutenant-Colonel Stalker* on the journey back to the Bombay Presidency, had the pleasure of showing the Governor-General, Lord Dalhousie, over Multan and explaining to him the details of the assault.

The 3rd Battalion marched to Lahore from Benares in 1850 under the command of Colonel Need and formed part of the garrison of the

1850.
3rd Battalion.

newly-annexed territory, remaining there until 1853, but the country quickly settled down and the battalion was not called upon for any action.

In the year 1852 hostilities again broke out in Burma, where the people had forgotten the losses they had incurred in the first war and

1852.
3rd Battalion.

offered repeated indignities to the British representatives and merchants.   Before the end of the year the war came to an end and resulted in the British annexation of the province of Pegu.   Early in the following year the 3rd Battalion sailed to Burma, under the command of Major Bush, and was once again employed in garrisoning newly-acquired territory. It was stationed at Thayet Myo, in the north of the annexed province, and furnished a number of detachments.   It did not take part in any of the major operations against dacoits, and returned to India early in 1857.

---

* Colonel Stalker was afterwards promoted to the rank of Major-General.   When Lord Elphinstone, the Governor of Bombay, was requested to name some officer attached to his own Presidency in whom the troops of all arms would have a common confidence to command the expedition to Persia, he named General Stalker.   He would have preferred to select Colonel Hancock—also of the 2nd Battalion, and then Adjutant-General of the Bombay Army—but ill-health prevented this.   Stalker was the senior of the available officers, so there were no heart-burnings from supersession, and it was believed that the appointment would be both a popular and a safe one.   " I hear favourable accounts of his good sense and temper," said Lord Canning, " and that is what is required for the service before him, which will require more of patient and enduring than of brilliant qualities " (Kaye and Malleson).   Sir James Outram was simultaneously selected for the same appointment in England, and eventually General Stalker sailed as second-in-command of the expedition, in which he served with great distinction ; but suffering from many worries in the intense heat of the Gulf, he committed suicide before the outbreak of the Mutiny.

CHAPTER V

THE MUTINY

Bibliography.—Regimental Records; State Papers preserved in the Military Department (official); Anderson's *Ubique*; *The Revolt in Central India* (official).

IN the beginning of the year 1857 the 1st Royal Battalion, under the command of Major H. W. Matthews,* was stationed at Barrackpore, with a detachment of three companies at Chittagong. During January a class was assembled at Dum Dum for instruction in the use of the new Enfield rifle, which was attended by Lieutenant Russell, Subedar Seobart Singh, one naik and four sepoys of the battalion. The drill for loading this rifle included biting off the card-board top of the cartridge with the teeth, a totally unnecessary relic of the days of the flint-and-steel firelock when, the musket being brought to the right side with the left hand for the purpose of priming, it was almost impossible to use the cartridge without the aid of the teeth. This custom of biting the cartridge had always been disliked by high-caste sepoys, who did not know who had previously handled the car-tridges, and was frequently evaded; men went through the form of biting the cartridge, but actually tore it immediately afterwards with the left hand.

While the course was in progress, but before any of the cartridges had been issued, a sepoy of another battalion, while walking through the rifle depot premises, was called to by a man attached to the magazine who asked to be given a drink of water from the sepoy's *lota*, or brass vessel; the sepoy refused, saying he did not know what the man's caste was. The man im-mediately rejoined in an impertinent manner : " You will soon lose your own caste, as before long you will have to bite cartridges greased with the fat of pigs and cows." This remark was much discussed and quickly became known to the Dharma Sabha, a Hindu religious organization in Calcutta, and was seized upon by the disaffected, who spread a rumour throughout the Bengal army that the sepoys were to be forced to lose caste in order to make them embrace the Christian faith. The majority of sepoys did not believe this report and would have made no

1857.

1857.
1st Battalion.

* See p. 32.

E
49

objection to biting the cartridges, but were genuinely afraid that their friends and relations would regard them as having lost caste and would subject them to the terrible penalty of social ostracism should they do so. Permission was immediately given to the officer commanding the depot at Dum Dum to obtain the ingredients for greasing the cartridges from the local bazaar, and for the sepoys themselves to mix them, so that they could be assured that there was nothing objectionable used, but the mischief was already done. Though the men were now perfectly assured that there was nothing objectionable in the grease, they dreaded the welcome they would receive on rejoining their battalions should they bite the cartridges, for the Brahmin sepoy dreaded becoming an out-caste. Loss of caste would make him an object of loathing and disgust and would bring shame and misery upon his wife and children besides depriving him of the consolation of his religion. When the cartridges were issued to the class, this dread of being regarded as having lost caste caused the men to demur to using them; but as they themselves had no longer any doubt regarding the purity of the ingredients used for greasing the cartridges, they followed the example shown by Subedar Seobart Singh, who was the first to come forward to use them.

Meanwhile the news of this had reached Barrackpore, and the propagators of sedition commenced to spread a report that the paper of which the new cartridges were composed actually contained the fat of pigs and cows in its composition. This paper differed from that previously used and was manufactured in England; it was glazed and shone like wax-cloth, so that the rumour earned a certain amount of credence. Some incendiarism took place and a number of men, particularly belonging to the 34th Bengal Native Infantry, whose lines were next to those of the 1st Royal Battalion, were plotting to mutiny.

In the month of February the detachment of the 1st Royal Battalion at Chittagong returned to battalion headquarters at Barrackpore, having suffered much from sickness; and the whole garrison, which consisted of four Bengal battalions, was paraded before the divisional commander, General Hearsey, who energetically and explicitly explained to the men the folly of the idea that Government wished to interfere with their religion. An act in Calcutta which resulted in two sepoys of another battalion being sentenced to fourteen years' imprisonment caused a second brigade parade, attended by the 1st Royal Battalion, and addressed by General Hearsey. In this address he stated that he expected orders to disband the 19th Bengal Native Infantry for an act of mutiny.

The disbandment of a battalion meant that all ranks were deprived of their means of livelihood. The sympathies of a large portion of the garrison of Barrackpore were with the men of the 19th, who were regarded as having refused to break their caste. The announcement of the approaching disbandment of the 19th caused a lot of talk among the men, and this was particularly the case with the 34th Native Infantry, many of whom were already disaffected, and whose lines were only separated from those of the 1st Royal Battalion by a street.

On Sunday, March 29th, soon after four o'clock in the afternoon, Mungul Pandy, a Brahmin sepoy of the 34th, thoroughly intoxicated and maddened by the talk of the sepoys in the lines, went towards the quarter guard of his battalion, calling out for the bugler. On seeing him he pointed his musket and ordered him to sound the "Assembly." This was not done, but the jemadar commanding the quarter guard, who was also a Brahmin, took no steps to arrest the sepoy, who continued to rave. Meanwhile, the Mohammedan naik of the quarter guard went off to report the circumstance to the British Sergeant-Major of the battalion, who sent him on to the Adjutant. The Sergeant-Major then ran to the quarter guard, and was shot at by Mungul Pandy. Shortly afterwards the Adjutant galloped up, and his horse was shot under him ; he picked himself up and drew a pistol from his holster and fired, but the shot did not take effect, and he drew his sword and rushed in, followed by the Sergeant-Major. Others then helped Mungul Pandy, and the two Englishmen, badly wounded, had their lives saved by a Mohammedan sepoy and made their way with difficulty to the house of the Sergeant-Major of the 1st Royal Battalion.

Meanwhile the men of the 1st Royal Battalion, hearing the shots but not knowing what was happening, had collected in front of their bells of arms, and the native officers of the battalion were doing their utmost to allay the excitement and prevent any panic, and had sent information to the Adjutant, Lieutenant Powell. Lieutenant Powell immediately rode up to the lines, where he saw the Adjutant of the 34th ; and after helping him into the Sergeant-Major's bungalow and finding out the situation, went at a full gallop to General Hearsey's bungalow, where he arrived with his hand and clothes partly covered with blood and reported the situation, followed immediately by Major Matthews, the Commanding Officer of the 1st Royal Battalion, who was also Field Officer of the Week. Major Matthews was ordered to take a message to the Colonel of the 34th and galloped back to the lines with Lieutenant Powell, followed shortly afterwards by General Hearsey and his two sons, who joined the group of officers, some mounted and some on foot, which had collected on the road between the two battalions. Seeing Mungul Pandy, the General immediately rode up to the guard, followed by his two sons and the group of officers and ordered the jemadar with his guard to follow him. The order was not obeyed, and the General rode at a quickened pace towards the mutineer, who then shot himself. He was not dead and so was taken to hospital for treatment. The General then rode to the lines of the 1st Royal Battalion, where the men, unarmed, were still collected in front of their bells of arms, the native officers having succeeded in allaying their first alarm. He reassured them that no person would be permitted to interfere with their religion and caste prejudices, and then rode away to the lines of the 34th Native Infantry.

A couple of days later the 1st Royal Battalion was present on the parade at which the 19th Bengal Native Infantry was disarmed and disbanded.

Shortly after this the same court-martial which had previously sentenced the two men to fourteen years' imprisonment was reassembled to try Mungul Pandy. It was entirely composed of native officers, and the president was Subedar-Major Jowahir Lall Tewary of the 1st Royal Battalion, two other native officers of the battalion also being members. The court sentenced Mungul Pandy to death, and he was hanged at dawn on April 8th on the brigade parade ground in the presence of all the troops not on duty. The jemadar who had commanded the guard was also tried by the same court, sentenced to death, and hanged in the presence of the troops.

On May 6th the 34th Native Infantry was disarmed, the men being stripped of their coats on parade and disbanded, the 1st Royal Battalion taking part in the parade.

During the months of April, May and June the 1st Royal Battalion was the only unit at Barrackpore allowed to furnish the guards over Government House.

Meanwhile, a party of 85 men of the 3rd Light Cavalry at Meerut had been tried for refusing to handle cartridges, saying they would get a bad name if they did. A native court-martial had sentenced them to imprisonment, and on May 9th these 85 men were paraded in front of the whole garrison of Meerut, who were kept standing motionless for more than an hour while the fetters were slowly hammered on the ankles of the prisoners by the artillery smith, each individual calling loudly to his comrades to rescue him. Next evening the jail was broken into, the prisoners rescued, and the Mutiny had started in earnest and quickly spread throughout Northern India.

At this time the 3rd Battalion was stationed at Ghazipore, where it had recently arrived from Burma under the command of Major Bush.

1857.
3rd Battalion. As the battalion contained only men willing to serve overseas at a time when this was regarded by many as breach of caste, it was very unpromising material for propaganda based on appeals to bigoted caste prejudice. Moreover, the battalion had only returned from Burma early in the year, and while overseas had been exempt from visits by the numerous agents who were spreading sedition throughout the Bengal regiments in India.

The men were loyal to their officers, and at no time was there the slightest doubt of their trustworthiness.

Ghazipore lies on the River Ganges just within Oudh territory, and some forty miles to the north-west is the city of Azimgarh. This was garrisoned by the 17th Bengal Native Infantry, and on June 3rd that regiment mutinied and, seizing the treasury and two guns, marched with them towards Lucknow. A detachment of the 3rd Battalion, together with a troop of irregular cavalry, the whole commanded by Captain H. L. Robertson of the 3rd Battalion, was sent to occupy the deserted cantonments. The country was swarming with bands of rebels, and the detachment was several times engaged with them, behaving very well, defeating the rebels whenever met and losing several of their own party.

The sepoys at Benares, to the south-west of Ghazipore, had followed the example of those at Azimgarh, whom they joined at Fyzabad ; but the station had been saved mainly owing to the presence of Colonel Neill with a detachment of the Madras Europeans. The mutiny of the sepoys at Dinapore, to the west of Ghazipore, however, made it necessary to withdraw the Azimgarh detachment and evacuate that cantonment. The detachment escorted back the remaining guns, and thenceforward the whole battalion was employed in protecting the lines of their officers and the other European residents of the district. The troop of irregular cavalry, which had accompanied the detachment to Azimgarh, then heard of the mutiny of their own regiment, and endeavoured to persuade the sepoys of the 3rd Battalion to join them in the murder of the Europeans and the seizure of the guns. Being unsuccessful in their attempt, they rode away and joined the mutineers at Delhi.

The conduct of the whole battalion throughout the Mutiny was most praiseworthy ; they guarded the civil treasury, Government stud and opium godowns until the arrival of a European detachment, and by their loyal bearing kept in check the bad characters of the city of Ghazipore.

The outbreak in the north had its repercussions in Barrackpore and Calcutta. Early in June an agitator, supposed to have been an emissary of the King of Oudh, attempted to bribe a sepoy of the **1857. 1st Battalion.** 1st Royal Battalion who was a sentry over the gate of the fort in order to obtain admission. The sepoy, Hannooman Doobe, reported the matter and the agitator was seized. By order of the Governor-General, Hannooman Doobe was promoted as a supernumerary havildar.

The public of Calcutta were thoroughly alarmed by the constant reports and rumours from the north, and were considerably disturbed in mind at the presence in their immediate neighbourhood of a fully armed Bengal battalion. Pressure was brought to bear upon the

Governor-General, and he, much against his will, issued orders for the disarming of the 1st Royal Battalion. On June 15th, 1857, the battalion was ordered to parade at six o'clock in the evening, when it was disarmed, the men behaving in an orderly, quiet manner. Rumours were quickly credited in those days of mental excitement, and one was started in Calcutta that the battalion had refused to lay down their arms, and this led to a certain amount of panic among the European population ; at the same time agitators succeeded in entering the lines of the battalion, and started to spread a report that the men had been disarmed in order that they might be easily disposed of and that European troops were marching against them. A panic occurred and a great number deserted, many of them leaving their dinners cooking on the fire. The Governor-General promising to pardon all who returned within three days, a great number came back.

The 1st Royal Battalion, although disarmed, furnished the guards over Government House throughout the year 1858, and was given back its arms on September 9th, 1859. During this time 29 Sikhs were transferred to the " Seikh Volunteers," and this, combined with the desertions after the panic and the losses due to sickness among the original Chittagong detachment occurring during a period when no recruits were received, caused the battalion to be very much reduced in strength ; so that, although a number of loyal men were transferred to it from the late 34th Native Infantry, it was, in March, 1859, re-organized in three companies.

While the two Bengal battalions remained comparatively inactive during the Mutiny, a number of their British officers were actively employed. The Gurkha force of 3,000 under Jung

1st and 3rd Battalions.

Bahadur reached Azimgarh on July 13th, and two days later were at Jaunpore, only about fifty miles west of Ghazipore, where was the 3rd Battalion, and in the heart of the disaffected districts. Both Captain C. L. Montgomerie and Lieutenant W. Battye of the 3rd Battalion were lent to the Gurkha force and served with it throughout the campaign, the latter receiving the thanks of Government for aiding Mr. Venables, a well-known indigo planter, in the capture and death of a noted rebel at Azimgarh. Captain Weston, also of the 3rd Battalion, was present throughout the siege of Lucknow. Lieutenant Annesley, of the 3rd Battalion, was in political charge of a force sent against the rebels under Tantia Topi in 1858. Lieutenant C. W. Hawes of the 1st Royal Battalion served as Adjutant of the Corps of Guides and Commandant of the Guides Cavalry before Delhi, and commanded the infantry of the Guides on several occasions during the siege, assault and capture, being present in every skirmish from June 9th until September 14th, 1857, and being wounded four times. After the capture he commanded the Guides

Cavalry in Brigadier Showers' flying column in the districts about Delhi, and in April and May, 1858, served in the expedition under Sir S. Cotton in the Eusufzai country as commandant of the cavalry and second-in-command of the Guides. Captain J. Dawson of the 1st Royal Battalion accompanied General Outram on his advance to Oudh.

The 2nd Battalion, belonging to the Bombay army, was not at first involved in the Mutiny, but took an active part in restoring order.

1857. **2nd Battalion.** While the majority of the ruling princes were loyal, their troops joined the rebels and the whole country lying between the Rivers Jumna and Narbada was in a state of rebellion, which was spreading south of the latter. The fort of Asirgarh, some fifty miles south of the Narbada river, was garrisoned by a detachment of the Gwalior contingent, a force raised in accordance with the treaty following the battle of Maharajpore,* and officered by British officers. In the month of July, 1857, this detachment mutinied ; but a British force arriving on the 22nd, the mutineers were disarmed and their leaders executed. Two companies of the 2nd Battalion were then detailed to garrison the fort in conjunction with two companies of Bhils. The Bhil Corps detachment did not behave well, for a large part of this aboriginal race† had resorted to their old habits and were taking advantage of the disturbed state of the country to raid the more settled districts. The Bhil disturbances spread south of the Narbada, and in January, 1858, a detachment of the 2nd Battalion consisting of 2 native officers, 4 havildars and 41 sepoys, under Lieutenant Fairbrother, was attached to a field force which operated against them in the Satpura Hills, the range which runs south of and parallel to the Narbada river. These operations were completely successful and resulted in the disturbances being confined to the north of the river.

During the first half of 1858 a force under Sir Hugh Rose advanced through Central India, captured Jhansi and Gwalior, dispersed most of

1858. **2nd Battalion.** the rebels and brought the regular campaign to an end, but a force of mutineers under Tantia Topi was still at large. Tantia Topi, the most successful of all the rebel leaders, had been brought up at Bithur, near Cawnpore, in the house of the ex-Peshwa of the Mahrattas‡ who had surrendered to the British during the campaign of 1817-18. When the ex-Peshwa died his vast wealth was succeeded to by his adopted son, known as the Nana Sahib, of infamous memory. Tantia Topi, who at the outbreak of the Mutiny was about forty-five years of age, acted as companion and aide-de-camp to his relative, the Nana. His army was called " The Army of the Peshwa," and displayed the standard of that obsolete authority.

After the successes of Sir Hugh Rose, Tantia Topi was forced south-ward and, arriving at Jhalra Patan, in the north of Malwa, was joined

---

* See p. 39.   † See p. 18.   ‡ See p. 14.

by the troops of Jhalawar State. He then marched south-east to Rajgarh, intending to try and reach Indore and raise Holkar's troops in rebellion. The 2nd Battalion, less its detachment at Asirgarh, was dispatched as part of a small force under Colonel Lockhart to cover Ujjain and so prevent Tantia Topi from reaching Indore ; it took up a position at Susner, thirty miles west of Rajgarh, but was not strong enough to attack the enemy. By September 14th, 1858, a junction was formed with two other forces at Nalkhera, ten miles to the south-east, and command of the whole column was assumed by Major-General Michel, who at once marched to Rajgarh and reconnoitred the enemy's position, which was on both banks of the river at that place. Next morning the column advanced, but it was found the enemy had marched during the night to a very strong position on the road to Biaora.

On approaching this position fire was opened on the cavalry who were covering the advance, and these retired when the advancing infantry came under artillery fire. The range being too great for the British artillery, the leading infantry were partially retired to await the arrival of the whole force, which was covering a large extent of road. The advance was then resumed, the rebels keeping up a well-sustained but ineffective fire from some eight heavy guns ; and on the British approaching their position they began to retreat. None of the advancing infantry were allowed to fire a round from their Minie rifles, so that no check occurred. After the column had advanced in this fashion for two or three miles, following the retreating rebels, two guns were brought rapidly into action in front of the skirmishers, and their fire soon threw the rebels into extreme confusion. Another advance and another dash forward of the artillery completed their defeat. Every minute guns, material and baggage were falling into the hands of the pursuers, and the remaining organized bodies of the enemy were charged by cavalry, who continued the pursuit for four or five miles. The rebel army, estimated at 10,000 men, was entirely dispersed, while the British casualties were negligible, only three men in the whole force being wounded. Captain Barrow of the 2nd Battalion was mentioned in despatches.

Tantia Topi fled eastwards to the valley of the Betwa river, marching through the densely wooded district of Maksudnagar, followed by General Michel's force, including the 2nd Battalion. Turning north towards Jhansi, Tantia's force split up, part making for Talbahat and Lalitpur, while he himself moved on Chanderi. This held out against the rebel attacks, and after three days he moved twenty miles southwards to Mangraoli on the left bank of the Betwa river. Here he was headed off from the north by two other British columns. General Michel was at Bahadurpur when he heard of the arrival of Tantia Topi at Mangraoli. He marched with a small column, which consisted of two very weak British battalions and the 2nd Battalion with 90 men of the 17th Lancers and four guns, before daybreak on October 9th, and on reaching Mangraoli was informed by his scouts that the enemy, to the number of about 5,000, was advancing some two miles off. The rebel advanced guard, 1,000 strong, was found close to the village of Barulpore, out of which a few shells drove them on to their main body, posted at the elevated village of Shahjehan Mau. The surrounding country was covered with high scrub in which the infantry could not see the enemy until close to them. The force then advanced, each regiment covered by its skirmishers.

The jungle was so thick that a column of the rebels got unperceived in rear of the support, when they were charged and cut to pieces by the 17th Lancers. The enemy stood to their six guns, which were taken by the infantry, and then dispersed, having lost some 300 killed. About 2,500 crossed the Betwa that night by a ford eight miles off near the Chanderi road. Captain Barrow was again mentioned in despatches.

Tantia fled towards Lalitpur, where he was joined by the rebels who had previously separated from him, and next day marched fifteen miles to Sindwaha. Information of this reached General Michel at midnight on October 18th at Narhat. The force marched at four o'clock next morning, and at half-past eight the rebels were found drawn up on a hill beyond Sindwaha on the road to Marauni. The battle opened with an attack by the rebels on the British cavalry, which was repulsed. Whilst this was going on the 71st and 92nd Highlanders, who only numbered 530 between them, came up in line on the British left, with the 2nd Battalion in their left rear, and drove the enemy up the hill. The rebels then tried to turn both flanks, and the horse artillery and cavalry were so hard pressed on the right by the enemy posted in a field of high corn that the 2nd Battalion had to go to their assistance. The 92nd had also to wheel to their left to meet a flank attack, but the 71st still advanced steadily and, going up the hill, drove the rebels back until the guns were captured by a combined movement of the two Highland battalions. The enemy then retreated at all points, constantly rallying and massing before the pursuit—which was slow owing to heavy ground—and as often dispersed by the guns. The pursuit was continued for about nine miles and was eventually checked by the difficult nature of the country and the division of the rebels into small parties. Five hundred of the enemy were left dead on the field, and Captain Barrow was again mentioned in despatches.

The battle of Sindwaha was followed by a number of rapid marches which resulted in the small British column, reinforced by a few cavalry-men and some artillery, discovering the enemy crossing its front at dawn on October 25th near Karai. As the infantry had marched an hour before the cavalry, the latter had only just come up in rear when the infantry, including the 2nd Battalion, having cut the enemy's line of march in half, had wheeled to the right and was advancing in skirmishing order. The enemy were very quickly dispersed as they had not formed up in order of battle, and they fled in three different directions.

This was the last action in which the 2nd Battalion took part during the Mutiny. The operations developed into the pursuit of the enemy by several different small columns, the 2nd Battalion following a party of the rebels to Hoshangabad on the Narbada river and then to Betul, while the garrison of Asirgarh barred the way to the south across the Tapti river. The force, which included the 2nd Battalion, was broken up in December, when the battalion returned to its peace station, Mhow. Tantia Topi was eventually captured by one of the columns on the night of April 7th, 1859, and was hanged at Sipri on the 18th.

Subedar Mendhye Sing and Naik Sooklall Sing of the 2nd Battalion were both subsequently admitted to the Indian Order of Merit as a recognition of their very valuable services rendered during the siege of Lucknow (G.O. 566 and 567 of 1859), but there are no records to show how they came to be in the garrison.

CHAPTER VI

BHUTAN AND THE SECOND AFGHAN WAR

Bibliography.—Regimental Records ; *Frontier and Overseas Expeditions from India* (official); Hanna's *The Second Afghan War*; *The Second Afghan War* (1878-80) (official).

A LONG series of outrages committed by the inhabitants of Bhutan, including the insolent treatment of a pacific mission in open durbar, resulted in an expedition being sent to that country in the end of 1864. Bhutan is an exceedingly mountainous country lying in the heart of the eastern Himalayas and extending from the plains of Bengal in the south to Tibet in the north. The military capacity of the Bhutanese was greatly under-estimated, and this resulted in several disasters occurring early in the following year. Large reinforcements were sent and a change was made in the chief command ; successful operations followed, but it was not until October that arrangements were completed for an advance into the interior by two columns, the left from Buxa to Panakha and the right from Dewangiri to Tongsa.

At this time the 1st Royal Battalion was again stationed at Barrack-pore, where it had recently arrived from the Punjab, and it was singularly well off for senior officers. The Commandant was Colonel Matthews, who had commanded during the Mutiny ; while the Second-in-Command was Lieutenant-Colonel G. Holroyd, who had distinguished himself with the battalion in Afghanistan and whose horse had been shot under him while he was performing his duties as Adjutant during the battle of Sobraon. Lieutenant-Colonel Holroyd was temporarily absent, officiating as commandant of another battalion, but his place was taken by Lieutenant-Colonel Pogson, the officer who had accompanied the force sent from Lahore to establish Rajah Gulab Singh in Kashmir. On October 13th the battalion commenced its march to join the left column of the Bhutan Field Force, moving by rail to Khoostea and thence by river steamer to Doobree, where it arrived on October 21st, 1865. Leaving Doobree on the 27th it marched through Cooch Behar to Buxa, where it arrived on November 6th. Here all baggage was stored, including camp equipage, no tents being allowed to be kept except such small ones as officers were able to include in their 160-pound kit.

59

The left wing of the battalion then moved to Pabree under Lieutenant-Colonel Pogson, where it arrived on November 10th after having spent a night at Tehinchula, and where it was later joined by Colonel Matthews and battalion headquarters. The right wing under Captain Shaw moved to Tehinchula on the 22nd. The men, having hutted themselves, were then employed in making a military road until shortly before Christmas, when the whole battalion was again concentrated at Buxa Dooar. Here, again, it was chiefly employed in road-making, but on March 2nd a detachment of 100 men was dispatched under Captain Shaw to garrison Darlinkote, a frontier post between Buxa Dooar and Darjeeling. The following day another detachment was dispatched under Lieutenant Boyd to relieve a wing of the 3rd Gurkhas at Pabsee. Peace was now restored, and on March 7th, 1866, the field force was broken up and the 1st Royal Battalion commenced its march through Cooch Behar to Jalpaiguri, where it was to be quartered, but was not rejoined by the detachment from Darlinkote until November 21st.

In the year 1878 affairs in Europe were so disturbed that a war between Great Britain and Russia seemed almost inevitable. At this time a Russian mission was received at Kabul, a sign of friendship which was denied to the British. It was decided that, after due notice, a mission should be dispatched to Kabul at all costs, and that if its progress were opposed the fact would be regarded as equivalent to open hostility. A mission was therefore dispatched from Peshawar in September with a strong military escort. Passage to Kabul being formally refused by the Afghan officials, the mission withdrew and an ultimatum was sent to the Amir. No reply being received to this, war was declared on November 20th.

1878.
1st Battalion.

Three separate columns advanced, called respectively the Peshawar Valley, the Kurram Valley and the Kandahar Field Forces. The 1st Royal Battalion, commanded at the time by Colonel Thompson, was stationed at Lucknow, and after various movements was eventually ordered to march from Rawalpindi to Peshawar. Arriving at Nowshera on November 14th, it was ordered to halt there and was posted to the 4th Brigade of the Peshawar Valley Field Force; the other units in the brigade, which was commanded by Colonel Browne of the 81st Foot, being the 51st K.O.L.I., and the 45th Sikhs. The force was commanded by Lieutenant-General Sir S. Browne, V.C., C.B., K.C.S.I.

The brigade left Nowshera on the 18th and joined the remainder of the division at Jamrud, the entrance to the Khyber Pass, on November 20th. The 45th Sikhs were then left to garrison Jamrud, and on the following day the force entered the Khyber Pass, three companies of the 1st Royal Battalion, under Captain Birch and Lieutenant Tate, the latter being an officer of The Buffs who was attached on probation, acting as rear-guard to the column.

About seven o'clock in the morning the firing of heavy guns was heard from the front, and about noon the battalion reached the western slope of the Shagai heights, from which an elephant battery of 40-pounder Armstrongs and a field battery of 9-pounders was shelling Ali Masjid fort, estimated to be about 2,300 yards distant. The battalion, less the three companies composing the rear-guard, was then ordered to line the crest of a height immediately in rear of the field battery and to the right of the heavy battery. It was therefore extended in line at one pace interval and lay down under cover of the crest. Shortly afterwards, " B " Company, under Captain Atkins, was advanced about eight hundred yards in order to prolong to the left the line taken up by the 51st Regiment and to protect a mountain battery. Both the positions assigned to the battalion were under fire from the enemy's guns at Ali Masjid fort as well as from some hostile posts occupied by both artillery and infantry on the right front, but the cover provided by the rocks was so good that no casualties occurred in the battalion, although one man of the 51st was killed and another wounded and several of the artillery were killed. The flight of the round shot and shell was continuous until dusk, and although the fort was considerably damaged the enemy returned shot for shot throughout the day.

That night the battalion bivouacked where it lay, two companies being detailed to piquet the heights on the right and rear in conjunction with the piquets provided by other units. There were now only two companies left with battalion headquarters, and at ten o'clock orders were received to send these off, under a British officer, to assist in bringing artillery ammunition up the pass. As the only officer available was the Adjutant, the Commanding Officer was left alone with the Medical Officer and hospital till daylight, when the companies returned with the artillery ammunition and the piquets were withdrawn.

At seven o'clock on the morning of the 22nd the heavy battery again opened fire on the fort, and " B " Company, under Captain Atkins, was ordered to accompany the 51st Light Infantry and advance in support of part of the 3rd Brigade to the assault. It was then found that the enemy had evacuated all their positions during the night and fled, and by nine o'clock the fort was occupied by a company of the 51st and " B " Company of the 1st Royal Battalion. The remainder of the battalion joined the 51st and bivouacked for the day on the left bank of the stream immediately under the fort.

The capture of Ali Masjid fort gave the British command of the Khyber Pass, and the 4th Brigade, including the 1st Royal Battalion, was part of the force employed in garrisoning this while the main body advanced into the plains of Afghanistan.

The three companies which had formed the rear-guard did not arrive at Ali Masjid until eleven o'clock on the morning of the 23rd, having been employed the whole of the previous two days and nights in bringing up the rear—chiefly artillery ammunition in wagons which had great difficulty in getting up the pass, drawn, as they were, by bullocks.

The following day the battalion, leaving two companies under Captain Atkins at Ali Masjid, marched three miles farther up the pass to Kata Kushtia, where it relieved the 20th Punjab Native Infantry. Here it was continuously employed in piqueting duties or in escorting convoys to the front, the escorts returning with the empty camels to Ali Masjid. On November 27th two companies were ordered back to Ali Masjid, where an attack in force was expected ; the attack did not come off, but the piquets round the fort were attacked both that and the following night, with the consequence that the remainder of the 1st Royal Battalion was recalled on the 29th. The battalion had only left Kata Kushtia six hours when a convoy passing that place was attacked by the Pass Afridis, who wounded a sergeant of the 81st Foot, believed at the time to have been killed, and killed five camel men, besides severely wounding a sepoy of the 27th Punjab Native Infantry. On news of this reaching Ali Masjid, two companies of the 1st Royal Battalion under Captain Birch and Lieutenant Boileau were ordered back to Kata Kushtia. Captain Birch and Lieutenant Boileau succeeded in recovering the sergeant of the 81st who, on being wounded, had run up the heights and defended himself from behind a rock where he was found in a very excited and weak state twenty-four hours later. The same day two companies, under Lieutenant Tate, were sent towards Jamrud to assist in getting in a large convoy which had been attacked in the pass. On the 30th a sepoy of the battalion was shot and killed by the enemy while on convoy escort under Lieutenant Tate.

The garrison of Ali Masjid was now composed of the 1st Royal Battalion and the 51st Light Infantry, and the escort, guard and piquet duties were excessive. Nearly the whole battalion was permanently on duty day and night from the end of November until December 10th, when the 45th Sikhs arrived at Shagai, some three miles away, from Jamrud and took a share in the duties.

About Christmas time the 45th Sikhs were replaced in the brigade by the 81st Foot, a battalion which had suffered considerably from sickness, and the brigade was transferred to the 2nd Division and placed under the command of Brigadier-General Appleyard, C.B. The 1st Royal Battalion was then ordered to march to Landi Kotal, ten miles further up the Khyber and the most advanced post of the 2nd Division.

On the evening of January 1st, 1879, everything was ready for the march next morning when at about ten o'clock the camp was suddenly attacked from its rear, the direction of Shagai. One of the first of the shots of the enemy killed a man of the battalion as he was in the act of rising from his bedding in the quarter-guard tent. The previously appointed alarm posts were then taken up, and after about an hour's firing the enemy withdrew without having done any further damage. As the night was dark and the enemy fired from behind rocks, which afforded excellent cover, it was supposed that none of them were hit.

On January 2nd the battalion marched to Landi Kotal, where it remained employed daily on escorting convoys up and down the pass, road-making and the other duties of lines-of-communica-

1879.
1st Battalion. tion troops. On February 25th the headquarters and 300 men of the battalion under Colonel Thompson were ordered to join in the second expedition to the Bazar Valley. The inhabitants of this valley, which runs roughly parallel to the Khyber and to its south-west, had been giving considerable trouble and had already been visited once by an expedition. The battalion marched at 6 a.m., crossing the Bori Pass, some 6,500 feet high ; the route was extremely difficult, passing through narrow rock gorges which, in several places, were wet and slippery so that the mules had to be unloaded and the loads carried by the men. It was not until 6 p.m. that the rear-guard arrived at Karamna on a tributary of the Bazar river, where the main body had arrived three hours earlier. Here the battalion joined a force under Brigadier-General Appleyard which had marched the same day from Ali Masjid. That day the eleven towers of Karamna were blown up, the battalion assisting in the arrangements by which this was effected.

The following morning the force advanced at dawn to Burj, where the towers were blown up, and then continued its advance to Chora, in the Bazar Valley, where it joined the main column, commanded by General Maude, which had arrived from Jamrud. On arrival in the Bazar Valley it was found that the villages were already in flames, having been fired by the hands of their inhabitants, a clear proof of their intention to resist the advance of the expedition. The united force was then moved to a strong position in the centre of the valley out of range of the hills—a necessary precaution, as during the ten days the battalion was in the Bazar Valley the camp and piquets were attacked every night. Frequent skirmishes occurred during the day, notably on January 29th, when the battalion, under Colonel Thompson, advanced to Hulwai to blow up the towers of that village and the tribesmen appeared in very considerable strength. The towers were successfully blown up, and although the return march was harassed by the Afridis, the battalion fell back in good order towards the camp, inflicting a loss estimated at twenty men on the enemy. Fortunately there were no casualties in the battalion.

The battalion then returned to Landi Kotal, where it arrived on March 6th, 1879. Landi Kotal is over 3,500 feet above the sea and in north latitude 34, consequently the winter temperature is severe and the thermometer in tents used frequently to read 24° F. in January and 28° F. in February. Nevertheless the general health of the battalion was good, and it enjoyed its stay in Landi Kotal. It was with many regrets that, on March 20th, it returned to Ali Masjid.

The Ali Masjid duties, night and day, were again excessive, and they were also very fatiguing : night piquets posted on very inaccessible hill peaks, where the wind blew so furiously that no tents could stand against it ; day escorts, for convoys of carts from the plains, that were often out much over the twelve hours of daylight. On one occasion the convoy escort, which always started at daylight, did not return to camp until 11.30 p.m., and it was no unusual occurrence for the men to be out till 8 or 9 p.m. This duty was daily both up and down the pass, and the night duties, which of course were additional, only gave the men slightly more than alternate nights in bed. The battalion had three months of this excessive hard work, and at this period the rations became inferior. The duties necessitated irregular hours of feeding on hastily cooked inferior food ; milk could not be obtained, and vegetables and lime juice in insufficient quantities only. The very high wind made tent life most disagreeable, especially in the hot weather, when it was almost impossible to sleep owing to the wind by night and the heat by day. During this period the battalion had several brushes with the Afridis, who frequently attacked convoys, piquets or cattle at graze, one sepoy being killed and another wounded. The damage inflicted on the enemy could never be accurately ascertained, as they always had the advantage of cover and ground, and generally took away their killed and wounded.

Towards the end of May cholera appeared at Ali Masjid and there were six cases in the battalion, five of which proved fatal, but as soon as the camp was changed it disappeared. On May 30th news reached the battalion that peace had been arranged, the Treaty of Gandamak having been signed, and in the end of June the battalion returned to India.

Meanwhile, the Kandahar Field Force had advanced by the Bolan Pass, and the 2nd Battalion joined a brigade commanded by Brigadier-General Phayre at Jacobabad about the middle of December, 1878, for service on the line of communications. The battalion, which was commanded by Colonel C. T. Heathcote, then, in conjunction with the 1st Bombay Grenadiers, spread gradually along the entire line of communications.

1878.
2nd Battalion.

Their presence soon ensured the safety of the convoys, and their labour in due time facilitated their movements ; for the two battalions so widened and repaired the road up the Bolan—modifying gradients, ramping ravines, bridging the river at many points and clearing away shingle and boulders along an aligned route extending for nearly seventy miles (a work which it took them six months of incessant toil to complete)—that, just at the very time when the mortality among the camels had thinned their ranks beyond all hope of replenishment, it became possible to replace them by bullock carts.

Before this road had been completed the Treaty of Gandamak was concluded, but it was decided, chiefly on account of the impracticability of retiring in the hot season through the plains between the Bolan Pass and Jacobabad, that the withdrawal of the British forces from Southern Afghanistan could not take place until the autumn. The battalion remained with its headquarters and one wing spread out between Quetta and Jacobabad and with one wing at Durwaza. The evacuation actually began on September 1st, when the movement was suddenly stopped by the news of an outbreak at Kabul on September 3rd and the massacre there of the British Resident, Sir Louis Cavagnari, and his escort of the Guides.

A demonstration was made by the troops at Kandahar in the direction of Kelat-i-Ghilzai, and Brigadier-General Phayre's brigade, including the 2nd Battalion, was ordered to relieve the

**1880.
2nd Battalion.** troops at Quetta and Peshin to enable them to advance to Kandahar. The brigade was unable to move until relieved in the end of January, and by that date a movement from Kandahar on Kabul had been decided upon. Accordingly the 2nd Battalion was ordered to advance to Kandahar, where it arrived on March 30th, 1880.

The 2nd Battalion was then distributed with its headquarters at Kandahar and with detachments at Mandi Hissar and Abdur Rahman, the two latter being under the command of Major Sidney Waudby of the battalion, who was also appointed commandant of the whole road between Kandahar and Quetta. On April 16th, whilst halted at Dabrai, a post two marches from Chaman, an attack was made on the post by Kakar Pathans. Major Waudby had with him only a dafadar and two sowars of the Scinde Horse, and two orderlies, Sonnak Tannak and Elahi Baksh, of the 2nd Battalion. In the course of the afternoon of the 16th warning of the impending danger was brought to Major Waudby by a Pathan and he, accordingly, barricaded the entrance to the post with bags of grain. The post consisted of a simple enclosure surrounded by a wall, four and a half feet high, with a small ditch outside ; its garrison, besides the five men with Major Waudby, was composed only of some Pathan levies, who deserted as soon as the

F

attack threatened. At 10 p.m. Major Waudby, who had been lying down to rest for an hour or two, after posting some sentries, arose and sent out two men to reconnoitre towards the low hills on the east of the post. They had advanced but a short distance when the enemy, apparently about three hundred strong, were seen coming over the hill. Major Waudby ordered his five men to reserve their fire, and the assailants were kept at bay for three hours, when the ammunition of the little party began to fail; the enemy then made a rush and succeeded in gaining an entrance. Major Waudby fought to the last, and was said to have killed several of the enemy with a hog-spear.

One sowar of the Scinde Horse made his escape at the last moment, shot down the foremost of his pursuers and got away to the neighbouring hills, from which he saw the post set on fire and the enemy making away with their plunder into the hills, where they quickly dispersed. Early in the morning the sowar observed a caravan coming from Chaman, and returned with it to the ruined post. The only person uninjured was a servant of Major Waudby, who could speak Pushto and had saved himself by reciting the Kalma. The dafadar was severely wounded and had been left for dead, but he afterwards recovered. The sowar got an Afghan dress from the caravan and went on through the hills to Kandahar to report the affair.

The best proof of the resistance offered by Major Waudby was that thirty dead bodies of tribesmen were counted ; and it was known that the assailants had carried away two dead bodies and many wounded.* Sepoys Sonnak Tannak and Elahi Baksh were granted, posthumously, the Indian Order of Merit. The hostile Kakars were so astonished and disheartened at the desperate defence made by only six men at Dabrai that they made no further attempt on any of the posts.

The whole of the Bengal troops left Kandahar in the end of March and moved towards Kabul, and the garrison of Kandahar consisted of **1880.** the bulk of a Bombay division, in the 2nd Brigade of which was the 2nd Battalion. During the months of April and May frequent rumours began to be heard of a new enemy, Sardar Ayub Khan, who was gathering forces in the direction of Herat. During July a force was dispatched from Kandahar to operate against Ayub Khan, and this was disastrously defeated on July 27th at Maiwand. News of this defeat was received at Kandahar very early on the morning of the 28th, and it quickly became evident that the whole population of the surrounding country was hostile, while the arrival of Ayub's victorious

---

* A British force which passed Dabrai shortly afterwards was surprised to find that the Afghan villagers living nearby were, contrary to their custom, taking great care of Major Waudby's grave. When asked the reason they replied : " An Afghan always respects the brave, and no braver man ever lived than the Englishman buried here." There is a memorial of Major Waudby in Bombay commemorating this fight. Waudby Road is called after him.

army could be expected within a few days. The cantonments were quite indefensible, and the day was spent in evacuating these and removing the baggage, sick and wounded into the citadel.

Shortly after dusk, when all the sick and as much as possible of the baggage had been removed from the cantonment, and when there were no signs of any more of the fugitives from Maiwand approaching, the whole garrison was withdrawn within the city walls and the gates were closed. The city of Kandahar is roughly a quadrilateral, and the walls were strengthened with barbed wire and sandbags. Various units were detailed to defend sectors of the walls, and the 2nd Battalion was detailed for internal defence and for the protection of the supply, transport and medical units, those not on duty forming part of the reserve in the citadel.

That night passed quietly, though a few shots were heard in the direction of the cantonments, possibly due to some unfortunate stragglers from Maiwand returning to find the cantonments in the hands of the enemy, and at about 10 p.m. the saddar bazaar was seen to be on fire. The first of Ayub Khan's soldiers were seen on the afternoon of July 30th, and from then on the working parties were fired on daily. There was a walled garden outside the western walls of the town which provided the enemy with cover, and on August 12th a party of the 2nd Battalion, together with some of the 7th Fusiliers, rushed this garden with the object of destroying the walls. Amongst the enemy who were killed on this occasion was the Governor of Farah, while the battalion lost eight sepoys wounded. One of these sepoys was very gallantly brought out of action under heavy fire by two Sapper subalterns.

All the adjacent villages were now occupied and being fortified by the enemy, who were completely investing Kandahar, and it was decided to make a sortie through the village of Deh Khwaja. This village lies to the east of the city and almost parallel to the city wall, in which there are two gates, the Bardurani in the north and the Kabul Gate about its centre. The distance from the former gate to the village is six hundred yards and from the latter nine hundred and fifty yards.

It was decided to attack on August 16th with three columns, all of which were to issue from the Kabul Gate. The first consisted of two companies of the 2nd Battalion and two of the 7th

1880.
2nd Battalion. Fusiliers, commanded by Lieutenant-Colonel Daubeny, and this was to advance to the south of the village and then through it to the north, driving out all the enemy met. The second column, commanded by Lieutenant-Colonel Nimmo, was to follow and conform to the movements of the first, but on reaching the village was to operate on the right of the first column. The third column, consisting of two companies of the 2nd Battalion and two

other companies, under the command of Colonel Heathcote of the 2nd Battalion, was to remain within the Kabul Gate awaiting orders. A cavalry brigade was to co-operate.

Artillery opened fire at 4.45 a.m., and at 5 a.m. the infantry advance started and succeeded in entering the south of the village under heavy fire half an hour later. An advance of all the troops through the village to the north would have left them open to counter-attack from the south, which was exposed ; consequently the two companies of the 2nd Battalion, which were under the command of Major R. J. Le P. Trench, were sent to occupy a small walled garden to the south while the Fusiliers advanced through the village. Meanwhile, the third column, commanded by Colonel Heathcote, advanced from the Kabul Gate and entered the village by its main entrance on the west, where it established itself.

While the advance of the Fusiliers was still in progress a large party of Ghazis attempted to advance from some nullahs in the south to counter-attack the village. Major Trench met them with three well-directed volleys, which turned them, when they were at once charged by the cavalry and driven back into the nullahs and broken ground. Soon after this, orders were received for Major Trench's companies, covered by the cavalry, to withdraw to the city. The cavalry withdrew to the Kabul Gate from which to cover the retirement, which then began. No sooner had the infantry left the walled garden than it was occupied by the enemy, who immediately opened fire. Major Trench and many of the men were killed, but eventually the companies succeeded in reaching the Kabul Gate.

The withdrawal of these companies and the cavalry left the south of the village open to the enemy, who immediately poured into it. The two companies of the Fusiliers belonging to the first column, as well as the whole of the second column, then debouched from the northern end of the village and withdrew to the north gate of the city, while Colonel Heathcote's column, including his two companies of the 2nd Battalion, commenced to withdraw towards the Kabul Gate. As soon as the retirement began the enemy again occupied the whole of the village and reopened fire, and to this the three columns were exposed, while the nature of the ground prevented their moving in anything but close formations. During this retreat the Adjutant of the battalion, Lieutenant F. C. Stayner, was killed.

At length, by 7.30 a.m., the disastrous retirement was completed ; firing had entirely ceased, and the enemy were seen streaming away from Deh Khwaja, carrying some of their dead with them. Although the enemy were believed to have suffered very heavily, the 2nd Battalion, besides the 2 British officers, lost 50 other ranks either killed or wounded.

While these events were occurring in Kandahar the two detachments of the battalion on the road to Quetta were left in a very exposed position. On the death of Major Waudby the command of these had been succeeded to by Major W. Jacob of the 2nd Battalion, and he was at the post of Mel Karez when he received news of the disaster of Maiwand, and was ordered to concentrate all the troops under his command at Chaman. He waited at Mel Karez for the arrival of the party from Abdur Rahman, and marched on the morning of the 29th to Dabrai. During the previous night a large body of Achakzais and Nurzais had collected round Mel Karez, and they followed the march of the detachment, constantly firing at it from a distance without doing any damage. After halting a few hours at Dabrai the march was continued to Gatai, and on July 30th Chaman was reached in safety without casualties, though the camp was fired into on the night of the 29th and the rear of the column was threatened by the tribesmen at starting. The march was a trying one for, besides the constant danger of attack, the want of water, especially during the last stage of seventeen miles from Gatai to Chaman, was keenly felt.

Both General Phayre, who was now commanding the line of communications, and the Commander-in-Chief expressed their appreciation of the soldier-like manner in which Major Jacob had executed the difficult task entrusted to him.

The Khojak Pass by this time had been occupied by a strong body of Achakzais, and the telegraph line between Chaman and Killa Abdullah entirely destroyed. The detachment of the 2nd Battalion moved out of Chaman the day after its arrival as part of a very small force which co-operated with another small force from the Khojak Post and attacked the enemy in the pass. After two days' skirmishing, the tribesmen were driven out with heavy losses, and the detachment returned to Chaman.

Meanwhile, the investment of Kandahar continued and the enemy kept up artillery fire daily. On August 24th a great commotion was observed amongst the Afghans, and by ten o'clock it became evident that they had broken up their camp and moved towards the Babawali Pass.* It was then learnt that a relieving British force had arrived at Kelat-i-Ghilzai from Kabul, and this had caused the Afghans to abandon the siege and concentrate their forces. On August 31st Lieutenant-General Sir Frederick Roberts arrived at Kandahar, and his army encamped east of the city, so bringing to an end the four trying weeks of siege.

The following day General Roberts moved out to attack Ayub Khan's forces. During the ensuing battle the 2nd Battalion formed part of a force which took up a position at Kalachi-i-Haidari at 8 a.m., where it remained threatening the Babawali Pass and watching the

* See p. 28.

Kotal-i-Murcha. The battalion took no active part in the fighting which ensued, when the hostile army was completely defeated and dispersed.

Shortly after this the battalion was sent, with the 3rd Bombay Cavalry, to reopen communication with Chaman and to restore the telegraph line. It then moved to Sibi, where it remained till early in 1881, when it returned to India. Colonel Heathcote was made a Companion of the Order of the Bath.

CHAPTER VII

BURMA, THE TOCHI, ASSAM, THE BOXER RISING AND SOMALILAND

Bibliography.—Regimental Records ; *Frontier and Overseas Expeditions from India* (official).

THE terrible conditions prevailing in Upper Burma in 1884 were having serious consequences to British trade. On one day in September

1884. 3rd Battalion. nearly three hundred men, women and children were massacred in Mandalay while high festival was held within the palace, theatrical and other performances being given night after night to distract the attention of the people from the horrors that were continually being committed around them. Meanwhile, the growing influence of the French at the court of King Thebaw was being used still further to depress British interests, and in August, 1885, the Burmese Government imposed an arbitrary fine of twenty-three lakhs of rupees on the Bombay-Burma Trading Corporation, a British timber company. The fine, whatever justification there may have been for it, was so large that it could not be paid, and must result in expelling large British interests from Upper Burma, so making room for further French influence, and it thus had a grave political importance.

The British Government insisted that British subjects should receive a fair trial, and requested that the order for the payment of the fine should be suspended until the matter had been fully and impartially investigated. The Burmese questioned the right of the British to raise the subject and refused point blank to agree to any arbitration or to suspend the payment of the fine. War was declared on November 10th.

Mandalay was captured during the cold weather of 1885-86, and during the following cold weather the country was reduced to order and

1887. 3rd Battalion. many of the internal troubles quashed. The 3rd Battalion arrived at Rangoon from Nowgong on March 31st, 1887, and the following day left there by rail for Prome. From there it moved up the Irrawaddy by steamer to Mandalay, arriving on April 7th, under the command of Lieutenant-Colonel C. H. Palmer.

In October information was received of the rising of a rebel Shewgabo prince. A force was dispatched against him under the command of

Colonel Symons, and this included 200 rifles of the 3rd Battalion under Lieutenant C. G. Hunter.   On November 1st the camps of the prince's *bohs* were attacked simultaneously by three columns, Lieutenant Hunter commanding the column which attacked the stockade of Boh Saga.   The rebels were utterly routed and the backbone of the rebellion broken.   The 200 rifles of the 3rd Battalion were then ordered to hunt the leaders of the now scattered rebels.   For some five months Lieutenant Hunter constantly patrolled the Pagyi Hills and Lower Chindwin jungles.   He met with various successes, including the capture of Boh Maung Khan, who was subsequently hanged, and his large gang.   It was through the exertions of this detachment of the regiment that the well-known Boh Sawbaw, who used to maraud with mounted dacoits, was finally captured.   Boh Saga's lieutenant and numerous minor *bohs* and small gangs were taken.   Finally Saga's and the Shewgabo's camps were captured, the capture including about 40 dacoits, 170 Burman guns and 160 *dahs*.   Saga and the Shewgabo escaped across the hills into the Chin country.   The troops were then withdrawn in April, 1888.

The battalion had left Mandalay in detachments, " A " Company and a portion of " D," under Lieutenant O. I. Obbard, for Kandat, and " B " Company with details of " C," under Major C. W. J. Hingston for Alon, both stations in the Chindwin district, the whole of which came under Major Hingston.

1888.
3rd Battalion.

The headquarters of the battalion with the remaining four companies and details moved in detachments to Pokoko from March 1st to 4th. On April 11th battalion headquarters moved to Alon and Lieutenant-Colonel Palmer took over command of the Chindwin.

It now became necessary to protect the newly-acquired territory from the attacks of the border tribes.   Burma is bordered on the north-west by mountain ranges running roughly north and south which separate Burma from India.   The western ranges bordering India are known as the Lushai Hills, and the eastern, bordering Burma proper, as the Chin Hills.   The Chins, who inhabit these hills, carried out several raids, taking away a number of captives.   In November, 1888, punitive operations were commenced.   The fact that all transport was carried by coolies necessitated the columns being small, and having to move in single file.   There was always danger from ambushes. Having carefully selected his spot, the Chin would lie up below the path and, after discharging his gun in the back of a man at such close range as to burn his clothes, would slip off his rock and dive down the hillside out of sight and out of all possible lines of fire.

The detachment of the 3rd Battalion under Lieutenant Obbard, together with a detachment of the 10th Madras Infantry under Major Leader of equal strength, moved to Kan, a small town on the Myittha river which borders the Chin country, while similar columns occupied other posts on the border. Kan was occupied without opposition, and the detachment of the battalion remained here while other columns entered the Chin country and, after a number of skirmishes, succeeded in securing the release of two hundred captives.

Meanwhile, Boh Saga mustered a large force and attacked the 10th Madras Infantry, the action resulting in the so-called siege of Gungaw, a village south of Kan on the Myittha river. A large detachment of the 3rd Battalion under Major Hingston advanced from Alon and marched straight across the mountain ranges to Gungaw, where it was the first to arrive. Saga had gone in the opposite direction to engage Colonel Macgregor, who was advancing with the 44th Gurkhas, but had left a large following on Major Hingston's line of advance. Colonel Macgregor and Major Hingston engaged the dacoits on the same day in December, 1888, and utterly routed them. Sepoy Soodha killed two dacoits single-handed, and Subedar Buta Singh also distinguished himself. Major Hingston was mentioned in despatches.

The force was then broken up, though a fort, known as Fort White, in the heart of the Chin Hills, was occupied, and the line of communications to it secured.

Throughout the following summer the Chins continued to give trouble by cutting telegraph wires, ambushing convoys and firing into British posts. These facts, coupled with the advisability of thoroughly exploring and opening out the narrow strip of territory which alone now divided British Burma from India, led to the undertaking, in the cold weather of the year 1889-90, of military operations from Burma and Chittagong into the country of the Chins and Lushais. The troops from Burma were to advance into the Chin country in two columns, the northern one starting from Fort White and the southern from Kan, while other troops held posts guarding the western frontier of Burma. The southern column was to meet the force advancing from Chittagong, constructing a road as they moved forward, and so linking Burma with India.

1889.
3rd Battalion.

Headquarters of the 3rd Battalion under Major Hingston, with Lieutenant Wright and 250 rifles, moved up the Chindwin river to Kalewa, the nearest point on the river to Fort White, whence Major Hingston moved to Kalemyo, half-way to Fort White, and assumed command of the whole valley. The whole of the battalion was then split up in posts and stockades guarding the frontier and the line of communications to Fort White. On January 29th, 1890, Captain Hunter, commanding at Sihaung, left that post with 60 rifles of the regiment and made a long and difficult march into the hills to punish the hostile and troublesome

1890.
3rd Battalion.

village of Hanta. On the 30th, after a sharp fight, the village was captured and totally destroyed, the enemy being so cowed that the withdrawal of the force was unopposed. Captain Hunter got a bullet through his pugaree, and Jemadar Mana Khan was subsequently granted the Order of Merit for distinguished gallantry in leading an assault on a stockade. This expedition of Captain Hunter's had a marked effect in quietening that part of the country.

On February 9th, 1890, Colonel C. L. Prendergast arrived and took over command of the battalion. Parties of the battalion then took part in several expeditions to punish Chin villages implicated in cutting the telegraph wires, and the men did a great deal of hard work in patrolling the Fort White line and harassing these marauders. Towards the end of April the last tribe of the Chins submitted. Each clan was allowed to rebuild its villages as soon as all slaves had been surrendered, and the campaign was brought to a close. The 3rd Battalion left Burma on May 9th, 1890, and arrived at Lucknow ten days later.

On June 10th, 1897, a political officer, Mr. Gee, left Datta Khel in the Tochi valley on the North-West Frontier of India with a strong escort to visit Maizar in connection with a fine which had been inflicted on the tribesmen for murdering a Hindu writer. On arrival in Maizar the maliks appeared quite friendly and, pointing out a site to halt at, offered to provide a meal for the Musalman sepoys of the escort. At midday the promised meal was produced and later the pipers of the 1st Sikhs began to play while the villagers gathered round listening to them. Suddenly the listeners withdrew and heavy fire was opened on the escort from all the surrounding villages. The escort was only able to withdraw to Datta Khel with great difficulty, all the British officers being either killed or wounded.

1897.
1st Battalion.

As the result of this treachery a punitive expedition of two brigades was sent up the Tochi valley, and the 1st Royal Battalion was ordered to join the second Brigade. The battalion arrived at Khushalgarh on June 25th and commenced its march to Bannu the following day. All the marches had to be performed at night owing to the excessive heat, and the battalion arrived at Bannu on July 3rd. There it remained halted until the 14th, when it marched to Miram Shah in the Tochi valley, leaving two companies *en route* at Saidgi. The battalion then took over the garrisoning of several posts along the lines of communication. The escort and guard duties at all these posts were very heavy and trying, and, in addition to these duties, parties of the battalion were continually scouring the hills for raiders. On July 16th a large gang of Mahsuds drove off some contract camels which were at graze without a guard near Idak, and " B " Company of the battalion, under Lieutenant Marshall, went in pursuit. Just at dusk the Mahsuds were attacked and the camels recovered, one sepoy being dangerously wounded and having to have his leg amputated. On August 3rd a band of Waziris opened fire on a post garrisoned by fifty rifles of the battalion. A small party, aided by the escort of a passing convoy, attacked the enemy, killed one, and drove them back without suffering casualties. Another gang of Mahsuds was dispersed by fifty men of the battalion on August 7th, one enemy being killed and three wounded. A small column of two companies commanded by Major Maxwell was overtaken by night when returning from a reconnaissance near Miram Shah on September 2nd, and fire was opened on it from a steep hill. One sepoy was killed as well as some transport animals.

All through the hot weather the health of the battalion was good, but with the approach of the cold weather the effects of the hard work in the worst part of the unhealthy Tochi began to be felt. By November it had so deteriorated that the battalion was ordered back to India, but not before the campaign had come to an end, a *jirga* having formally submitted on November 15th.

Two years later, in December, 1899, the 1st Royal Battalion was stationed at Dorunda in Assam. On the 24th and for two or three nights following some natives were shot with arrows by Mundahs in the Ranchi bazaar, and several attacks had also been made by them on the police in the district. At the request of the civil authorities, on December 29th a party of 2 native officers and 82 rank and file under the command of Captain H. J. Roche marched to Khunte, twenty miles south of Dorunda, and worked in concert with the Deputy Commissioner through the surrounding country.

1899.
1st Battalion.

On January 7th an organized attack was made by some two or three hundred Mundahs on the police station at Khunte which resulted in a constable being killed. Accordingly a further party, consisting of Lieutenants Middlemass and Vandergucht, 2 native officers and 134 rank and file, the whole under the command of Lieutenant-Colonel Westmorland, marched to Khunte. On January 9th a gang of about 150 insurgents were found to be in occupation of the Sait Rakab hill, three miles north of Saiko, and these were attacked by Captain Roche with a party of 1 native officer and 40 rank and file. The insurgents defied the troops, and after being fired on for some little time were dispersed at the point of the bayonet with a loss of 15 killed and 8 wounded.

The troops subsequently worked in several places through the disaffected portion of the district and furnished guards for various mission stations. By February 5th, after much hard marching, they had all returned to Dorunda.

At this time there was a great scarcity of rain in China, a scarcity which had lasted for two years and which resulted in a failure of the crops. A secret society, known as the Boxers, proclaimed that this was due to the influence of foreigners, and that until all foreigners were removed the rain would be withheld. The mysterious powers which these Boxers professed to possess appealed to the imagination of the young men and boys of the country, while the prospect of rapine and loot attracted all the ruffians, so that their numbers rapidly increased and they became able openly to defy and terrorize the provincial officials, while they were secretly encouraged by the Manchu party, who were the actual rulers of the land. Constant outrages were committed against both Chinese Christians and foreigners, and the legations at Pekin were surrounded. A mixed force of various nationalities advanced from Tientsin, and the legations were relieved on August 14th, 1900, and the city occupied, but the rising had not been finally suppressed. The 1st Royal Battalion arrived at Hong Kong on September 1st, 1900, where it disembarked and went into camp on Stonecutter's Island, having been posted to the 3rd Brigade of the Chinese Expeditionary Force. Here it was joined by the commandant, Lieutenant-Colonel Westmorland, and shortly afterwards re-embarked and sailed for Wei-hai-wei, in the province of Shan-tung, where it arrived on September 22nd.

[margin note: 1900. 1st Battalion.]

The nearest point on the coast to Pekin is the port of Tientsin, from which ran two railways, one direct to Pekin and the other north-east to Mukden. This latter crosses the Chinese frontier into Manchuria* at the seaboard town of Shan Hai Kuan. Field-Marshal Count Von Waldersee was now appointed Commander-in-Chief of the allied forces in China, and he immediately decided that Shan Hai Kuan should be occupied. The battalion, leaving No. 1 Double Company under the command of Major MacCartney for duty at Wei-hai-wei, sailed again on October 1st and arrived at Shan Hai Kuan, in the province of Chih-li, on the evening of the 2nd, where it disembarked without opposition the following morning. At Shan Hai Kuan there are several forts, and here also the Great Wall of China meets the sea. Headquarters of the battalion was located in what was known as No. 4 Fort, which it shared with some Japanese. A detachment also occupied the north gate of the city in conjunction with a party of French belonging to the 1st Regiment of Zouaves. There were also detachments in the railway station and No. 1 Fort, both of which were shared with troops of all the nationalities present.† On October 15th Fort " A " which was situated beyond the Great Wall, was occupied by No. 4 Double Company under Major C. F. G. Young, where it was subsequently joined by No. 1 Double Company on its arrival from Wei-hai-wei about the middle of October.

---

* Now called Manchukuo.
† Germans, Austrians, French, Italians, Japanese and Russians.

For nearly two months the battalion was employed mainly on working parties, though throughout the winter and spring detachments moved out on reconnaissance either alone or with other troops. At first the climate was pleasant, similar to autumn weather in England, but towards the middle of October it began to get much colder and occasionally snow fell on the hills to the north. On the 21st frost at night began, and on November 1st there was a quarter of an inch of ice on the ponds in the morning. From the beginning of December all water was frozen solid, while a couple of months later the sea was frozen for miles out. The cold did not affect the health of the battalion, which was excellent throughout. The men were most friendly with the Japanese, for whom they conceived a genuine liking. With other foreign troops they maintained amicable relations, with the exception of some quarrels with drunken French Zouaves, which resulted in one sepoy being wounded with a bayonet and two Zouaves badly hit with sticks.

Some seventy miles down the railway line towards Tientsin is the railway station of Lan Chou, and in October a greatly exaggerated report was brought in by the Russians that this had been attacked. A detachment of the battalion, taken from all companies, moved out on the 16th under the Commandant, together with Russian, German and French troops. The force detrained some sixteen miles north of Lan Chou, and the following day, which the majority of foreign troops spent in burning villages, the detachment of the 1st Royal Battalion, together with some Russian infantry, marched to the town of Yung Ping Fu ; and on the 19th the detachment, without the Russians, marched to Lan Chou railway station. No enemy were met and all the villagers were very friendly to the British. The party returned to Shan Hai Kuan on the 21st.

On April 20th a small party of the 4th Punjab Infantry was driven back by a gang of robbers, well armed with small-bore, breech-loading rifles ; and on the following day a detachment of 100 men **1901. 1st Battalion.** of the 1st Royal Battalion with a Maxim machine gun, under the command of Major Young, with Lieutenant P. H. Dundas and Lieutenant Hunter, I.M.S., left for Funing to join a small force operating against the robbers. The gang occupied the town of Tao To Ying and the surrounding villages, which were attacked on April 23rd. The enemy put up considerable resistance, but eventually the town was captured and the enemy fled, the battalion losing one non-commissioned officer and two men wounded, the non-commissioned officer later dying of his wounds.

Towards the end of May the battalion moved to Ching Wang Tao and took over the posts at eight stations along the railway line, and three more in the middle of June. On July 1st it left Ching Wang Tao by troop train and embarked for India on July 3rd.

From April to December, 1903, a double company of the 3rd Battalion, under Captain E. G. Wright and Lieutenant G. C. C. Clarke,

**1903.
3rd Battalion.** was stationed at Gangtok in Sikkim for duty on the lines of communication of General Younghusband's expedition to Lhassa.

During the same year Subedar Bhairo Gujar, 4 naiks and 18 sepoys of the 2nd Battalion went to Somaliland as mounted infantry. On

2nd Battalion. December 19th, at the action of Jidballi, the subedar saw Sepoy Dhana Gujar dismounted and hard pressed. He returned alone and, under the fire of the enemy horsemen, mounted him on his pony and carried him out of action, for which he was admitted to the 3rd Class of the Order of Merit. He was later awarded the 2nd Class of the Order of British India for conspicuous bravery in the same campaign.

In May, 1912, Major Pocock, Captains Boxwell and Lecky and Lieutenant Daly, with 320 men of the 2nd Battalion, moved to

**1912.
2nd Battalion.** Berbera in Somaliland. The detachment supported the Camel Corps during a punitive expedition in the interior, but did not take part in any fighting.

To face page 78

9th Jat Regt.

CHAPTER VIII

FRANCE, 1914

Bibliography.—Regimental Records.

IN August, 1914, the 1st Royal Battalion was stationed at Secunderabad, and on the 10th of that month, six days after the declaration of war with Germany, it received orders to mobilize as a unit of the 19th (Dehra Dun) Brigade of the Indian Expeditionary Force.

1st Battalion.

Owing to the raids being carried out in the Indian Ocean by the German cruiser *Emden*, transports could only safely move in convoys adequately escorted : it was, therefore, not until September 20th that the battalion, under the command of Lieutenant-Colonel H. J. Roche, sailed from Bombay on the H.T. *Arankola*, one of a convoy of twenty-nine transports escorted by H.M.Ss. *Swiftsure, Fox* and the Royal Indian Marine ship *Dufferin*.

The battalion arrived at Marseilles at 7 a.m. on October 12th, where it was ordered to exchange its rifles and ammunition and then march about nine miles to a camp at La Valentine. It was about 3.20 p.m. before the battalion could commence its march, which led through the city, where the battalion was very cordially received by the public ; but it was for the most part over rough cobble, and the last mile of the road was hilly and in very bad condition, so that it was trying to men who had spent nearly a month on board ship. The result was that camp could not be pitched that night and it was necessary to bivouac in a damp valley after a dispiriting march—ominous of what was ahead.

On the afternoon of October 17th the battalion marched from La Valentine and entrained in very wet and stormy weather at the Gare d'Arenc, alongside the quay where it had landed, the men travelling in covered goods wagons, forty to a wagon. Halts of three hours' duration were made each night for cooking, and early on October 20th the battalion arrived at Orleans, where it detrained and encamped on a muddy plain at Les Greues, about a mile and a half from the station. Here it was possible to get a little practice on the range with the new rifles and also to carry out some route marches.

The battalion left Orleans on October 27th shortly after midnight and detrained at Merville at 1.30 p.m. on the 28th, where it went into its first billets on the eastern outskirts of the town, the Indian ranks in sheds and workshops, the British officers in cottages. The latter who, by order of the corps commander, were wearing safas instead of helmets, were not cordially received until their identity was established by the French interpreters. That afternoon the battalion had its first glimpse of the enemy in the form of a German monoplane which flew over the billets at a great height.

The following day the battalion marched to Vieille Chapelle, where it arrived at 1 p.m. and was ordered to go into temporary billets ; but at 6 p.m. further orders were received that the Dehra Dun Brigade was to relieve the 7th (British) Brigade in the trenches that night.

Owing to counter-orders regarding the route received after the brigade had started, it was 2.30 a.m. before the battalion arrived at the trenches. The ground was wet and slippery, there was no communication trench, and while the relief was taking place the enemy opened a very heavy fire. The brigade was disposed opposite Neuve Chapelle on, and to the east of, the main Estaires–La Bassée road in the following order from the right : 1st Seaforth Highlanders, the 1st Royal Battalion, 1/9th Gurkha Rifles, 2/2nd Gurkha Rifles. Brigade headquarters at Vieille Chapelle. The battalion dispositions were : No. 1 Double Company (Lieutenant-Colonel A. J. Jamieson and Captain A. C. Anderson) on the right, No. 3 Double Company (Captain R. C. Ross) in the centre, No. 4 Double Company (Captain F. G. Moore) on the left, with No. 2 Double Company (Major P. H. Dundas and Lieutenant E. C. Liptrott) in support at Pont Logy, where battalion headquarters was established. The machine-gun section (two guns under Captain J. P. Gilbert) was in the left sector.

Three double companies (hereafter called companies) had relieved portions of three war-worn and depleted battalions of the 7th Brigade. The trenches taken over had been hastily prepared, were not continuous, and in the left sector the parapet had been undercut for shelters, with the result that it fell in during the first rain, leaving the trench a wide shell-trap. By a coincidence this was the only sector of the three which was not subjected to shell fire. There were no communication trenches, no second or third line, and no arrangements for latrines. The company in support lay up for the day in a ditch partially concealed by a hedge, and in the early hours of darkness commenced work on a support trench.

At 11 a.m. on the 30th the battalion had its baptism of shell fire, the trench line being subjected to shrapnel and the houses on either side of the La Bassée road to high explosive. Battalion headquarters and the aid-post which had occupied houses during the hours of darkness had, on the advice of their predecessors, forsaken them for haystacks during the day, and both had narrow escapes during the morning shelling. At 3 p.m. the enemy again shelled the trenches with shrapnel, and just before dark made an attempt to advance, but were soon checked by cross-fire from the 1st Royal Battalion and the Seaforths. During the day the battalion lost 2 killed and 2 wounded.

During the following day the enemy carried out much the same time-table, but the resultant casualties were heavier, the battalion losing 17 wounded ; while on November 1st 1 was killed and 9 wounded.

Heavy gun fire was opened on the trenches at 7 a.m. on the morning of November 2nd, and at 9 a.m. it was reported that the 2/2nd Gurkhas were being seriously attacked and subjected to severe minenwerfer fire ; Captain Ross with " C " Company, being then in support, moved to their assistance. By 12 noon the 7th Dragoon Guards and 34th Poona Horse also arrived, and the line, though bent back, was kept intact. " C " Company returned at 8 p.m., and the casualties in the battalion during the day consisted of 24 wounded.

During this first period of the battalion in the trenches it was shelled regularly twice a day, particularly by one field battery which had an accurate estimate of the range, while the British guns were handicapped by want of ammunition. Battalion headquarters was twice set on fire by shell fire. When the weather was fine a German monoplane would fly over in the direction of Richebourg out of range of rifle fire and apparently unmolested. Though not large on any one day, the casualties were consistently reducing the strength of the battalion, the heaviest occurring on November 5th, when 4 were killed and 23 wounded. Subedar Shib Lal was the first Indian officer wounded, followed two days later by Jemadar Tulsa, severely wounded. There was a good deal of rain and fog, and it was generally very cold in the early hours of the morning. The men began to suffer from swollen feet, and Lieutenant L. M. Peet* was evacuated to hospital with this complaint, which developed into rheumatic fever and practically finished his active soldiering.

At this time the atta ration, the staple food of the men, ran short, and they were issued with one-third of this ration supplemented by bread, biscuit and tinned mutton. Some of the older men, especially those who had served with the battalion in China, and the younger, driven to it by hunger, accepted the substitute, but the majority were inclined to use the bread and biscuits as cobble stones in the wet trenches till disciplinary action was taken. The discovery that on the outside of the mutton tins was the head of a cow caused the whole lot of this to be thrown away, the explanation that this was merely the trade-mark of the company being not sufficiently convincing.

On November 14th the battalion was relieved in the trenches and

---

* Later Judge-Advocate-General in India.

G

withdrew to Zelobes, half a mile west of Vieille Chapelle. Here it was
billeted by companies in farm-houses ; the inhabitants were full of
hospitality but embarrassingly curious, despite which fact a bath and
change of clothing after fifteen days on end in the trenches, were much
enjoyed. The change of clothing was absolutely necessary, as vermin
had begun to show themselves, a phase of warfare which had not
hitherto been experienced by the battalion.

The rest was brief, as early on November 16th orders were received
to march at 9 a.m. to Gorre to join the Bareilly Brigade, and on arrival
at Gorre further orders were received to leave cooking parties, baggage
and transport in billets there and march to a farm-house at a cross-
roads on the Rue de Béthune with a view to an attack that night near
Festubert.

At this time the enemy's system of progress was to sap forward from
his front-line trench and then join up the sap-heads, so forming a new
front line. There were two of these saps in particular about two
hundred yards apart on the front held by the 4th Cavalry and 107th
Pioneers which were becoming a nuisance, and these it was decided to
destroy. The general plan was that a party of infantry should occupy
the enemy's trench from which these saps started while a party of
engineers followed up and destroyed the saps, half an hour being allowed
for the work. " B " Company, 125 strong, was detailed for the task,
with 60 of the 1st Sappers and Miners under Captain E. H. Kelly, R.E.,
and Lieutenant E. O. Wheeler, R.E. There was to be no preliminary
bombardment, but fifteen minutes after the advance commenced the
artillery of the section was to open on the rear German trenches.

" B " Company extended in the front-line trench opposite the line
to be captured, Major Dundas with the right half and Lieutenant
Liptrott with the left, and advanced at 9 p.m. with orders not to fire
until the enemy's main trench was reached. As it cleared its own wire
a heavy cross-fire was opened on it from the German saps, and some
casualties resulted. Some of the enemy in the saps were dealt with on
the way, but the greater part of the company pushed on to its objective.
At sixty yards or so a deep drain was crossed which, on the right, was
intersected by the sap but on the left bore away obliquely, and this was
used for the approach of the sappers. About the same distance on
the main trench was reached, evidently an old British one, as it had
originally been prepared to fire in the opposite direction. Germans
were seen retiring from it and also running along it to the right and left.

The mouth of the right sap was closed. A party under No. 1548
Havildar Badlu moved out to the right, clearing the trench, while
another under Jemadar Inchha Ram worked back along the sap,
clearing it to the drain in rear. Both were severely wounded, but
continued to carry on. Lieutenant Liptrott extended to the left

beyond the original frontage till he met the enemy who had retired along the trench in that direction. Here he established a block and kept them off, but the mouth of the left sap was not found. Shortly before 10 p.m. enemy guns opened fire and the signal to withdraw was given. Parties were detailed to work back along the saps; the left one was empty, but a few Germans were found bottled up in the right sap and were dealt with.

During the withdrawal Subedar Kanha (II) and a wounded German prisoner were killed, and Subedar Neki (II) was mortally wounded by a fragment of shell and was carried in by Lieutenant Liptrott, assisted by a sepoy. The casualties during the operation were 1 Indian officer and 12 other ranks killed, 2 Indian officers (of whom one died) and 21 other ranks wounded. Major Dundas received the D.S.O., Jemadar Inchha Ram the Military Cross, Havildar Jai Lal the Indian Order of Merit, Havildar Badlu and Sepoy Risal the Indian Distinguished Service Medal, while Lieutenant Liptrott was mentioned in despatches and the battalion was congratulated by the Corps Commander.

The battalion then remained in the trenches, while the enemy became particularly aggressive as a result of the raid and increased his sapping activity, covered by intermittent shelling and bombing, which became heavier as the saps approached the battalion front line. To cope with the sapping hand-grenades were introduced. These consisted of either jam- or tobacco-tins filled with explosive, or of slabs of explosive tied on to a piece of wood with a handle to it; a length of safety fuse led out of a detonator in the explosive. This had to be cut to the estimated required length and then lit, which in rain and wind was no easy matter.

The first experiments with improvised mortars were also carried out in the battalion trenches during this period. Two were produced, one of metal, the other apparently of hoop-iron. The projectile was an 18-pounder cartridge cut down and filled with explosive and a detonator; a short length of instantaneous fuse connected the detonator with a length of safety fuse. The propellant was black powder, ladled into the mortar in a tobacco-tin, with a length of safety fuse shorter than that of the projectile. Length of fuse and quantity of charge required were found by trial and error. The method of firing the mortar was to light both fuses and walk round the nearest traverse to observe results. This weapon was invented by Major P. J. Patterson, R.F.A., and was known as " Patterson's Pulveriser for Portly Prussians."

The experimenting officer professed himself quite satisfied with the results obtained, and carried off the better of the two mortars, leaving the other for use by the battalion. His experiments had begun at night and had ended in daylight, when the smoke of the black powder disclosed the whereabouts of the new engine of destruction.

The immediate result was a retaliation by shell fire which buried and, it is believed, destroyed the remaining mortar—a loss regretted by no one in that portion of the line.

The retaliation also had the effect of blocking a communication trench which joined a building known as " The Glory Hole "—untenable by day, but held by a piquet at night—to a piquet in the front-line trench. On November 20th, while this was in process of being cleared, a brief shelling, accompanied by rifle and machine-gun fire and bombing, took place, and some of the enemy were seen advancing across the open towards the communication trench. This move was checked by rifle fire, but for the time being the piquet was isolated. Three men were killed and one severely wounded while trying to reach it, and it was only by tearing down a machine-gun barricade and moving along a previously abandoned portion of trench that reinforcements reached the piquet. While using his revolver on the advancing Germans Lieutenant E. C. Liptrott was shot through the head. He managed to walk out of the trenches and was sent at once to Field Ambulance, but died of his wounds at Boulogne on November 26th.

Two days later, on November 22nd, it was reported that the enemy were gathering in the irrigation drain between the two trench systems. Captain A. C. Anderson reinforced the piquet nearest to the drain, and was himself throwing hand-grenades when one burst in his hand and killed him.

That evening the battalion was relieved in the trenches by the 34th Pioneers and moved into brigade reserve at the cross-roads on the Rue de Béthune, about three-quarters of a mile west of Festubert ; but at half-past seven the next morning, November 23rd, received orders to move up in support of the centre section of the Bareilly Brigade, where a portion of the front line had been blown in and captured by the enemy.

Two nights before snow had fallen, and this had been followed by a frost, so that the whole ground was covered with frozen snow.

" A " and " C " Companies were the first to arrive in the section, and were ordered to the left and right respectively to watch those flanks. " B " and " D " Companies and the machine-gun section were then ordered by the commander of the section to counter-attack. The only information available was that the enemy, after springing one or more mines, had advanced and cleared the trenches to right and left by bombing, but nothing was known of the extent of his gains or of the number or position of our troops still in front, and in the need of the moment there was no time to arrange for artillery support.

At 11.30 a.m. the two companies started, " D " Company finding the firing line and supports, with its right on the road which led to the main communication trench, " B " Company in local reserve, with the machine-gun section moving in the ditch bordering the road. The second-line trench, on which the battalion had been working the six previous nights, was reached without loss. In it were two companies of the 34th Pioneers, under Major Cullen, from whom it was ascertained that some of our own troops were still holding a more forward position in a ditch some four hundred yards on.

A joint advance was then made from the second line, the two companies of the 1st Royal Battalion still in the same formation. It was subjected to heavy rifle and machine-gun fire, to which there was little reply owing to uncertainty regarding the positions still held. The advance was checked in a ditch some three hundred and fifty yards from the enemy's new line and parallel to it. Here were found portions of the 34th Pioneers, 9th Bhopal Infantry and 58th Rifles, who had been hanging on ever since they had been forced out of their original line. Major Cullen having been severely wounded in the advance, Major Dundas was now the senior officer in the front line. Captain F. G. Moore was severely wounded in the head by a sniper while trying to get up ammunition for his company. The attacking lines of the 1st Royal Battalion moved forward in the broad daylight across the snow-covered ground without the least hesitation, and the rushes from objective to objective were carried out with the greatest *élan* and determination. Not until the front line was within the last hundred yards, with half its British and Indian officers knocked out and the numerous German machine guns pouring into it an increasingly intense and murderous fire, was the advance brought to a stop just as darkness fell.

Major Dundas was wounded in the arm, Subedar Kanha (I) and Subedar Neki (I) were killed, and Jemadars Shiu Lal and Jug Lal wounded, 40 Indian other ranks of the battalion were killed and 104 wounded. The enemy continued to keep up a heavy fire for some little time after it became dark, which delayed reorganization. Lieutenant-Colonel Roche had moved up with the second line, and after dark it became very difficult for him to keep in touch with the situation in front and he decided to go forward, accompanied by the Adjutant, and see things for himself. There was then little firing or noise, and it was difficult in the darkness to find anything to guide him or to distinguish between friend and foe. He was about to get into the first trench he came to when he was challenged at short range in German and immediately fired at, the bullet just grazing his nose. Realizing his mistake, he hurriedly retraced his steps and got back to his own men. He then found that he was not accompanied by the Adjutant, Captain L. G. Dudley. Meeting the Quartermaster, Lieutenant A. B. McPherson, who had gone in search of him, he told of the escape he had just had and asked if Captain Dudley had been seen. Lieutenant McPherson then went in search of Captain Dudley, and finally came upon him lying in an unoccupied trench. He had a very large wound in the chest. With the aid of Captain Gilbert and some men he was got into a stretcher and taken to hospital, and died at Gorre early next morning.

Lieutenant-Colonel Roche then ordered the leading lines to maintain their position. The 1st Gurkhas had recaptured a portion of the trench held by the Germans, and a part of " C " Company of the 1st Royal Battalion was sent up a communication trench on the right to support a movement being made under Major Cassels and Captain Buckland of the 1st Gurkhas to attack along the trench with the aid of bombs. Lieutenant C. J. Cockburn of the 1st Royal Battalion, with two or three men of " C " Company, then joined Major Cassels and, reinforced by Captain E. H. Kelly of the Sappers, the little party made very considerable progress by means of that extremely useful system of aggression which afterwards became known as " bombing along a trench " until their supply of bombs was exhausted. This was probably the first time this system was used. Major Cassels was badly hurt and almost blinded by an enemy bomb which wounded him in a dozen different places. Lieutenant Cockburn, who received the Military Cross, escaped with a graze, Captain Buckland being also slightly wounded.

During the evening Subedar Ram Bhagat had been wounded, and at about midnight the 107th Pioneers arrived to relieve the remnants of the 34th Pioneers, the 9th Bhopals and the 1st Royal Battalion, which marched back into billets at 4 a.m.

The battalion had now lost fifty per cent. of its British officers, 10 out of its 15 Indian officers, and its strength was under 300 Indian ranks. It moved into billets at Le Hamel on November 27th, when the necessary reorganization was undertaken.

On December 3rd the battalion again moved forward into billets on the Rue de Béthune as brigade reserve, and commenced providing fatigue parties for carrying and digging every night, in the performance of which four men were killed and six wounded. Then, on the 11th, it was moved to Cse. Duraux, where it again came under the orders of the Dehra Dun Brigade. By this time the battalion, though still much under strength in Indian ranks, had received considerable reinforcements, and that evening it relieved the 2/3rd Gurkhas in the trenches.

The battalion was now holding about three hundred and fifty or four hundred yards of trench with three companies, while one company was in local reserve at battalion headquarters, situated at Richebourg l'Avoue on the Rue du Bois. In the centre of the battalion front was a rather awkward salient. The first day or two were compara-tively uneventful, though throughout the 14th and 15th the whole Indian Corps maintained a steady, controlled fire in order to keep the enemy tied to his trenches while attacks were carried out on other parts of the front.   On the early morning of the 19th the Leicestershire Regiment delivered an attack on the enemy trenches, and by 7 a.m., being in touch with the 1st Royal Battalion at the salient, were reported to have captured two machine guns and two prisoners and occupied about one hundred and fifty yards of trench ; but later, in the face of heavy bombing attacks, they were forced to yield up, yard by yard, the trenches they had taken, and under cover of darkness they finally withdrew.

On this day Captain J. P. Gilbert, the machine-gun officer of the 1st Royal Battalion, was wounded in both legs.*

There was considerable rifle fire during that night, and early on the 20th a German mine was blown up and, under minenwerfer and shell fire, an attack was made against the 2/2nd Gurkhas on the right of the 1st Royal Battalion.   On the right of the 2/2nd Gurkhas were the Seaforth Highlanders, with the Highland Light Infantry beyond them.   Both the 2/2nd Gurkhas and the Highland Light Infantry were forced out of their trenches, leaving both flanks of the Seaforths in the air.   The right of the 1st Royal Battalion was left in the air by the withdrawal of the majority of the 2nd Gurkhas ; this consisted of " C " Company under Captain Ross, and Lieutenant-Colonel Roche at once sent up " A " Company from the reserve and instructed Captain Ross to hold on at all costs, using part of " A " Company to strengthen his flank.   The remainder of the 2nd Gurkhas, under Captain Bethell, were also organized under Captain Ross's command.   At about 2 p.m. the 1/9th Gurkhas arrived and were put at Lieutenant-Colonel Roche's disposal.   He ordered them to get into position echeloned behind the right flank of the 1st Royal Battalion.   A similar situation arose on the right of the gap, where the 58th Rifles had been brought up and echeloned to the rear of the left of the Seaforths ; thus communication was more or less established, although there were no trenches connecting the 9th Gurkhas with the 58th, there having been no second-line trenches originally.   Late in the afternoon and during the early hours of the night the 41st Dogras and the Black Watch arrived, and were employed by Lieutenant-Colonel Roche in digging a second line.   Next morning Captain Bethell's company of the 2nd Gurkhas was withdrawn and the right flank of the 1st Royal Battalion was readjusted.

On the evening of the 21st, at 7 p.m., a brigade of the 1st British Division counter-attacked, the 1st Royal Battalion assisting them by fire.   The attack was made over ground which the attackers did not know, and in the dark, so it is uncertain how far it progressed, but its

---

* Captain Gilbert, when convalescent from his wounds, was ordered to India to take over command of the battalion depot. He sailed in the s.s. *Persia*, which was torpedoed and sunk. Both Captain Gilbert and his wife were drowned.

effects were neutralized by a sudden heavy attack by the enemy which was launched before 9 a.m. while there was a heavy mist. The British brigade was compelled to withdraw through the rear positions held by the 58th, 41st and 9th Gurkhas.

That evening the 30th Lancers, under Lieutenant-Colonel Mason Macfarlane, arrived and reported to Lieutenant-Colonel Roche, who by this time had the better part of two brigades under his command. This regiment, with the remainder of the Black Watch, was employed in strengthening the line which had been commenced by the 41st Dogras, while the brigaded machine guns of the Garhwal Brigade, under Captain Lodwick of the 3rd Gurkhas, were ordered by Lieutenant-Colonel Roche to take up a position near the junction of the Rue du Bois and Chocolat Menier road to support the left flank of the 1st Royal Battalion.

By means of these fresh troops it was possible to complete the new lines which had been mapped out by Captain C. A. Bird, R.E., and although there was a good deal of minenwerfer firing during the day no further attempt to advance was made by the enemy.

On the morning of the 24th Lord Cavan, commanding the 1st Guards Brigade, arrived at the headquarters of the 1st Royal Battalion and discussed the situation with a view to relief, and that night the battalion was relieved and marched back about three miles to Richebourg St. Vaast, having lost 13 other ranks killed and Jemadar Jai Chand and 75 other ranks wounded, besides Captain Gilbert, during this, its last spell in the trenches in 1914.

Chapter IX

FRANCE AND EGYPT, 1915

Bibliography.—Regimental Records.

THE early days of 1915 were employed by the 1st Royal Battalion in reorganizing after its heavy losses, and several inspections of the battalion were carried out, during one of which, on January 4th, General Sir James Wilcocks, commanding the Indian Corps in France, said that the name of " Jat " had been greatly enhanced by the behaviour of the battalion since it had been in France and would not be forgotten. On the 7th Field-Marshal Sir John French also congratulated the battalion on its behaviour.

1915.
1st Battalion.

On January 29th the battalion moved into the front-line trenches. It remained there for three days of comparative quiet, losing Jemadar Badlu (I) killed and Jemadar Chandgi and six sepoys wounded before being relieved on February 1st. It then remained behind the trenches, usually in a state of constant readiness to move at short notice, until the 27th, when it relieved the East Lancashire Regiment on the line of the La Bassée road from near Pont Logy to a point a few hundred yards north of the junction of the Rue du Bois and the La Bassée road—a frontage of about six hundred yards. The trenches were cut into the road in order to avoid the water which filled the whole trench held in November, and were in very bad condition ; the few traverses had been much cut into to make shelters for the men during the winter, while the parapet was so low it needed a great deal of work to make it possible for men to walk along the roadway behind in safety. There was no second line. Work was greatly hampered by the extreme narrowness and slipperiness of the roadway, while a hostile machine gun, which could not be identified by day, caused a number of casualties among men moving out of the trenches at night to collect materials, such as bricks, in rear of the trench line. Altogether, from the time the battalion entered the trenches until the evening of the 9th, 7 men were killed, 2 died of wounds and 40 were wounded.

On the 7th orders were received that the Garhwal Brigade was to carry out an attack from the line held by the Battalion, and that the trench was to be made suitable for offensive action. Accordingly, shelters were knocked down, parapets thickened, roadways broadened, and on the night of the 9th ladders were placed in position for use by the attacking troops, bridges were placed at frequent intervals across the ditch east of the La Bassée road, and the wire entanglements in front of the trenches were cut, the wire being drawn between the stakes towards the enemy.

At 3.30 during the night the Garhwal Brigade commenced arriving in the trenches, and at 7 a.m. manned the trenches in place of the 1st Royal Battalion. Half an hour later the British artillery commenced a heavy bombardment of the enemy's wire entanglements which lasted for ten minutes, gradually increasing its range for a further twenty minutes over the enemy's line of trenches and rear positions ; simultaneously heavy rifle and machine-gun fire was opened from the front line. At 8.5 a.m. the bombardment ceased and the Garhwal Brigade immediately attacked ; there was little or no fire and there were no apparent obstacles. The Germans surrendered at once. By 9.30 practically the whole of the Garhwal Brigade had gone forward, and the enemy began shelling the line held by the 1st Royal Battalion with light howitzers and shrapnel. By 9.50 information was received that the Garhwal Brigade had gained the whole of the enemy's line except two hundred yards, and had taken over a hundred prisoners ; while the 8th Division, on the left, had reached Neuve Chapelle church.

As soon as the Garhwal Brigade was clear the 1st Royal Battalion had commenced the construction of two communication trenches forward to the captured line, but was compelled to abandon work on the southern one temporarily. This work was recommenced at 12.30, but Captain T. L. Ovens (11th Rajputs, attached to the battalion) and three men were hit, with the consequence that the work was again postponed, although the northern trench was completed by 3.30 p.m. The southern was eventually dug under cover of darkness, but was not fully completed until 4 a.m. on the 12th. The battalion did not take part in the subsequent attacks during the battle of Neuve Chapelle, which were held up by the River Des Layes, but was employed mainly in trench-digging under shell fire and in collecting rifles and material, including a large quantity of correspondence and papers in the German trenches.

At 5.30 p.m. on the 13th the battalion marched out of the trenches, arriving two hours later at Vieille Chapelle, where billets had been allotted, but within a quarter of an hour was ordered back to the trenches as an enemy counter-attack was expected. Food was being cooked in the farm at Cour St. Vaaste, and as the battalion marched back past this farm-house quantities of chappaties were handed to the men, who carried them back to the trenches up the Richebourg road through a great mixture of units and transport, where the enemy's shells added to the confusion. The night passed without incident and the battalion was back in billets by half-past ten the following morning, having lost, since the commencement of the Garhwal attack, 13 Indian other ranks killed and 1 British officer (Captain Ovens) and 60 other ranks wounded.

After a period of rest and reorganization at Paradis the brigade again moved into the trenches at Pont du Hem, the battalion being in brigade reserve in billets on the Estaires road. Lieutenant-Colonel Roche, who had been made a Companion of the Order of the Bath, was temporarily in command of the Brigade, and the battalion was commanded for a few days by Captain Twiss (3rd Battalion, attached). The period was one of quiet, and the battalion was employed mainly in digging while the British officers made themselves acquainted with the trench system and, as far as possible, with the ground in front. On the 30th the battalion was relieved, and arrived again at Paradis on April 1st, where it again came under the orders of the Dehra Dun Brigade.

This period of rest was notable for two events, the first being a visit by General Sir Douglas Haig, who was met by all commanding officers, and the second an inspection by Field-Marshal Sir John French, who made a congratulatory speech which was translated into Hindustani by the Brigade Commander, Brigadier-General Jacob.* The weather was greatly improving, which added to the comfort of the battalion.

On April 12th the battalion again moved forward, but remained in brigade reserve until the 28th, when sectors were exchanged with the Garhwal Brigade and the battalion was ordered to hold the line in front of the Rue du Bois along with the 1/9th Gurkhas. At 4 a.m. the following morning the enemy started bombing very heavily into the Orchard Redoubt, where " D " Company was in support and in rear of the main trench. The British guns replied with a very little shelling. There were only two casualties in the battalion, one other rank being killed and one wounded. At 4.30 a.m. on the 30th the enemy again started bombing the Orchard, though not so heavily as on the previous day, though their artillery was more active than usual, and during the following night they made an unusual amount of noise working in front of their parapet and digging.

On May 1st at about 4.30 the Germans suddenly opened a very heavy bombardment with their artillery and bomb guns. The first-line trenches were practically unaffected, but the rear face of the Orchard, the Rue du Bois and the ground immediately south of it were very heavily shelled. At the same time machine guns opened with short bursts of fire along the top of the parapet of the front line. The bombardment was kept up until 5.20, in spite of reply from the British guns.

---

* Now Field-Marshal Sir Claud Jacob.

The actual damage done was very slight considering the intensity of the fire, and there were no casualties in the battalion. The extent of the ground covered by the bombardment, coupled with the feverish excitement among the German working parties during the previous night, pointed to the fact that the Germans had been expecting an attack in the early morning and had hoped to catch the assembled attacking troops with their fire. A German aeroplane then appeared over the line and the remainder of the day was quiet.

Little occurred during the following two days, and on the 5th two companies in the front line were relieved by the 4th Seaforths—the third being relieved on the night of the 6th by the 2nd Gurkhas—and moved to Vieille Chapelle, where they remained during the 7th and 8th. One company was still in the Orchard and headquarters in the Rue du Bois. On the 8th Lieutenant-Colonel Roche, C.B., was admitted to hospital sick, and did not again rejoin the battalion, command of which devolved upon Major E. A. F. Redl (113th Infantry, attached).

At 5.30 a.m. on May 9th an attack was made on the German trenches by the 2nd Gurkhas, the 1st Royal Battalion moving up to be in support. Two platoons of the 1st Royal Battalion were ordered to operate on the right of the 2nd Gurkhas so as to maintain connection with the brigade on the right. Before the attack was launched bottles of bicarbonate of soda were passed round for the soaking of anti-gas masks. The two platoons on the right advanced with the Gurkhas in two lines. The first moved forward under Captain D. Dudley (91st Punjabis, attached) and Subedar Lekh Ram, and was practically wiped out, Subedar Lekh Ram being killed and Captain Dudley so severely wounded that he died soon after. All the rank and file were either killed or wounded. The second line also suffered severely, Lieutenant Hibbert (44th Infantry, attached) being severely wounded and Jemadar Nanwa Singh wounded. The attack was held up by heavy machine-gun fire and was not pressed so that the remainder of the battalion was not called upon to advance. During the afternoon the battalion was relieved in the trenches by the Black Watch and withdrew without casualties, although the ground traversed was heavily shrapnelled by the enemy. The total casualties during the day among the rank and file were 22 killed, the bodies of 18 of whom were not recovered, and 30 wounded.

The battalion then moved into billets near Vieille Chapelle, and on the 17th received an unexpected and unofficial visit from His Royal Highness the Prince of Wales, who arrived driving his own car and stayed for about a quarter of an hour discussing the situation and inquiring into the part taken by the battalion in the recent attack. Major Redl was struck off the strength of the battalion on May 20th, and command devolved upon Captain R. G. Baker (82nd Punjabis, attached) for a few days until Captain R. C. Ross returned from short leave in England and took over command.

On the 23rd the officers of the battalion were taken round the trenches occupied by the 1/4th Gurkhas with a view to relieving that battalion, and Lieutenant N. L. Inkson (Indian Army Reserve, attached) was wounded. The battalion moved up the following night. The line was an unusual one. In front of the front-line trench there was a hill which obstructed the view from the enemy, and this made it possible to keep one's head above the parapet without fear of rifle fire and even to walk about outside the trench ; the shelling, however, was so heavy that the communication trenches were not made use of. While the relief was being carried out the battalion was heavily shelled, but no casualties occurred, and the front line was occupied by a company composed of all the men left of the original battalion, in support of which was a company composed of reinforcements received from the 113th Infantry, who were occupying an old German trench. A third line was held by a company composed of drafts received from the 87th Punjabis, while the fourth company, which was in reserve north of the Rue du Bois, consisted of reinforcements from the 82nd Punjabis. During the night there was a great deal of shelling, mostly with light shells, but at 4 p.m. on the 25th the enemy heavily shelled the Rue du Bois and Albert road with 6-inch shells. During the three days the battalion was in these trenches it was more heavily shelled than it had been since the previous November, but the trenches gave good protection and the casualties were few, although battalion headquarters was practically demolished on the 26th. After four days in the second-line trenches near St. Vaast post, where a new type of respirator, which was subsequently found to be ineffective, was received, the battalion again returned to the front line until June 2nd. The casualties from shelling during these ten days in the trenches amounted to 6 killed and 40 wounded.

Three more spells in the front-line trenches from June 17th to June 23rd, June 29th to July 3rd, and July 7th to July 10th, then took place, during which no events of outstanding importance occurred. The casualties in the battalion during the first of these periods of " all quiet on the Western Front " were 1 killed and 19 wounded ; during the second, 2 were killed and 1 Indian officer (Subedar Harnarain Singh, who subsequently died from his wounds) and 32 other ranks were wounded. Second-Lieutenant W. A. Doyle-Kelly (Indian Army Reserve, attached) was also slightly wounded. During the third spell 11 other ranks were wounded.

On July 20th, while the battalion was in billets near Calonne railway station, a bomb accident occurred, mortally wounding Second-Lieutenant Seppings-Wright (Indian Army Reserve, attached) and one sepoy and wounding four others.

On August 8th the battalion relieved the 2/8th Gurkhas in trenches to the north of Neuve Chapelle. Little happened during this spell in the trenches, which was chiefly remarkable on account of a patrol of the battalion bringing in eighteen German rifles, varying in dates from 1891 to 1915. The casualties were 19 wounded.

On the 14th orders were received for the battalion to be ready to move at short notice to Marseilles, and it embarked on the H.T. *Erinpura* before 5 a.m. on the 20th, parting with regret from its interpreter, Monsieur Henri Le Gras, who had been with the battalion since its first arrival in France without a day's absence or sickness. He had been invaluable and had almost become one of the regiment.

Amongst the complimentary farewell messages received, that from Brigadier-General C. W. Jacob stated that " The battalion had a very hard time during October, November and December. Fighting hard with hardly any rest, it has kept its good name. Its losses have been very heavy and there is very little of the 6th Jats left, but it went through everything with credit, and never gave way. Never once was it forced back. In all its attacks against overwhelming odds and decimating machine-gun fire it did more than it was thought human beings were capable of."

The battalion arrived at Port Said on August 26th, 1915, and left immediately for Kantara, which it reached the same day and where it joined the 31st Indian Infantry Brigade. At Kantara each battalion was encamped in rear of the portion of the perimeter allotted to it and was responsible for its security. By day each battalion furnished an observation post, and by night a double sentry was posted every two hundred yards along the perimeter. In addition to this, an outlying piquet slept, fully dressed, immediately in rear of the perimeter and stood to arms for half an hour before dusk and dawn. There was also a night outpost position of six piquets furnished by each battalion in turn. The battalion also provided a detachment for duty on an armoured train.

After October 14th detachments were sent off to various posts, but the battalion took part in no fighting before leaving Egypt on December 5th.

FRANCE

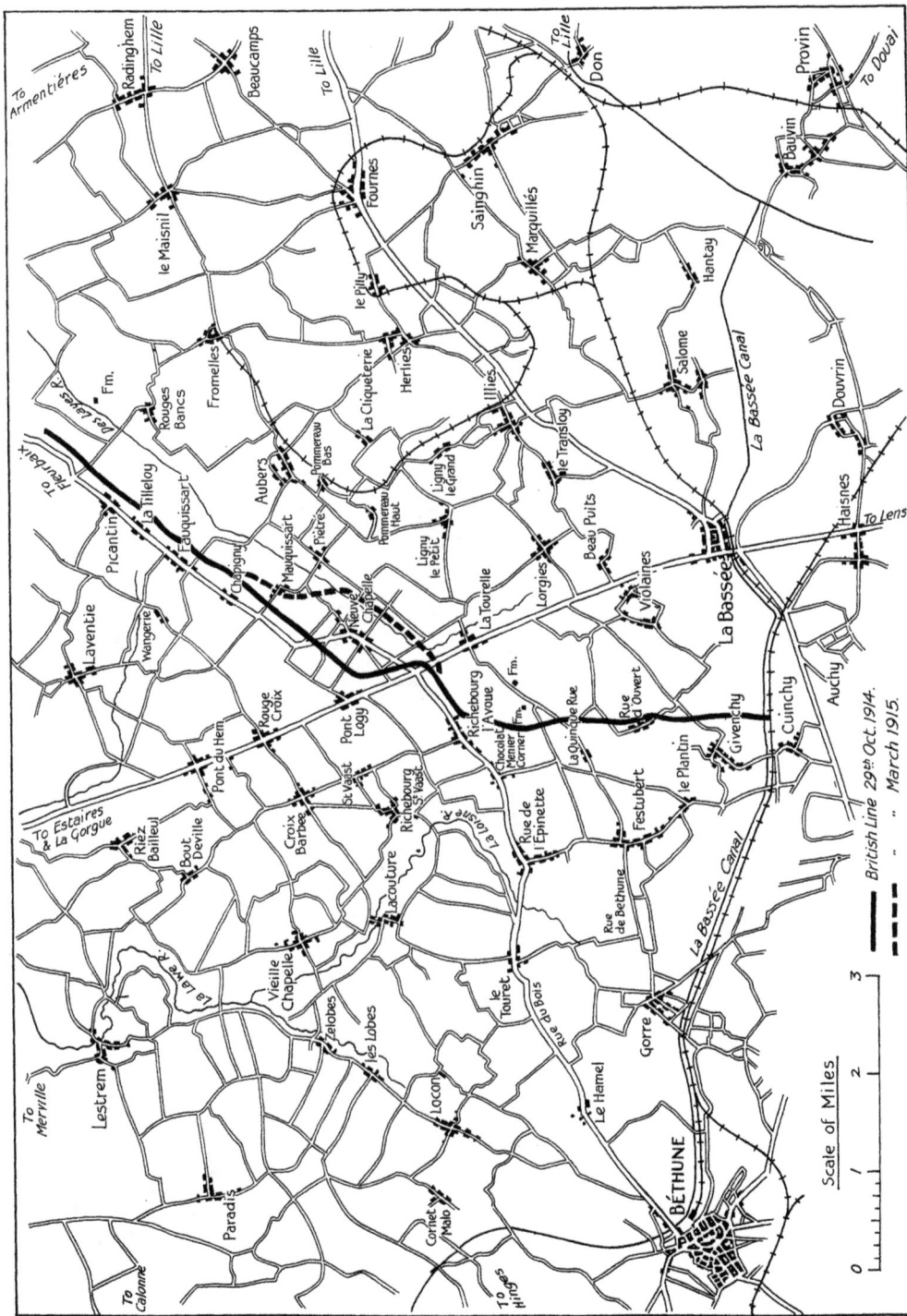

British Line 29th Oct. 1914.
" " March 1915.

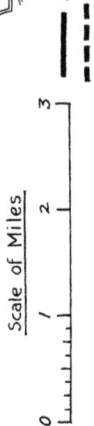

Scale of Miles

0 1 2 3

9th Jat. Regt.

CHAPTER X

THE ADVANCE TO CTESIPHON AND THE SIEGE OF KUT

Bibliography.—Regimental Records.

In 1914 the 2nd Battalion was stationed at Ahmadnagar, and during September received orders to mobilize as part of the 17th Brigade of
1914.
2nd Battalion.
the 6th Indian Division. It sailed from Bombay on November 19th, 1914, and disembarked at Basra on December 7th. The port of Basra is situated on the right bank of the Shatt-al-Arab, the great river formed by the junction of the Tigris and the Euphrates. On each bank of this river there is a dense belt of date palms, about three miles wide, with an undergrowth of vines, pomegranates and other fruits, intersected by numerous creeks and irrigation channels. Beyond this cultivated area lies the open desert. The city of Basra is on the outer edge of this belt bordering the desert and some distance from its suburb of Ashar on the river bank to which it is connected by a creek. During the early part of December the battalion was employed in garrisoning this city, which had recently been captured, and was split up for the purpose in four detachments ; but on the 17th it moved to Magil, on the bank of the river a short distance upstream of Ashar, where many of the incoming transports were unloaded, and here it encamped among the palm trees. Here Captain Boxwell, who had a knowledge of the Arabic language, was taken from the battalion and appointed Military Governor of Ashar, and for his services in this capacity he eventually received the C.I.E.

The Euphrates river has, in comparatively recent times, changed its main course and in the olden days it joined the Tigris at the town of Qurna, some forty miles upstream from Ashar. This town had surrendered to the British on December 8th, but a Turkish force had taken up a position on the Ratta creek about four miles to the north on the left bank of the Tigris. Here there is no belt of palm trees. The ground is an open, flat, stoneless plain, very fertile but uncultivated, hard in dry weather, but forming a peculiarly adhesive mud after rain.

On January 10th, 1915, the 2nd Battalion moved upstream and joined the 17th Brigade in a large perimeter camp on the left bank of the
1915.
2nd Battalion.
Tigris at Muzaira, opposite the town of Qurna. Here it was sniped every night, but no casualties occurred.

95

On January 20th a reconnaissance in force was carried out towards the Turkish position by the 17th Brigade, assisted by H.M.S. *Odin* of the Royal Navy. The 2nd Battalion was in brigade reserve, but one company was detailed as left flank-guard. The reconnaissance approached to within about eight hundred yards of the hostile position before withdrawing, when the flank-guard became merged in the firing line and came under fire from the Turkish trenches. This visit to the enemy was returned a few days later when the enemy made a night attack on Muzaira. The attack was ineffective, though a few casualties occurred on each side. The only loss suffered by the 2nd Battalion was the mess cask of rum which, in the words of the Mess President, " was shot in the bung and bled to death unobserved during the night." No further operation was undertaken, the brigade remaining in its perimeter camp at Muzaira. On February 28th the battalion crossed the river to Qurna, the reputed site of the Garden of Eden, where it remained until March 7th, when it was detached from the 17th Brigade and ordered back to Basra to form part of the 16th Brigade under Brigadier-General W. S. Delamain at Shaiba.

Shaiba lies nine miles south-west of Basra, but between the two is a tract of low-lying ground which at the time was flooded. The water was the overflow from the new channel of the Euphrates, which joins the Shatt-al-Arab at Kurmat Ali, six miles above Ashar. The flood varied in depth from one foot to four feet, but could not be waded as there was a creek through it impossible for men on foot to negotiate ; and the battalion, instead of moving direct to Shaiba, marched six miles across the flood to near the desert town of Zubair and then four miles along the edge of the flood, arriving at Shaiba on the evening of March 10th.

Here the force, consisting of one cavalry and two infantry brigades, was in an entrenched camp among a few buildings and groves of tamarisk trees, protected on three sides by a single line of trenches with no depth and on the fourth by the flooded area.

On April 11th news was received that a Turkish army was advancing with a view to the recapture of Basra, and that night the battalion remained in a state of readiness, all tents being struck and men and officers sleeping on the ground. At dawn a series of shots rang out, and away on the horizon were seen hordes of people assembled, probably two thousand yards away. These were the Turkish advanced troops accompanied by a host of Arabs.

All that day the battalion remained in the trenches watching the enemy, who did not venture within fifteen hundred yards of the position, which the open plain made very difficult of approach. That night consisted of one long, dreary watch, broken by bursts of rapid fire from the battalion and others at an enemy who occasionally came close and ventured to test the barbed wire.   The morning of the 13th broke to show that the Turks had withdrawn to their original positions of the day before and that they had entrenched themselves crudely. During the night Major-General Melliss had arrived from Basra by boat and taken over command of the forces at Shaiba.

Although the majority of the Turks were out of rifle range, there was one detachment occupying a position of considerable tactical importance some thousand yards from the British trenches.   General Melliss first sent the cavalry to drive these enemy back, but their move having proved unsuccessful, the 24th Punjabis were sent out.   The 24th, by operating against the Turkish flank, succeeded in dislodging the majority of the enemy ; and the 104th Infantry, together with two companies of the 2nd Battalion, under the command of Major J. R. Darley, moved out to clear up the remainder.   The enemy retired with some loss, leaving behind a few prisoners and two guns, without offering serious resistance.   The casualties in the battalion were very slight, though Lieutenant Haddon was hit on the head by an enemy shrapnel bullet, and a clerk, Havildar Arjun, was shot through the nose, the bullet entering at one side and coming out again at the other.   Apart from this action, the 2nd Battalion did little on the 13th, being generally confined to the trenches.

Contrary to expectations, the following night was dead quiet ; not a shot was fired, and it was believed in the battalion that the Turks and Arabs had withdrawn altogether.   Soon, however, information was received that the Turks had dug themselves in, in a very strong position, some six and a half miles south of Shaiba at a place called Barjisiyeh Wood.

General Melliss at once decided to move out of Shaiba and attack the enemy's position, and at nine in the morning the force advanced with the 18th Brigade on the right and the 16th on the left, commanded respectively by Generals Fry and Delamain.   The 2nd Battalion was in the 16th Brigade, of which the other battalions were the 2nd Dorset Regiment, 24th Punjabis and 117th Mahrattas.   The force advanced in line of battalions in column, with the cavalry protecting the right flank, until it reached the top of a long rise which slopes gradually down to Barjisiyeh Wood.   Here the battalion began to suffer casualties, which was not surprising in view of the fact that the ground was flat with no cover anywhere.   At about 2 p.m. Major G. N. L. Labertouche, who was commanding the leading company, was mortally wounded.   The battalion Medical Officer, Captain Harper Nelson, I.M.S., lifting the wounded officer on his back, carried him half a mile to the rear of the firing-line and thus out of the danger zone, then returned to the front line, where he continued to tend the wounded until the end of the action, for which he received the Military Cross.   Eventually

H

three and a half companies were entrenched in a crude manner within about three hundred yards of the Turks, the remaining half-company being kept in local reserve by the Commanding Officer, Lieutenant-Colonel Chitty. A message was then received by Lieutenant-Colonel Chitty from the Dorset Regiment saying that they were running short of ammunition. Five mules, loaded up with small-arms ammunition and led by three men of the mule corps and three of the 2nd Battalion, were promptly sent forward to what looked like certain death. Without hesitation they advanced; three of the men were killed as well as three of the mules, the remainder being badly wounded, but the Dorsets got their ammunition.

By four o'clock in the afternoon no one could advance any farther, and things began to look very gloomy. There was no hope of any reinforcements, and neither could the force remain in its position indefinitely without water and with ammunition running short. To add to the discomfiture of the battalion, away on the left, some three thousand yards distant, was a body of about two thousand armed Arab horsemen standing by and waiting to see which side was going to win the day and ready to loot and murder the defeated.

At about five o'clock, just as orders were being issued by the commander for a withdrawal, it was observed that the enemy were abandoning their trenches and were clearing off *en bloc* in the direction of their base at Nasiriyah, some fifty-five miles up the Euphrates. At once the British troops were up and into the Turkish trenches, where 700 prisoners were taken besides ammunition, arms and the whole enemy camp, which had been abandoned.

No pursuit was possible; the troops had had a long, hot, thirsty, tiring day, ammunition was running short, and there was nothing to be done except withdraw towards Shaiba; but the battalion returned with the knowledge that it had helped to gain a decisive victory. The casualties in the battalion were Major Labertouche, Subedar Baijnath Tiwari, Jemadar Sheo Lal Singh and 22 other ranks killed, and Major D'Oyly, Lieutenant Haddon, Subedar Uma Rawat, Subedar Sheikh Abdul Shakoor and 90 other ranks wounded. The Turkish commander, Sulaiman Askari, later committed suicide. The battalion was thanked by General Delamain, who expressed his admiration for the determination with which it had pushed home an attack over open ground against a stubborn enemy who had the advantage of position and men.

The complete defeat of the Turkish army threatening Basra made it no longer necessary for the 2nd Battalion to remain at Shaiba, and on April 21st it marched back to Basra and rejoined the 17th Brigade at Qurna on the 30th.

Some distance to the north of Qurna the country was, by this time, under water, though here and there a yellow sandhill stood above the flood. The main Turkish position was some eight miles from the advanced British position at Qurna, though in front of this was a curtain of small islands, all of them occupied by the enemy. The only possible way of getting at these Turks was in small, shallow-draught boats known locally as *bellums,* and the month of May was mostly occupied by the battalion in learning the art of punting and in being instructed in *bellum* tactics and drill. Ten men could be put in one *bellum,* and sixteen of these were allotted to each company, the machine guns being mounted on rafts. A quarter of the *bellums* were armoured, but it was found impossible to propel these through the weeds.

At 6.80 on the morning of May 81st the battalion, in conjunction with two other battalions of the brigade, moved to attack the advanced enemy positions, supported by artillery fire both from the naval guns and those in the Qurna position. The artillery fire was particularly accurate, and the foremost Turkish position, an island about a hundred and fifty yards long, was entirely hidden in clouds of fumes from which great mountains of earth shot up. The effect of this was utterly to demoralize those Turks watching from positions in rear, and they put up white flags half an hour before the battalion could reach them. The attack on the main position was to have been made on June 1st, and at dawn the battalion continued its slow advance in *bellums* under cover of artillery fire ; but the enemy had fled, and the town of Amara surrendered to Major-General Townshend, who had recently taken over command of the 6th Division, a couple of days later. So ended the remarkable battle known to the force as " Townshend's Regatta," the only serious casualties being due to heatstroke among the British battalions.

For two weeks the battalion was encamped at Ezra's Tomb, the remarkable blue dome of which is the outstanding architectural feature of this stretch of the Tigris, and then, after a short spell at Qala Salih, it moved to Amara, where it arrived on June 80th, 1915.

After the capture of Amara the Turks withdrew to the neighbourhood of Kut and prepared a strong position about eight miles downstream of that town on both banks of the Tigris.

The capture of Baghdad was now contemplated, and early in September the battalion moved to Ali Gharbi by ship, the whole of the 6th Poona Division being concentrated there by the 11th. The following day the battalion marched with the majority of the division up the left bank, halting for the night in the Musandaq reach, while the Turkish detachment which had been at Shaikh Saad fell back to their main position at Es Sinn. The march was continued daily without opposition till the 15th, when Abu Rumman was reached ; but owing to the great heat, which was as much as 116° F. in the shade, marching only took place from dawn till 8.30 in the morning. At Abu Rumman the division crossed the river and bivouacked on the right bank until September 26th.

On September 26th the whole force advanced about four miles to Nukhailat, the 18th Brigade moving by boat and disembarking on the left bank of the Tigris, while the remainder, including the 2nd Battalion, advanced up the right bank.   Every endeavour was made to cause the enemy to expect the attack to be delivered on the right bank, and a camp was pitched here and left standing throughout the subsequent operations.   A bridge of boats which had been at Abu Rumman was then dismantled and again constructed at Nukhailat, out of sight of the Turks.   That night the newly-pitched camp was shelled by the enemy, but no attack was made.

On the morning of the 27th the 2nd Battalion and the Oxfords, the whole under the command of Major Darley, advanced on a broad front with the Oxfords on the right and the 2nd Battalion on the left.   This was solely intended as a demonstration, while the 18th Brigade, on the left bank, advanced to within three thousand yards of the enemy's position and entrenched.   That evening the remaining two brigades, including the 2nd Battalion, crossed the river, every endeavour being made to prevent noise, and that night commenced a night march behind the 18th Brigade with a view to getting on the extreme left of the Turkish position.   A halt was made at a post known as Clery's Camp, where the force bedded down until 1.30 a.m. on the 28th.

At 1.30 a.m. the advance was resumed, guided by a Sapper officer. The 17th Brigade, including the 2nd Battalion and two battalions of the 16th Brigade, were intended to form the assaulting force under General Hoghton.   The going was perfect, absolutely sound and quite level ; there was a full moon, and the sky was full of stars.   To the west of Clery's Camp lay a marsh known as the Suwada marsh, and some six thousand yards* to the north of this lay another smaller one known as the Ataba marsh.   The route it was intended to follow led first north and then north-west, skirting the southern edge of the Ataba marsh, up to which the Turkish trenches did not reach, and so passing along the defile between the two ; but the column turned too far to the north and passed east of the Ataba marsh, and it was not until this had been passed at about 5.30 a.m. that the mistake was realized through the fact that there was then a marsh on three sides of the column.   During the march a small standing patrol of Turkish cavalry between the two marshes had been passed unobserved, and as light broke these opened

* The positions and extent of these marshes constantly change.   The distance, 6,000 yards, is taken from the map, prepared from aeroplane photographs and amended according to the latest information, which was actually in use at the time of the operations.   Another account says the marshes were two miles apart.   If this latter statement is correct and the map was wrong it would fully account for the column being lost.

fire at long range, doing very little damage, but adding to the doubt as to the exact position of the column.

The remainder of the 18th Brigade under General Delamain then developed a containing attack against the left flank of the enemy along the route originally intended to have been followed by General Hoghton's column, while General Hoghton made a detour right round the Ataba marsh with the object of attacking the enemy's trenches from the rear. After getting into a position well in rear of the enemy, a long halt was made until about 9 a.m., when an attack was developed against the enemy's trenches extending northwards from the Suwada marsh. There were two lines of attack. The 103rd Mahrattas, supported by the Oxfords, were directed on the northern end of the hostile trenches, while the 2nd Battalion, supported by the 22nd Punjabis, was directed on redoubts to the south, with orders to conform to the movements of the 103rd. The northern column naturally met the advance of General Delamain's troops from the opposite direction, and the two entered the Turkish trenches practically simultaneously.

The 2nd Battalion meanwhile captured a Turkish gun position and a redoubt. A further advance was then attempted on the next redoubt up the fire trench which connected the two, but this was caught by enfilade fire and for a quarter of an hour to half an hour was completely checked. Eventually Major Darley organized an advance from the first redoubt across the open which swept over all the defences in this section of the enemy's position, and the whole fight in this quarter was over by about 1 p.m. The 2nd Battalion was then left behind to hold the captured ground while the remainder of the force reorganized.

By this time the men were greatly exhausted. They had been on the move except for two or three long halts since 10.30 the night before. They had no water except what was in their water-bottles and in the *pakhals* with the first-line transport, as the water in the marsh was undrinkable.

On the 29th Kut-al-Amara fell into British hands, while the 2nd Battalion with the rest of the 17th Brigade remained to clear up the battlefield. During the action Captain G. T. Nicholson and Jemadars Pehlad Singh and Sheikh Mohomed were killed, while Captain J. McG. Taylor and Lieutenant H. Parsons were wounded.

After the battle of Es Sinn the Turks withdrew to the neighbourhood of Ctesiphon, where they took up a position in two lines some two or three miles apart astride the Tigris. Their front line was chiefly on the left bank of the river, where there were five miles of defences which consisted of a series of fifteen redoubts connected by a continuous line of trench. All the redoubts and trenches were low-sited and were invisible except at the closest range, while the redoubts were protected with wire. The first two miles were in a narrow loop of the river almost impossible to attack.   About the centre of their position was a feature known as High Wall, which was actually the ruins of an old city wall and which formed two sides of a rectangle running south-west and south-east from the point of junction, the former being about eight hundred yards long and the latter six hundred.   This was an extremely important tactical feature, varying in height from twenty to twenty-five feet and giving very good observation.   From High Wall the trenches ran for one mile in a north-north-east direction to a redoubt known as the Water Redoubt, which stood on a small mound only some three or four feet above the surrounding country.   Thence the fire trench continued some three thousand yards to two redoubts at the extreme northern end of the line which became known as Vital Point.

Little was known of the Turkish second line, but between the two and near the river was the famous Arch of Ctesiphon, conspicuous for miles round, with a village near it on the river bank and the village and tomb of Suliman Pak.

The 18th Brigade had followed the retreating Turks as far as Aziziya by boat immediately after the battle of Es Sinn, and after a considerable period the remainder of the division marched to that place, the 2nd Battalion arriving on October 10th.   The next month was spent in preparations for the attack.   The 2nd Battalion advanced up the left bank of the Tigris to El Kutuniya on November 18th, where it crossed the river, and on the 20th, after again crossing, reached Lajj, nine miles from Ctesiphon.   For the attack the division was organized in four columns, the plan being that the 17th Brigade, including the 2nd Battalion, should pin the enemy to his ground by means of a holding attack against the portion of his front between High Wall and the Water Redoubt, while the 16th and 18th Brigades should encircle his left flank ; a fourth column, composed mainly of mobile troops, was to operate on the outer flank of the encircling columns. There was no reserve.

At 2 p.m. on the 21st the 17th Brigade, including the 2nd Battalion, advanced five miles along the Baghdad road and then went down to the river bank to fill water-bottles.   Here the brigade was shelled by our own ships, who had not expected the column to be diverted to the river. At 10 p.m. the advance was renewed until midnight, when a halt was made.

At 6 a.m. on the 22nd the Brigade deployed on a fifteen-hundred-yard front, the Oxfords being on the right and the 2nd Battalion on the left, supported respectively by the 48th Pioneers and the 22nd Punjabis.   The position of the Turks could not be seen.   Only the great Arch of Ctesiphon stood up as a landmark, and the left of the advance was directed on this.   The advance against the invisible enemy was carried out slowly and cautiously and did not draw fire from the hostile trenches.   At 9 a.m. the battalion received orders to push home the attack.   Artillery support was impossible owing to the mirage, and when the battalion arrived within seven hundred yards of the Turkish trenches it came under powerful rifle and oblique machine-gun fire from High Wall.   The battalion machine guns engaged the enemy on High Wall, but suffered severely from gun fire. The leading companies attempted to advance by rushes, but the whole brigade attack, now very much scattered, became checked.

Meanwhile, another brigade had had a partial success and had succeeded in capturing Vital Point.   In order to exploit this the G.O.C. 17th Brigade received orders to move on Vital Point, which meant moving to a flank within effective rifle range of an entrenched enemy. Leaving the machine guns of the 2nd Battalion and two companies of the 22nd Punjabis to keep up a rapid covering fire, the battalion moved to the right, following the Oxfords across the open plain.   The Turks, seeing their opportunity, opened the heaviest possible rifle, machine-gun and shrapnel fire, inflicting very heavy casualties which included Lieutenant Parsons and Captain Fagan killed and Major Darley, Captain J. G. Lecky, Lieutenant A. de St. Croix and Lieutenant Keeling wounded.   Greatly reduced in strength, the battalion reached the meagre cover of a shallow ditch some two hundred yards east of the Turkish line in the neighbourhood of the Water Redoubt, where for a time its advance was arrested.   Shortly before midday a final assault was made which carried the Water Redoubt.

By this time there was great confusion in the brigade, units being hopelessly mixed and wide distances separating various parts of the battalion which were not in touch with each other.   Lieutenant Haddon, who was the senior officer with one of these parties, then received an order that the battalion was to sweep south and capture the next redoubt, which he did by bombing down the connecting trench.   From here a further advance, in conjunction with details from other battalions, captured four field guns.   In an attempt to reorganize the battalion, Lieutenant Haddon then found that there remained only 2 British officers, 1 Indian officer and 82 other ranks.

Meanwhile a vigorous counter-attack was made by the enemy against one of the encircling columns which met with considerable success, and to take the pressure off this column the 17th Brigade was ordered to abandon the sweep south and advance on Qusaiba. This order was received by Captain Brickman, who did not know that Lieutenant Haddon's detachment existed, and he, with the majority of the remains of the brigade, advanced towards the enemy's second line. The sound of the heavy fighting which resulted was heard by Lieutenant Haddon who, after sending a message to brigade headquarters informing them of his action, abandoned the captured guns and moved towards the sound. He was fired on from Ctesiphon village, but not being attacked, continued his advance, collecting more detachments from other regiments on the way, and soon became involved in the attack upon the Turkish second line, which was not pressed home.

At dusk firing died away completely on both sides, and at about five o'clock in the evening the battalion received orders to withdraw to the Turkish first line, where it occupied the trench between High Wall and Water Redoubt, but was again ordered forward to occupy the high ground by Ctesiphon Arch, which subsequently became known as Gurkha Mound, and to hold it until relieved. At about eight o'clock that night it was relieved by the 2/7th Gurkhas and withdrew, first to Water Redoubt and then to Vital Point, where the whole 17th Brigade was collected for the night.

The night and most of the following day passed quietly and the battalion was occupied in reorganizing and evacuating the many wounded, but that evening at about seven o'clock a Turkish counterattack developed against Vital Point. The enemy succeeded in getting within six hundred yards. The position was extremely serious, as there was a great shortage of ammunition, but the enemy were themselves disorganized and, although they continued to attack until 2 a.m. on the 24th, were completely unsuccessful.

The casualties in the battalion during the battle of Ctesiphon were 2 British officers, 4 Indian officers and 59 other ranks killed (59 other ranks later died of their wounds), while 5 British officers, 5 Indian officers and about 387 more other ranks were wounded, the majority of these casualties having occurred during the oblique march across the enemy's front.

The following day the battalion received orders to destroy all arms and equipment which were lying about, while the wounded were evacuated in mule carts, which entailed great suffering. Apart from this the next two days passed quietly, both sides preparing to retreat, and on the 25th the battalion received a sudden order to retire. The withdrawal began at 8.30 that night, the force leaving the camp standing with a view to deceiving the enemy, and the battalion arrived at Lajj at 3 a.m. in a deluge of rain. Next night another withdrawal was made, and the battalion arrived at Aziziya at 4 a.m. on November 27th. Aziziya was the advanced base, and here a halt was made for two days before the retreat was again continued, everything being left in position except the first- and second-line transport.

The pursuing Turks left Aziziya at about three o'clock on the afternoon of the 30th, their infantry believing that their advance was covered by their cavalry, although these were actually engaged in looting the stores abandoned by the British at Aziziya. The result was that at about 8 p.m. that evening the Turks advanced upon the British camp, believing the lights to be those of their own cavalry. When fired on they withdrew and encamped in the desert, all the lights of the British camp being extinguished. The 2nd Battalion had previously been detailed to act as escort to the baggage on December 1st and, working in the dark, the transport was all successfully started off by dawn, the movement being covered by a brilliant counter-stroke made by the remainder of the division against the pursuing Turks. The baggage, escorted by the 2nd Battalion, continued its march all that day and most of the following night, and reached the town of Kut-al-Amara at 10 a.m. on December 2nd, some twenty-four hours before the remainder of the division.*

The town of Kut is situated in a bend of the River Tigris on the left bank, the main course of the river here flowing from the south-west to the north-east, with the result that the north-west front of the town is exposed to the open plain while the other three fronts are protected by the river. The river itself required watching as it contained numerous shoals over which it was possible for the enemy to wade at low water. Such defences as existed across the loop had been designed merely for protection against marauding Arabs, and the battalion was kept constantly at work night and day strengthening these defences, being badly handicapped by shortage of tools and also by the fact that it was ordered to economize its ammunition, with the result that the Turks were able to dig in at close range and hinder the digging parties at work with fire to which they could not adequately reply. Gradually the Turkish trenches drew nearer until, in one place, they were within fifty yards of those held by the battalion.

On the morning of December 24th a mine was sprung outside the battalion sector, but did no harm. At noon that day the Turks assaulted, and Captain H. E. Haddon was killed by a bomb, the enemy breaking through the first line, which was subsequently recaptured. The battalion having by this time been very severely knocked about, it was withdrawn into the town of Kut itself, but took over part of the river front, where outpost duties became very onerous with the depleted numbers available.

---

* " An Indian battalion was leading. The men were dusty, haggard, bedraggled and almost unbelievably weary. Their grimy faces and sunken bloodshot eyes conveyed the impression that they were men who had descended into hell, seen what was there, and returned. Doubtless they imagined that life could hold no greater hardships than those they had endured since that evening twelve days ago when, full of high spirits, they marched away from Lajj, hoping their next halt would be in Baghdad. They were wrong—the dead they left behind them were the lucky ones.

" As I watched those men, the remnants of what had been a magnificent regiment, dragging themselves past the line of blockhouses—it could not be said they were marching—a lump came into my throat and I turned away." (Shalimar, in *Blackwood's Magazine*, August, 1931.)

By the end of January, 1916, it was raining heavily and the River Tigris commenced to rise. Night after night every available officer and man who could be spared from the defences was employed in building up the embankment, which prevented the river from overflowing and flooding the town. Food supply then ran short. To keep off scurvy, regular parties were sent out to collect a weed which grew freely in the neighbourhood, and which was cooked and eaten as spinage.

**1916.
2nd Battalion.**

In March the river rose in earnest and flooded out the whole Turkish front line as well as most of the British. There was then little danger of attack. Fuel was obtained from large stores which were in Kut, horses and mules were eaten as food. Towards the end of the siege the ration was 4 ounces of flour and ¾ lb. of horseflesh ; then even this gave out, and from April 22nd to the 25th emergency rations were eaten. The daily death rate was now appalling. On April 28th and 29th arms and equipment were destroyed and ammunition thrown into the river, and that day the garrison of Kut surrendered and the 2nd Battalion went into captivity.*

---

* It is impossible to attempt to give an account of the misfortunes of the gallant survivors of the battalion while in captivity. British officers were separated from their men and the latter were forced to march, under the most brutal conditions conceivable, to their prisons. Many did not survive the march. For an authoritative and well-documented account of the treatment of the prisoners the reader is referred to Sir Arnold Wilson's *Loyalties, Mesopotamia*, 1914-1917, published by the Oxford University Press.

Chapter XI

THE RELIEF COLUMN

Bibliography—Regimental Records.

THE 1st Royal Battalion, under the command of Captain R. C. Ross, sailed from Suez in the s.s. *Jeddah* on December 5th, 1915, and dis-
1915.
1st Battalion. embarked at Basra on the 19th, when it immediately commenced marching, as part of a mixed column, towards Kut. It arrived at Ali Gharbi, on the left bank of the Tigris, on January 3rd, and there was posted to the 21st Brigade under Brigadier-General Norie, the other units in the brigade being the Black Watch, 9th Bhopal Infantry and 41st Dogras.

On the 6th the brigade moved forward eighteen miles to Musandaq, some few miles from Shaikh Saad. On the morning of the 7th the
1916.
1st Battalion. battalion left camp at about 8 a.m. as advanced guard to the brigade. At about ten o'clock the brigade was halted in rear of the reserves of the 19th Brigade, at the same time coming under shell fire. The River Tigris here flows from west to east, and a line of Turkish trenches appeared to stretch for a mile or so at right-angles to the river and then to curve eastwards with a big sweep. The 35th Brigade was already engaged, and this was detailed to hold the enemy near the river while the 19th Brigade, supported by the 21st, was to make a decisive attack against the enemy's left flank.

In accordance with these orders the battalion with the rest of the brigade moved about eight hundred yards to the right. No sooner had this been done than at half-past eleven fresh orders arrived and the battalion, together with the Black Watch, was ordered to attack the main position, filling in the gap between the 21st and 35th Brigades. The advance had to be carried out over a bare, open plain without any appreciable covering fire, as there was very little artillery available. Within a quarter of an hour the leading companies had come under a withering machine-gun and rifle fire from the concealed trenches, and as the advance was continued the other companies, following at a distance of two hundred and fifty yards, also began to suffer severely. The advance was finally brought to a halt some three hundred yards from the Turkish trenches, and here the battalion remained until dusk,

107

when it withdrew about two hundred yards to an irrigation ditch which it converted into a trench, the Black Watch and the Seaforths on the left and right of the battalion taking up more or less the same line. Lieutenant C. J. Cockburn, M.C., who had been with the battalion throughout the fighting in France, was killed by a bullet through his forehead. Second-Lieutenant W. E. Godwin (Indian Army Reserve, attached), 3 Indian officers and 62 other ranks, of whom 21 at the time were reported missing, were killed. Captain R. C. Ross, Captain M. E. Coningham (96th Infantry, attached), Captain A. B. McPherson, Captain J. Gordon (Indian Political Service, attached) and Second-Lieutenant Doyle-Kelly (Indian Army Reserve, attached), 10 Indian officers and 315 other ranks were wounded. Captain F. W. A. Wells, who now took over command, was also slightly wounded, but did not report sick.

Great difficulty was experienced in getting the many wounded back with the few stretcher-bearers available, owing to the heavy fire which the enemy continued to maintain. Sub-Assistant Surgeon Purgan Singh, I.O.M. was invaluable in attending the wounded of all regiments under fire, and for his great gallantry was admitted to the 1st Class of the Indian Order of Merit. Captain Ross received the Distinguished Service Order,* Captain Gordon and Captain McPherson received the Military Cross, and five Indian ranks received the Distinguished Service Medal.

During the following day the battalion consolidated its position and, although heavily sniped, had no casualties ; that night it threw back its right flank and joined up with the 9th Bhopal Infantry, the left being still joined up with the Black Watch. Sniping occurred again during the night, and one man was wounded while out with a burying party.

Early on the morning of the 9th it was discovered that the Turks had abandoned their position, leaving snipers behind. These were soon rounded up except one party of fifty men who were discovered crawling along one of the trenches ; machine-gun fire being brought to bear on them, they put up a white flag and surrendered. The brigade then marched forward to Shaikh Saad, where it encamped with the rest of the division and remained the following day. The battalion was now organized in three companies only owing to the heavy casualties which had occurred.

On the 11th the brigade advanced some five miles, and on the evening of the 12th moved to a position of assembly, where it arrived at about 11 p.m. and bivouacked for the night. The enemy were believed to be holding a deep wadi or nullah at right-angles to the river, and it was

---

* As Captain Ross was subsequently awarded the D.S.O. for his earlier services in France his award for the battle of Shaikh Saad appeared in the *London Gazette* as a bar to the D.S.O.

the intention that the 21st Brigade should feel for the enemy, hold them, and enable the 19th and 35th Brigades to work round their flank. Accordingly, the brigade marched at 6 a.m., the battalion being in reserve five hundred yards in rear of the 9th Bhopals. On crossing the big nullah, which was not occupied as had been believed, the battalion came under heavy shell fire and a certain amount of small-arms fire, from which a few casualties resulted. Verbal orders were then received that the battalion was to reinforce the right flank of the Black Watch, which it did, remaining with the Black Watch until dark. The rifle fire all this time was fairly severe and it was almost impossible to see any enemy, although the battalion machine-gunners were able to bring fire to bear on small bodies of the Turks retiring. At dusk the battalion entrenched in continuation of the line taken up by the Black Watch, putting out battle outposts and refusing its right flank. The casualties in the battalion during this action were 6 killed and 36 wounded.

By the morning the enemy had gone, and the battalion acted as advanced guard to the brigade, which moved forward some three miles, when it came under shell fire. It was then withdrawn a thousand yards, and the whole division went into camp until the 19th.

Heavy rain began falling on the 16th. This, besides making the ground a quagmire, caused great difficulties in cooking. The total allowance of firewood was only one pound per man, and this now was soaked, the result being that men ate only half-cooked rations and a number became ill. The hospital was a ship on the river, and this contained many wounded, some of whom had not had their wounds dressed since the 7th.

At 6 p.m. on the 19th the brigade marched out of camp to occupy a line of trenches situated eleven to twelve hundred yards in front of the Turkish position at Hannah. The 1st Royal Battalion brought up the rear of the column and came under heavy shrapnel fire before reaching its section of the trench, seven men being wounded. In the evening the battalion advanced through the trenches on its front, held by the Hampshire Regiment and the 97th Infantry, and dug itself in on a front about seven hundred yards long and about five hundred and fifty yards from the enemy's position. During this advance and while digging it was heavily fired on and four men were killed.

On the 20th the battalion remained in this trench, Subedar Lakhi Ram and four other ranks being wounded ; and during the following night the 2nd Black Watch advanced through the battalion and dug themselves in about three hundred or three hundred and fifty yards from the enemy's position.

The battalion was now very seriously reduced in numbers. The fighting strength at dawn on January 21st was approximately : British officers, 6 ; Indian officers, 5 ; and other ranks, 170. These numbers included Second-Lieutenant O'Connor, the Quartermaster, and Jemadar Net Ram, Transport Officer, who were not present in the trench. Jemadar Sultan, being Machine-gun Officer, did not take part in the subsequent advance against the Turkish position. The only three Indian officers available were Subedar-Major Dalpat Singh, Jemadar Bhart Singh and Jemadar Ram Lal, and the latter, who was on the extreme right, came under the orders of the 97th Infantry in the course of the advance.

Rain had been falling almost continuously for five days and the ground was sodden, making it difficult to move. The country was absolutely flat, devoid of natural cover, and the enemy's trenches were well concealed. As the Turkish right flank rested on the Tigris and their left flank on the impassable Suwaikiya marsh, they could not be attacked in flank. The Black Watch were now in a trench some three hundred to three hundred and fifty yards from the enemy's front line, with the 41st Dogras on their right. The 1st Royal Battalion was about two hundred yards in rear of the Black Watch, with the 37th Dogras on its right.

Orders were received for the battalion to support the Black Watch and join them in their trench under cover of an artillery bombardment. This was done at 7.45 a.m., and very heavy casualties occurred during the advance, the Commanding Officer, Captain Wells, and Jemadar Bhart Singh being among the many wounded. At 7.55 the bombardment lifted to the Turkish second line and the Black Watch charged the right of the enemy, where they were believed to be particularly strong, and the few of the 1st Royal Battalion left unwounded followed closely. This advance, in order to reach the enemy's right, had to be diagonally across their front, which caused the two battalions to become separated from the two battalions on their right, who advanced straight to their front until stopped by hostile fire. The officers, not being encumbered with rifles, could move more quickly over the heavy mud, and most of them got ahead of the men, who were longer exposed to the devastating fire. Although no pause was made, heavy losses were again suffered. About thirty men of the Black Watch were the first to reach the wire entanglements, which consisted of two fences about three feet high and about eight feet apart. These had been so damaged by the artillery that they were useless as an obstruction. About fifteen to twenty Turks got out of their trenches, but did not wait to meet the attackers. A sort of running fight ensued, and very shortly the men of the Black Watch entered the trench.

A few individuals of other battalions which had been in rear of the 1st Royal Battalion succeeded in getting forward, and the total number who entered the Turkish trenches were about forty of the Black Watch, one captain and three men of the Hampshire Regiment, five or six of the 97th Infantry, and four British officers, one Indian officer and six other ranks of the 1st Royal Battalion (Lieutenant Neale, 1st Brahmins, attached ; Second-Lieutenants G. Ives, Johnson and Dawn, Indian Army Reserve ; Subedar-Major Dalpat Singh, Pay Havildar Jug Lal, Havildar Chandgi, Naik Hardwari, Lance-Naik Matu, Sepoy Harnam and one other man whose name is not known). The man whose name is not known was sent back with an urgent message for reinforcements, but was killed before he had gone a few yards.

The Turkish trenches were very strongly built. The trench itself was six to seven feet deep and the parapet and parados were three feet high. There was a firing platform and the parapet was loop-holed. There were frequent traverses. A deep communication trench, which zig-zagged and had many traverses, connected the Turks' first and second lines where they rested on the river. Two machine guns and much ammunition as well as rifles and men's kits and a few bombs were found in the trench, where also there were ten or twelve dead Turks. The trenches were quite undamaged by artillery fire, though there were craters made by shells just beyond them and much shrapnel in the trenches themselves. The shrapnel appeared to have been effective, judging by the number of rifles and men's kits left behind, as these presumably belonged to men killed or wounded who had been taken back to the second position. A very noticeable thing was the cleanliness of the trench ; there was no refuse of any kind lying about, and even the fireplace in each section of the trench had been carefully cleaned of all ash.

About a hundred and fifty yards of trench from the river was occupied, then there was a gap, and the remainder of the Turkish line was still held by the enemy. The Black Watch undertook to hold the right ; the men of the Hampshire Regiment, those of the 97th and the Jats the left. The communication trench was blocked in two places, and one bomber with six bombs, belonging to the 1st Royal Battalion, and five men with rifles were posted behind the first obstruction.

The Turks kept up a heavy rifle fire from their second position, and some casualties occurred, Second-Lieutenant Johnson being shot through the head while observing the Turkish position. One of the machine guns found in the trench was placed in position on the parados and operated by men of the Black Watch ; the other gun could not be got to work. A reconnaissance was then made by the enemy from the right as well as along the communication trench, and both fell back before the fire which was brought to bear on them.

When the trench had been occupied for about an hour and a quarter the Turks counter-attacked in overwhelming strength. They advanced simultaneously along the communication trench and from the right across the open, throwing bombs and firing down from the parados at the men in the trench.   This was replied to by rifle fire, but hardly effectively, as very soon the men in the trench got crowded together and there was great confusion.   At this time Lieutenant Neale was shot at point-blank range.   The only hope of escape then lay in running the gauntlet of the Turks on the parados and endeavouring to get back to the British trenches.   Several tried, some were shot, but a few got away.   About a hundred yards in front of the Turks' trench was a small nullah, and there those who escaped took shelter.   In this nullah were about fifteen men, and one by one they left the nullah and crept back about two hundred yards to the trench from which the Black Watch had charged earlier in the morning.   This trench was crowded with men of three or four battalions, many of whom were wounded. Second-Lieutenant Dawn, Havildar Jug Lal and Lance-Naik Matu were killed ; Naik Hardwari and Sepoy Harnam were both severely wounded.

The total casualties during the day in the battalion were : Killed, 3 British officers and 20 other ranks ; wounded, 1 British officer, 1 Indian officer and 135 other ranks.   That night the relics moved back to the camp at Ora ; and, joining up with the Quartermaster's establishment and the machine-gunners, the battalion had a total strength of two British officers—Second-Lieutenant G. Ives, who commanded, and Second-Lieutenant O'Connor, the Quartermaster— with approximately twenty Indian ranks.

An Order of the Day was published as follows :—

" I cannot speak too highly of the splendid gallantry of the Black Watch, aided by a party of officers and men of the 6th Jats,* in storm- ing and occupying the enemy's trenches.   The advance had to be made across a perfectly open bullet-swept area against sunken loop-holed trenches in broad daylight and their noble achievement is one of the highest.   They showed qualities of endurance and courage under circumstances so adverse as to be almost phenomenal."

Captain Wells and Second-Lieutenant Ives were awarded the Military Cross, and all the Indian ranks who entered the Turkish trench were admitted to the 2nd Class of the Indian Order of Merit " for their very great devotion and pluck in the attack on the Turkish position."

The battalion was joined on the 29th by Lieutenant-Colonel W. FitzG. Bourne from the 3rd Battalion, who had been appointed Commandant, and on February 1st took part in a reconnaissance, although its total strength consisted of twenty rifles and one machine gun.

---

* Subsequently amended to include other battalions which had taken part in the attack.

During this period a system of trenches reaching from the river to the Suwaikiya marsh and facing the Turkish trenches at a distance of about nine hundred yards was constructed, and on February 9th the battalion, which had received a small reinforcement, moved into the rearmost line, called Pioneer Trench, as reserve to the 21st Brigade. From the 9th to the 14th the battalion remained in Pioneer Trench, the weather being appalling for the first two days. Torrents of rain fell, and the discomfort was added to by a great shortage of rations, British officers, owing to their small number, being the worst sufferers in this respect. Bread, of course, was unobtainable, and the biscuits issued in lieu were very hard and unpalatable. The meat ration was insufficient. There being only three officers,* one seven-pound tin of bully beef was issued and expected to last for three days in the mud of the trenches. There were no vegetables of any sort, and for the next three months it remained a saying that an issue of jam was the first signal received that the battalion was to take part in an attack. Later the weed which proved so useful to the garrison in Kut grew up between the trenches and was freely eaten. The Indian ranks were only slightly better off. The time was mostly spent in improving the trench and cleaning out the mud from the communication trenches, and, though bullets passed overhead and the trench was occasionally shelled, no casualties occurred until the night of the 14th.

The battalion then commenced the construction of a new fire trench in front of the existing first line, and remained there until the 18th, losing one killed and six wounded. It was then relieved and returned to Ora.

On the night of the 21st the battalion, which by then had a strength of about eighty and had been joined by Captain W. L. Hailes from the Depot and Lieutenant T. M. Layng from the 3rd Battalion, marched round the Suwaikiya marsh and took up a position with the rest of the brigade on the flank of the Turkish position, but separated from it by the marsh. Shelters were constructed before dawn at wide intervals to give protection against the enemy's artillery. During the day a demonstration of crossing the marsh in the enemy's rear was made. There was no intention that this should be more than a demonstration to distract the enemy's attention from more important movements on the right bank of the river, and consequently when the leading battalion had only advanced a short distance into the water it halted and then withdrew. The 1st Royal Battalion, being in reserve, did not move at all. It was intermittently shelled during the day, but the hostile shrapnel mostly burst high in the air and did little damage, one man only being wounded.

---

* Second-Lieutenant O'Connor, being Quartermaster, was not present in the trench. The third officer was Captain R. J. K. Potter, 117th Mahrattas, who was temporarily attached to the battalion.

I

During the night the danger from a large party of hostile Arabs, known to be in the neighbourhood, was regarded as being greater than that from the Turkish shell fire, consequently the whole brigade concentrated into a small space on the edge of the marsh, protected by a line of piquets. The brigade remained on the border of the marsh until after dark on the evening of the 26th, spreading out during the day to avoid loss by shell fire and concentrating at night to safeguard itself from the Arabs. No casualties occurred, and the battalion acted as rear-guard to the column on its march back to Ora, where it remained until the 29th.

From February 29th until March 4th the battalion was in the front-line trench, by then within three hundred yards of the enemy's parapet, and was employed in preparing another trench some fifty or sixty yards in front of the existing one. The casualties during these four days were one killed and eleven wounded. From the 4th until the end of the month the battalion was sometimes in the front line and sometimes in the support trenches, with a rest of a week from the 14th to the 20th in camp at Ora. During this period there were usually two or three killed or wounded each day that it was in the front line. On the 24th the battalion lost its Medical Officer, Captain D. H. Rai, M.C., I.M.S., who had served with it since it first sailed to France and had distinguished himself by his gallantry on numerous occasions ; he was transferred to a field ambulance and relieved by Captain J. W. Jones, I.M.S.

During the night of March 31st the battalion was relieved in the reserve trench by the 13th British Division. This had just arrived in the country, and great precautions were taken to prevent knowledge of its arrival reaching the enemy. Consequently the battalion was forbidden to pitch any tent or bivouac which might be seen by hostile aircraft and so give information that the number of troops at the front had been increased. A torrent of rain, which continued until the 2nd, started while the relief was being carried out, and everywhere the ground was covered with two or three inches of mud. In the dark the battalion moved to about a mile behind the reserve trench, where it halted and endeavoured to make itself as comfortable as the very adverse circumstances permitted, and after about two hours it was found that within a mile the standing camp of the 19th Brigade was empty. The battalion consequently moved into these tents, the machine guns remaining in the front-line trench. The battalion remained in this camp until the evening of the 4th, preparing for an advance. First- and second-line transport was taken over and surplus kit was loaded on a *mahailah*, or native sailing boat.

On April 4th at 8.40 p.m. the battalion, with a fighting strength of 5 British officers, 5 Indian officers and 146 other ranks, moved forward again to Pioneer Trench. A few bullets were coming over, and one man was hit just before getting into the trench.

The trench system was now occupied by the 13th Division in the front line and the 7th Division in rear, the battalion being the reserve battalion of the rear brigade of the 7th Division. At 4.55 a.m., without any preliminary bombardment, the 13th Division delivered what was intended to be a surprise assault. The hostile trenches were found to have been evacuated except for a small rear-guard, and the whole Hannah position was captured without difficulty. The 1st Royal Battalion was then detailed to salvage the ground.

One of the first articles found in the hostile trenches was a large notice in French : " Welcome to the 13th Division. We shall meet again on another battlefield ! " That night the battalion bivouacked on the Turkish position and marched forward at 2.55 a.m. on the 6th.

By this time the rest of the brigade was in the Turkish trenches at Fallahiya. The battalion moved forward in the dark, through the Fallahiya position, in support of the 19th and 28th Brigades against the Turkish position at Sannaiyat. This, like that at Hannah, had its right flank on the Tigris and its left protected by the impassable marsh. At about 5.30 a.m. the leading troops came under very heavy rifle and machine-gun fire, and their advance was quickly stopped. They could neither advance nor retire across the open plain in daylight under the hail of bullets, and an attempt to reinforce them would have been useless. The battalion was therefore ordered to entrench, which it did under shell fire.

On the following day, April 7th, the 19th and 28th Brigades having withdrawn, the 21st Brigade was ordered to advance as far as possible and dig in. The battalion was now organized in two companies, each about sixty-five strong, with a weak headquarters. It was leading on the left of the brigade with its flank on the river ; this had now risen considerably and in many places overflowed the protective embankment, with the consequence that a lot of the ground advanced over was covered with two or three inches of water. The enemy were bursting their shells high in the air and their gun fire did very little damage, but every shrapnel bullet falling in the water caused a splash and this, combined with the very heavy machine-gun and rifle fire, caused the patches of water to appear absolutely impassable. The battalion moved forward in two lines of a company each with head-quarters between, the latter being accompanied by two British signallers, who laid a telephone wire as the advance moved forward until one was killed, when the survivor carried on by himself. The battalion advanced until it was within six hundred yards of the Turks, when a ditch was found and occupied and later converted into a fire trench. During the advance heavy casualties occurred, mostly in the

support company.   Owing to a bend in the river, the front which the
battalion was now holding was very great for its strength—a state of
affairs made worse by the heavy casualties.

It was then seen that the protective embankment of the river in
front of the position occupied had been broken; the water was overflowing, and there was a probability that the trench held would be
flooded, though not until after dark.   Accordingly a British officer and
a small party of men were sent out with entrenching tools to try to
repair the breach, but owing to casualties it was found impossible even
to reach the breach by daylight; the attempt was therefore postponed
until after dark.   The battalion remained where it was throughout
the day, improving the trench, and as soon as it was dark a party
again went out to repair the embankment.   Shortly before nine o'clock
it was recalled, and at nine o'clock the enemy were heavily bombarded,
to which they replied with extremely heavy rifle and machine-gun fire,
evidently believing the bombardment was a prelude to an attack.
As soon as this had died down the battalion was relieved by a British
composite battalion composed of the Norfolk and Dorset Regiments
and moved back into brigade reserve.   During the day the battalion
had lost a third of its strength in killed and wounded, although there
were no casualties among the officers, either British or Indian, and a
message was received to say that the brigade commander had been
pleased to see that the battalion, despite its previous losses, had
advanced as gallantly as it ever did in France.

The whole of the following day, April 8th, the battalion remained
in brigade reserve.   On the 9th an attack was made on the Sannaiyat
position by the 13th Division, the 7th being in readiness to support
them.   The attack was a complete failure and the battalion, still in
brigade reserve, was not required to move.

By this time a regular system of trenches had again been formed,
and on the 10th the battalion relieved part of the 28th Brigade in the
advanced lines, where it remained for the following two days.   During
the first night heavy rain fell, causing several inches of water to collect
in the trenches.   A party of the battalion under a British officer spent
the second night in "no man's land" burying the dead of the 13th
Division; no casualties occurred, and the battalion was then relieved
and again moved into reserve.

The water of the marsh on the right flank of the British was very
liable to move and the whole marsh to change its position with the
wind, and there was a possibility that it might even join the river,
completely flooding the whole country.   In order to prevent this an
embankment was built near its edge.   On the 12th the marsh started
moving towards the trenches, and the battalion was employed in
strengthening the embankment near the reserve trenches, working

in daylight under shrapnel and long-range machine-gun fire. The embankment gave way near the front-line trench, which was flooded, but the troops on the spot managed to save the second line by blocking the communication trenches. That night the battalion was sent forward and commenced to dig a new front line, moving back into reserve on the 14th for a single day before returning to the front line, where it remained till the 18th, one company being in the trench begun on the night of the 12th and the other about a hundred yards in rear. As when the new front line was begun cover was needed in a hurry, it was dug immediately in rear of the trench which had been flooded out. The parados of the latter was used as a parapet to the new line, which had therefore to conform to the old trench ; where a traverse existed there was a wide curve in the new trench, resulting in an awkward alignment. Moreover, it could not cross the old flooded communication trenches, as this would have let the water in ; consequently, to get from one part of the front line to another it was necessary to get out in the open and jump the broad, flooded trench within some five or six hundred yards of the Turks. There was no communication trench between it and the second line, though this was prepared before the battalion left.   During all this time two or three casualties were occurring daily, and parties of reinforcements, composed largely of men discharged from hospitals, were constantly joining.

On the 18th the battalion moved into support in the third line, and the following day the marsh again moved towards the trenches, breaking the embankment at about three o'clock in the afternoon.   This time it was not found possible to confine the water to the front line, and the whole trench system was flooded to a depth of three feet above the fire step. The first and second lines were evacuated by the battalions in them, and the third line became the firing line. The battalion remained in three feet of water under heavy rifle fire until ordered to withdraw at 8 p.m., when it moved to the reserve trenches, which were not connected with the rest of the trench system, returning to the reconstructed third line on the 21st.

Orders were received for an attack to be delivered on the 22nd by the 19th brigade on the left and the 21st Brigade, including the 1st Royal Battalion, on the right. Owing to the previous heavy casualties among British officers, instructions had been received that when a battalion was ordered to take part in an attack a proportion of its British officers was to be left behind, and these were not to go forward until their presence was rendered necessary by casualties or until the end of the engagement. As the result of this the only British officers present in the trenches at dawn on the 22nd were Lieutenant-Colonel Bourne, Captain R. J. K. Potter (117th Mahrattas, attached) and Second-Lieutenants R. L. O'Connor and T. P. M. O'Callaghan

(Indian Army Reserve) as well as the Medical Officer, Captain Jones. The ground between the trenches near the marsh was so flooded that at the last minute the 21st Brigade was ordered to remain in support of the 19th. The battalion was in the third line, with behind it the 8th Gurkhas, a battalion newly arrived in the country and up to full strength, which had replaced in the brigade a composite battalion of Mahrattas.

A slow bombardment of the enemy's trenches was followed by an intense bombardment at 7 a.m. The noise of this bombardment caused a soldier of the Highland battalion of the 19th Brigade to lose his mental balance ; he rushed down the communication trench with a bomb in each hand with the safety-pins drawn out. On reaching the dug-out in which the officers of the 1st Royal Battalion were receiving their final instructions, he imagined himself to be among the enemy. He immediately threw one bomb, which wounded Lieutenant-Colonel Bourne and Second-Lieutenant O'Connor and which rendered Captain Potter temporarily shell-shocked so that he had to withdraw from the action. The Highlander had loosened his grip on the second bomb, which consequently was just about to explode, and was in the act of throwing it when Captain Jones jumped on him, snatched the bomb out of his hand and flung it over the parapet. For his gallantry on this occasion Captain Jones received the Distinguished Service Order. Lieutenant-Colonel Bourne would probably have been killed but for the timely action of Second-Lieutenant O'Callaghan who, realizing the first bomb was about to be exploded, pushed him into a corner of the dug-out. The battalion then came temporarily under the command of Second-Lieutenant O'Callaghan.

After the 19th Brigade had advanced, the leading battalion of the 21st Brigade, the composite battalion of the Norfolks and Dorsets, advanced to the enemy's trenches, and the 1st Royal Battalion, moving in support across the open, reached the front-line trench of the British system. During this advance Second-Lieutenant O'Callaghan was slightly wounded, a bullet passing across both his shoulder-blades and making four holes in his shirt as he was bending over. The wound was not sufficient to make him leave the battalion.

Most of the 19th and the leading battalion of the 21st Brigade had now penetrated the enemy's trenches, but in crossing some of the old Turkish trenches, which had been flooded out, their rifles became clogged with mud. The enemy delivered a counter-attack and the British composite battalion was driven back into its original position, which now became crowded as it was already occupied by the 1st Royal Battalion and the 9th Bhopal Infantry. During this counter-attack and under very heavy fire one of the two machine guns of the 1st Royal Battalion, working under the orders of the brigade Machine Gun Officer,

Captain Martin, was moved from the front-line trench across the open to a saphead, a distance of about a hundred yards, whence it was able to fire on the attacking enemy without hitting the retreating British battalion. During this movement three men were hit and all the belt boxes.

The battalion was now rejoined by Captain Potter, who assumed command, and by Captain Hailes, who had moved up on hearing that Lieutenant-Colonel Bourne had become a casualty. A large number of what at first appeared to be white flags, but which were later seen to bear the red crescent (corresponding to the red cross of Christian nations), then appeared in the Turkish trenches. Firing died down and stopped and Turkish stretcher parties advanced out of their trenches to pick up the wounded. Parties of the English regiment also went forward, and an unofficial armistice occurred. Where the noise had previously been deafening there was then silence, and men sat on the front-line parapet eating their midday meal away from the mud. The casualties for the day among the Indian ranks of the battalion were 2 killed and 17 wounded out of a total strength of 173.

The brigade then moved into the reserve trenches, where it remained until the 24th, and that night crossed the Tigris by bridge to the right bank and bivouacked at Abu Rumman, where it became corps reserve. Kut having surrendered on April 29th, the battalion marched to Fallahiya on May 1st, and there it took over a fleet of *mahailahs*, or large sailing boats, which it had been instructed to escort to Basra. The strength of the battalion was then 6 British officers, including the Medical Officer, 7 Indian officers, including the sub-assistant surgeon, and 123 other ranks, who began an extremely pleasant and restful journey down the river. For months the battalion had never been out of range of the hostile field guns, and had usually been within rifle range. The contrast between life in the muddy trenches amongst the continuous noise and the utter peace of drifting down the river with the current was emphasized by the relief from constant strain. The battalion arrived at Basra on May 14th, and went into camp at Makina Masus, a short distance from the port.

Chapter XII

CAPTURE OF KUT, THE LINES OF COMMUNICATION, RAMADI AND KHAN BAGHDADI

Bibliography—Regimental Records.

DURING the time the 2nd (Mooltan) Battalion was besieged in Kut there were a number of men belonging to the battalion scattered about in various hospitals and convalescent depots on the lines of communication, and there were also a number of recruits under training at the depot in India. As these became available they were first employed on road-making, but later, on June 6th, 1916, were organized as a battalion. This, which eventually took the place of the battalion captured in Kut, was known at first as the 2nd Battalion 119th Infantry, and was constituted at Amara under the command of Lieutenant-Colonel T. M. Heath. For some months it suffered from a lack of officers, there being only six British and three Indian, while the majority of the rank and file were little fitted for promotion and were in very bad physical condition. The battalion remained in the neighbourhood of Amara and Fulaifila until October 21st, the time being necessarily employed mainly in training, enlivened by the necessity of guarding against marauding Arabs whose boldness was only equalled by their ingenuity. One night a party of Arabs succeeded in entering the camp and taking away a horse belonging to Second-Lieutenant H. O. Crowther. Barbed wire, loosely attached to posts and several feet thick, was cut and a passage made through it opposite the centre of the mule and horse lines.

On October 22nd the battalion arrived at Shaikh Saad by boat. Here the Arabs were as enterprising as they had been at Amara and fire frequently had to be opened on them—fire which on one occasion, December 6th, lasted throughout the day. On December 20th the battalion moved to Imam al Mansur, where it was joined three days later by Lieutenant-Colonel J. R. Darley, who took over command. The battalion was now at the front.

The Tigris, flowing mainly from west to east, makes two big bends to the south some five miles apart. The western of these is known as the Shumran bend, while the eastern, in which lies the town of Kut, is known as the Kut bend. Between the two the bend to the north is called the Dahra bend. From the Kut bend the river flows roughly north-east to Sannaiyat and Hannah. The bend of the river to the east of Kut, where it commences to flow north-east, is called the Khudhaira bend. From opposite the town of Kut a canal, known as the Shatt-al-Hai, flows south-east to the Euphrates. At this time the Turks still held the Sannaiyat position and the whole of the north bank of the river westwards. On the south bank they held a strong position across the Khudhaira bend, both flanks resting on the river. They also held the junction of the Shatt-al-Hai with the Tigris, and their line extended from there across the Dahra bend to the Shumran bend.

Imam al Mansur, where the 2nd Battalion arrived on December 20th, lay on a light railway which reached the Shatt-al-Hai at Atab, some five miles south of Kut. Throughout the month, during which much rain fell, the battalion was employed in improving redoubts on the outpost line from Atab to Imam al Mansur as line-of-communication troops.

On January 10th and 11th, 1917, the leading troops attacked the enemy in the Khudhaira bend and suffered severe losses without being able to dislodge the enemy. As a result of this the **1917. 2nd Battalion.** 2nd Battalion was ordered to replace temporarily a battalion which had suffered particularly severely in the 8th Brigade, 3rd Division. Operations were then commenced against the enemy in the Khudhaira bend by means of a systematic advance accompanied by constant bombardment over a long period, and from January 11th to 18th there was a series of short advances, frequently entailing hard fighting by comparatively small forces, and gradually the Turkish advanced posts were driven back. By the evening of the 18th the line was within two hundred yards of the Turkish main position, and arrangements were made for an assault next morning. During the night the enemy evacuated their trenches and withdrew across the river.

Towards the end of January orders were received to create an impression among the enemy of constant movement eastwards and of reinforcement of the Sannaiyat position, and with this end in view the 2nd Battalion, together with the 47th Sikhs, commenced moving at 4.30 p.m. on the 24th. The two battalions moved by platoons at two hundred yards' interval through the Sinn banks towards Abu Rumman, returning under cover of dark.

The remainder of the month was occupied mainly in intensive training, and on February 2nd the battalion moved into the trenches near the mouth of the Shatt-al-Hai. Orders were received that the role to be adopted was an offensive-defensive with digging forward. The enemy were to be made apprehensive of an assault and as many of them contained as possible, but no assault was to be delivered. The enemy did not appear to have any wire, but patrol work was difficult owing to the bright moonlight and the absence of irrigation cuts or scrub.   Two days later the battalion left the trenches and became part of the corps reserve.

On the evening of the 19th the battalion relieved the 59th Rifles on the Tigris near Maqasis.   Here the front line of trenches occupied lay between the river and the protecting embankment and faced the enemy who were on the north bank of the river.   Four days later the III Corps, after successful operations, succeeded in crossing the River Tigris at the Shumran bend, thus threatening the rear of all the enemy between Sannaiyat and Shumran and forcing them to withdraw.   The 7th Division, which was facing the Sannaiyat position, was ordered to press the enemy vigorously, and the 8th Brigade, including the 2nd Battalion, was ordered to move in support.

The battalion, having crossed the river, moved up its bank at 7.30 p.m. on the 23rd, bivouacking two hours later, but prepared to move at half an hour's notice.   The following day it moved to the north of the Ataba marsh to protect the right flank of the 7th Division, and at 8 a.m. on the 25th it again advanced, halting at 4 p.m. and forming an outpost line, all the men being very tired.   The night passed quietly, and on the following day the whole brigade was ordered to concentrate at the west end of the Shumran bend.   The battalion arrived there at 8 p.m., and was at once ordered to occupy strong bridge-heads at Hai and Shumran bridges and to come again under the orders of Tigris defences as line-of-communication troops.

During the remainder of March the battalion remained in the vicinity of Kut, and at the end of the month was distributed with headquarters and half the battalion at Imam al Mansur and half at Shumran.   While the main army continued its advance towards Baghdad it became necessary to reorganize the defences on the line of communication, and on April 1st the half-battalion at Imam commenced to withdraw towards Shaikh Saad.   Imam was evacuated, and the half-battalion marched to Sinn, the retirement being covered by cavalry.   During this movement Arabs advanced under cover of a white flag and treacherously opened fire.   The next day the strong point at Dujaila was evacuated.   There were two to three thousand Arabs in the vicinity all day, on whom fire was opened, and who were eventually driven off by armoured cars ; but they continued to hang about in the neighbourhood of the column, with the result that there was firing from the camp all that night, and several Arab wounded were observed crawling away at dawn.   Just as the withdrawal was about to continue at 6.30 in the morning the camp was attacked by two thousand mounted Arabs, who were driven off by artillery and machine-gun fire.   From then the march was continued until the 9th, when

KUT-AL-AMARA

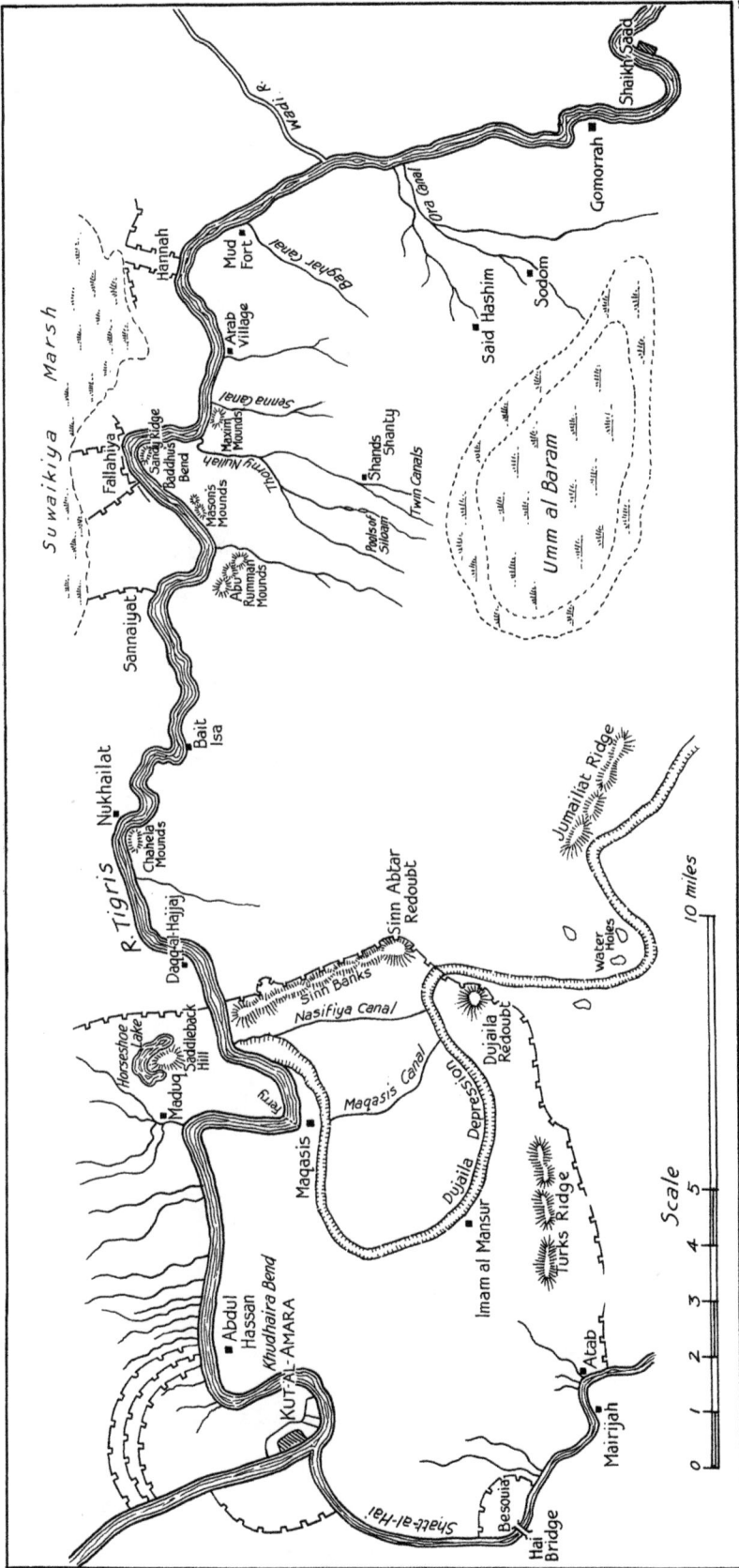

Suwaikiya Marsh

R. Tigris

Wadi R.

Hannah
Mud Fort
Arab Village
Baghar Canal
Ora Canal
Shaikh Sad
Gomorrah
Sodom
Said Hashim
Senna Canal
Maxim Mounds
Mason's Mounds
Sannaiyat
Fallahiya
Sandy Ridge
Paddhus Bend
Abu Rumman Mounds
Thorny Nullah
Pools of Siloam
Shands Shanty
Twin Canals
Umm al Baram

Bait Isa
Nukhailat
Chahela Mounds
Daqqat-Hajjaj
Horseshoe Lake
Saddleback Hill
Maduq
Maqasis
Sinn Banks
Nasifiya Canal
Sinn Abtar Redoubt
Ferry
Maqasis Canal
Dujaila Redoubt
Dujaila Depression
water Holes
Jumailiat Ridge

Abdul Hassan
Khudhaira Bend
KUT-AL-AMARA
Imam al Mansur
Turks Ridge
Atab
Mairijah
Besouia
Hai Bridge
Shatt-al-Hai

Scale
0 1 2 3 4 5   10 miles

9th Jat Regt.

To face page 122

Shaikh Saad was reached, without further opposition, though Arabs were seen in the distance who occasionally sniped the camp at night.

Half the battalion remained at Shaikh Saad until the 16th, when it moved to Baghaila by boat, the other half remaining at Shumran, where it suffered much from sickness.   Eventually, in June, the whole battalion was united at Baghaila and left there by boat on the 29th, arriving at Baghdad on July 2nd.   On July 27th Lieutenant E. Nunn, Indian Army Reserve (attached), died in Baghdad from the effects of heat.   The battalion remained in Baghdad, performing line-of-communication duties, for over a year and then, in September, 1918, moved by train to Baquba, where it relieved the 36th Sikhs in various posts, remaining there until the armistice was signed with Turkey and hostilities ceased.   Eventually it returned to India in 1920, and arrived at Ahmadnagar on May 19th.

1918.

On arrival at Basra on May 14th the 1st Royal Battalion was joined by Major (temporary Lieutenant-Colonel) P. H. Dundas, D.S.O., who assumed command, and having received a number of reinforcements it was posted to the 41st Infantry Brigade.

1916.
1st Battalion.

In a previous chapter mention has been made of the flooding of the whole country between Shaiba and Basra through the overflow of the River Euphrates.   In order to prevent this recurring an embankment had been built, known as the Shaiba bund, and this was being endangered by a large rise in the river level.   From May 16th until June 12th the battalion was employed working on this bund, repairing and strengthening it.   All parades and training, of which the battalion with its large number of recruits stood in great need, had to be stopped. The prevailing wind, known as the *shamal*, blew from the northwest, and while this was blowing the days were bearable, but were quite indescribable when the wind veered to the south and blew clouds of dust about.   There was a plague of flies during the day and of midges and sandflies in the night, though mosquitoes were not so numerous as might have been expected.

The battalion was rejoined by Lieutenant-Colonel Bourne on June 16th, and remained in the neighbourhood of Shaiba and Basra until April 18th, 1917.   During this time the construction of a railway from Basra to Nasiriyah across the desert was undertaken, and detachments of the battalion were employed in guarding the construction parties and in building and garrisoning blockhouses to protect the completed line.   From April 18th till June 26th the battalion was concentrated at Nasiriyah, and then it moved to Baghdad, where it arrived on July 7th and 8th in very hot weather. Orders were then received to march to Faluja on the Euphrates.   The march was carried out during a heat wave when the temperature was

1917.

higher than at any other time during the campaign in Mesopotamia. The battalion marched the first night across the desert to Nuqta, a distance of about twenty-four miles. At Nuqta water was obtainable, but the place had nothing else in its favour. The water contained salts, and there was a plague of flies, while mosquitoes and sandflies abounded. The next night the battalion did the shorter march of about twenty miles to Faluja. The men were very fit, and the battalion arrived well closed up and marching with a swing. On the 14th the battalion marched to Dhibban, then known as Zin-el-Zibban, on the right bank of the Euphrates, where it took over the outposts from the 93rd Infantry.

Dhibban was a bare bit of ground on the bank of the river with a ridge of rocky, bare hills round it. Between the river and the hills ran the Aleppo road. Across the river the ground was green with vegetation, and there was a belt of grazing ground on the right bank both upstream and downstream from Dhibban. Fruit and eggs were plentiful. The battalion was alone here at the foremost point held by the British on the Euphrates.

At this time the Lewis gun was introduced into the battalion for the first time, and the organization of platoons became one section of bombers, one of Lewis gunners, one of rifle grenadiers and one of riflemen. There were no machine guns in the battalion, as these had been removed and organized in separate machine-gun battalions.

The Turks were holding a strong position at Ramadi, two short marches up the Aleppo road, and towards the end of September the 42nd Infantry Brigade advanced through Dhibban, followed by the 12th Brigade. On 26th September the battalion marched from Dhibban in rear of the 12th Brigade, and arrived at Madhij at about 11.30 a.m., where it went into bivouac. Next morning the sound of artillery in action was heard, the guns with the 42nd Brigade ranging on the Turkish position. All that day the battalion remained at Madhij, and that night, marching independently of other troops, it moved forward to McCudden's Point, a place where some low hills approached the river bank. Between that point and Mushaid Ridge, a small range covering the town of Ramadi, lay a flat, open desert destitute of cover, but the night was dark and nothing could be seen.

After arrival at McCudden's Point the battalion marched a thousand yards on a compass bearing half-left across the desert, where it was joined by the 90th Punjabis and 43rd Erinpura Regiment, the whole forming the reserve under Lieutenant-Colonel Bourne, with Captain McCalmont as his staff officer. Before dawn the rattle of musketry was heard in front, and as dawn appeared the battalion could see Mushaid Ridge on its right being heavily shelled. Later the 90th Punjabis and 43rd Erinpuras were sent forward while the 1st Royal Battalion remained in reserve, moving with divisional headquarters.

The battalion took no active part in the action beyond furnishing 150 rifles under Lieutenant C. T. W. Dunsmure, Indian Army Reserve of Officers (attached), as escort to guns.   Some men were also sent under a British officer, to dig on a continuation of the Mushaid Ridge in an endeavour to draw the enemy's fire, but the Turks were too busily engaged to take any notice of them.   All through the following night the guns were firing slowly and there were occasional bursts of musketry, the firing being heaviest at about 5 a.m., when the Turks, having found themselves surrounded, attempted to fight their way out up the Aleppo road.

In the morning, the whole Turkish force having surrendered, the battalion was moved a few hundred yards to the crossing over the Habbaniyeh escape, a canal connecting the very brackish Habbaniyeh lake with the Euphrates, and here it remained until the afternoon, when it did an extremely dusty march into Ramadi city and took over charge of the prisoners.   The battalion was billeted in the serai and adjoining buildings, the prisoners at first being in the attached courtyards.   At first there was considerable difficulty with the prisoners owing to their thirst and hunger, but after the first night they settled down and showed themselves exceedingly good and willing workers. Their kit and equipment were in very bad condition, but they looked well fed and were physically fine men.

Gradually the prisoners were evacuated and on October 2nd the battalion left Ramadi and, until February 3rd, was stationed in three posts in the neighbourhood of Dhibban on both banks of the Euphrates.   The battalion was now a unit of the 50th Brigade in the 15th Indian Division, and by February 21st the whole of this brigade was concentrated at Madhij.   On that day the battalion marched on operation scale to Ramadi, and the next day to Khan Abu Rayat, fifteen miles further up the Aleppo road.   By the 24th the whole brigade was in bivouac at Uqbah, eight miles upstream of Khan Abu Rayat, and the most advanced British position on the Euphrates. Two days later a hostile aeroplane bombed the river front and one sepoy of the battalion was wounded.

On March 8th information was received that the Turks had evacuated the town of Hit and their position on the Broad Wadi.   This was first received from two Turkish deserters who surrendered to " C " Company of the 1st Royal Battalion, and was afterwards confirmed by the Flying Corps.   At 5 p.m. the battalion received an hour's notice to precede the brigade in support of armoured cars and occupy a ridge four miles north-west of Uqbah along the road.   At midnight the battalion was joined by the remainder of the brigade and marched to within three miles of Hit.   In the evening the brigade, under cover of artillery fire, advanced on Hit and reached the town without opposition at 10 a.m.

1918.

The town of Hit is built on a hill on the river bank, and immediately inland of it are flat, odorous bitumen fields. To the north-west of these and running at right-angles to the river are some low hills in which was situated the main Turkish position, known as the Broad Wadi position. The battalion continued the advance and reached the Broad Wadi position, which was also found to have been evacuated. The position had been well prepared with numerous fire and communication trenches, and a large quantity of timber had been used in its construction. One machine-gun emplacement existed in what appeared to be a natural cave with an exit behind the trenches, and which fired through a small hole underneath them. At noon the battalion went into bivouac on the bank of the river a mile upstream of the town, and on March 11th advanced with the remainder of the brigade to Sahiliya, seven miles upstream.

At 9 p.m. on the night of March 25th–26th the battalion marched with the remainder of the brigade up the Aleppo road, one company of the battalion acting as advanced guard. The objective was the enemy's main position at Khan Baghdadi, where he was to be pinned to his ground to enable the 7th Cavalry Brigade to outflank him from the west, take his position in rear and cut his one artery of communication, the Aleppo road. Some distance in front of the enemy's main position some trenches were known to exist across the road, which were called the " P " trenches. These were believed to be lightly held during the day and not held at all or only very lightly by night. The column halted at 12.45 a.m. at the Wadi Falij, some two miles short of these trenches, and " A " Company, under Captain W. L. Hailes and Second-Lieutenant B. R. Godley, was sent forward east of the Aleppo road, with orders to occupy the " P " trenches if not held and to brush aside opposition and seize them if lightly held. One company of the Oxford and Buckinghamshire Light Infantry was sent forward on the left of the road, and a company of the 24th Punjabis on its left, with similar orders. No bombs or Lewis guns were taken by any of the three companies.

The company of the 1st Royal Battalion moved forward in two lines of sections in file, and when it had advanced nearly two miles a challenge rang out in the dark and a few shots were fired. A charge was delivered and a few sangars and small trenches were found empty, but fire was then opened on the company from some high ground ahead. A second charge was made, when two machine guns suddenly opened fire from the left across the road at very short range, killing four men outright. From the fact that the fire of the two machine guns was uninterrupted, it was evident that the company on the left of the road, with whom touch had been lost immediately the first charge was launched, was no longer advancing; and as the company had no rifle grenades, it was unable to silence the machine guns, which were posted on a bluff about fifteen to twenty feet high and sheer. The left of the company was therefore compelled to withdraw a short distance until protected from the Turkish fire by the lie of the ground. Meanwhile, on the right, after a short hand-to-hand fight in the trenches, the Turks withdrew. Extremely heavy machine-gun fire was then opened and maintained upon the whole company front, but did little damage, for the night was dark and the cover good. A number of tracer bullets were seen flying far overhead.

Meanwhile, the main column, which had halted in column of route on the main Baghdad–Aleppo road some two miles back, was unexpectedly fired on by two hostile field guns. This caused considerable confusion, one man and two mules being wounded, and the battalion had to leave the road hastily and take cover behind some adjacent sandhills.

On the situation in the " P " trenches becoming known to brigade headquarters, orders were sent for " A " Company to withdraw, and it rejoined the battalion at 4.45 a.m., having lost four killed and six wounded.

At 9.30 a.m. an attack was launched by the whole brigade group, the 1st Royal Battalion being on the left, " B " and " C " Companies leading, " A " and " D " Companies in support. Slight opposition was met with from the " P " trenches, but only a half-hearted resistance was offered, the Turks either retreating or surrendering. Thirty Turks surrendered to " C " Company from these trenches. By twelve noon the battalion had advanced some three miles with a few casualties, the Turks fighting a weak rear-guard action until they reached their main position. The two leading companies were then held up by rifle, machine-gun and artillery fire, " B " Company having three killed and ten wounded, including Jemadar Salig.

Arrangements were then made for a deliberate attack upon the enemy's main position. The 42nd Brigade moved up on the right of the 50th Brigade between it and the River Euphrates. The 50th Brigade was disposed with the 24th Punjabis on the right, the Oxford and Buckinghamshire Light Infantry in the centre, and the 1st Royal Battalion on the extreme left of the whole line. The 97th Infantry were in brigade reserve. At 5.30 p.m. the attack was launched under very heavy covering fire from machine guns and less heavy from artillery. " A " and " D " Companies were leading, with " B " and " C " Companies in support. The Wadi Baghdadi—the dry bed of a stream with its banks sheer walls of rock fifty feet high—having been crossed, oblique machine-gun fire was opened on the battalion from some high ground to the left front. " C " Company, under the command of Captain A. B. Fletcher, attacked this position and captured

14 officers, 250 men and 2 machine guns. The main position was reached without loss and the Turks surrendered wholesale, 12 officers, 171 men, 4 machine guns and 4 field guns being captured by " A " and " D " Companies. These two companies then advanced to a second position, which was found to have been evacuated, and all four companies then remained where they were until after dark. At 2.30 a.m. the battalion, together with the rest of the brigade, continued the advance along the Aleppo road to the Wadi Hauran, where the remainder of the Turks, having been cut off in their retreat by a cavalry brigade, surrendered before the arrival of the infantry.

For gallantry during the battle of Khan Baghdadi Captain Hailes, Lieutenant (Acting Captain) C. K. Tester and Lieutenant T. C. McCarthy received the Military Cross. Sepoys Girdhala, Lakhi, Dodh Ram and Udmi received the Indian Distinguished Service Medal.

This was the last engagement in which the Regiment took part during the Great War. The 1st Royal Battalion remained on the Euphrates until after the Armistice, returning to India in April, 1919.

CHAPTER XIII

NORTH-WEST FRONTIER, MESOPOTAMIA AND
THE BLACK SEA

Bibliography—Regimental Records.

THE 3rd Battalion was stationed at Jhansi on the outbreak of war with
Germany, and left that station in November, 1914, for Bannu on the

1914.
3rd Battalion.

North-West Frontier, where it arrived on the 12th.
On the 29th news reached Bannu that a lashkar of
Khostwals was preparing to attack Miram Shah, a post
in Northern Waziristan occupied by militia. The battalion, leaving
a depot at Bannu, moved up the Tochi valley as part of a movable
column, and established a perimeter camp outside the militia post.
Orders then arriving that it was to remain at Miram Shah pending
further developments, it moved into the houses of the serai, the walled
courtyard which normally served as a rest camp for trading caravans.
These buildings had been looted and partially burnt by raiders on
November 29th.

The battalion remained in occupation of Miram Shah until
January 17th. During this period parties of the battalion were

1915.

constantly engaged in demonstration marches and operations,
but did not come into collision with the tribesmen. It then
returned to Bannu, where it arrived on the 19th.

On March 2nd the battalion again left Bannu with the movable
column, arriving at Miram Shah two days later, where it constructed
a perimeter camp. Again detachments were engaged in reconnaissances
without actually engaging in hostilities until the 25th, when hostile
tribesmen threatened the withdrawal to camp of one of the piquets.
The following day the column moved out of camp in three forces.
Headquarters of the battalion under Lieutenant-Colonel H. E. Lowis
with 300 rifles accompanied Force " A," which also included headquarters and a similar detachment of the 52nd Sikhs. Force " B "
consisted of 150 rifles of the 3rd Battalion under Lieutenant C. W.
Farquharson and a similar number of the Sikhs, and was detailed to
act as a reserve. Force " C " consisted mainly of militia.

Force " A " left camp shortly before seven o'clock in the morning,
and the battalion was given as its objective a sangared hill. Owing

K   129

to the conformation of the ground it had first to advance over an open plain and then cross a series of ridges with steep forward slopes and steeper reverse slopes. There was a section of guns with Force " A," which opened fire soon after seven o'clock. The leading companies advanced by rushes, covered by the artillery fire and by that of the company in local reserve. The tribesmen left both their advanced positions and their second positions before " C " and " D " Companies rushed up and seized them. The enemy were then in full retreat and were caught as they retired by the fire of Force " C," which appeared crowning the hills to the south-west. The battalion suffered no casualties, only two occurring in the whole column, while the tribesmen were estimated to have lost about eight hundred killed and wounded out of a total of about ten thousand. A reconnaissance carried out the following day showed that they had fled across the border.

For their good work on this day Lieutenant-Colonel H. E. Lowis was mentioned in despatches, Subedar-Major Nand Ram received the Order of British India, Class II, and No. 2399 Sepoy Pirdan received the Indian Distinguished Service Medal.

Headquarters of the battalion returned to Bannu from Miram Shah on October 2nd, and as the battalion marched down the Tochi road it relieved the garrisons of seven posts in the Tochi and took over the Bannu outposts.

On March 22nd, 1916, a detachment of the battalion was called out to effect the capture of an agitator known as the " Ber Fakir " in the neighbourhood of Lakki. The detachment detailed consisted
1916. of Captain J. B. Haines, 2 Indian officers and 100 other ranks. Captain Haines also attached to his force an Indian officer and 10 sowars of the 2nd Gwalior (Imperial Service) Lancers, then on detachment at Lakki outpost. The superintendent of police at Bannu with 14 armed police and certain civil officials also accompanied the force. The arrangements made were completely successful and the Fakir and his chief supporter were arrested without a shot being fired, although surrounded by threatening crowds.

Until November, 1917, the battalion was employed alternately either in the garrison of Bannu or as part of the movable column at
1917. Miram Shah. During this period numerous drafts were sent off as reinforcements to other units overseas, but the battalion itself was not engaged in any fighting, though columns frequently had to move out. On May 31st Second-Lieutenant E. S. Boyton-Smith with 100 rifles formed part of a column which marched to Tutnarai. This post had been captured from its small garrison of militia by a few Mahsuds through a stratagem. The column met with no opposition and reoccupied the deserted post, the detachment of the battalion returning to Miram Shah on June 2nd.

On November 5th the battalion received orders to mobilize for service in Mesopotamia. It embarked at Karachi on January 1st, 1918, on the transport *Ekma*, under the command of Lieutenant-Colonel C. G. Robson. The battalion arrived at Basra at noon on the 7th where it transhipped to paddle-steamers and moved up the Shatt-al-Arab to Nahr Umr, where it disembarked and went into standing camp. On the 14th it commenced leaving Nahr Umr by river boats, and arrived at Baghdad ten days later, where it was posted to the 55th Brigade.

1918.

For the first half of February the battalion was engaged in constructing the railway embankment at Conningham's Post and between Hanaidi and Diyala, and after this was engaged in ordinary training at Kadhimain. On March 7th a party of one Indian officer and 46 rifles under Captain Standen and Lieutenant G. Christie carried out a raid on a small Arab encampment with the object of searching for arms, ammunition and other goods stolen from Government. Certain Government property, including rifles and ammunition, was recovered, the Arabs concerned being arrested.

In March the battalion moved to Samarra, where it continued to be employed in line-of-communication duties and in training. On May 5th a detachment of fourteen Lewis guns of the battalion under Captain Standen joined a " mobile van column " which operated from Samarra under Lieutenant-Colonel Bridges. This column joined the 7th Cavalry Brigade at their camp below Beit-el-Khalifa, and on the following day moved to Daur, twenty miles up the river from Samarra. On the 7th Captain Standen's detachment acted as advanced guard, following the Daur–Tekrit road to Nukhaila springs, but was held up by impassable roads. The next day the column moved along the old Turk road along the skirt of the Jabal Hamrin ridge, when twelve mounted men were seen, who disappeared into the hills after firing a few shots. During the following three days reconnaissances were carried out towards Fatha, the gorge formed by the Tigris in forcing its way through the Jabal Hamrin range, sixty miles from Samarra ; a strong natural defensive position, about which it was desired to gain information in view of impending operations. During the first two days signs were seen of a Turkish camp on the right bank of the river and shelters on the north-east slopes of the Jabal Hamrin hills, but there were no signs of life in the Turkish position on the left bank. On the third day touch was at last established with the Turks on the left bank and a few shots exchanged, sufficient to prove the Turks had not evacuated Fatha. On the evening of the 16th the detachment rejoined the battalion.

On July 5th a party of 450 men under Lieutenant L. J. Montgomerie and Second-Lieutenant G. N. Buckton moved to Alajik for road construction. The battalion continued engaged in line-of-communication duties without taking part in any operations until September 28th, when it entrained at Samarra and moved to Baghdad and thence, on October 4th, to Makina near Basra. It then embarked in two transports, the *Huntspil* and the *Barjora*, and sailed on October 24th and 28th.

After transhipping at Port Said, the detachment on the *Barjora* having moved there by rail from Suez, the battalion was again united at Uchantar, near Salonika, early in December. During the voyage information was received that the Turks had signed an armistice on November 3rd, which caused the men to hope for an early return to their homes in India. The next six weeks were spent in the neighbourhood of Salonika, devoted to peace-time training, camp duties and working parties. Rain was incessant, and the muddy camp became a wet and miserable place. Everyone was glad when, on February 17th, the battalion again embarked, this time on the transport *Katoomba*. Surprisingly, it was a most beautiful day; so the battalion saw the last of Salonika under good conditions. The following day the battalion reached the port of Constantinople, and on the 21st disembarked at Batoum on the Black Sea.

The country of Trans-Caucasia, lying south of the Caucasus mountains and stretching from the Black Sea to the Caspian, comprises two

1919.   former provinces of Imperial Russia—Georgia in the west, with its port of Batoum on the Black Sea ; and Azerbaijan in the east, with its port of Baku on the Caspian. The two ports were connected by a railway, and half-way between the two lay Tiflis, the capital of Georgia, and formerly a great Russian cantonment. When the revolution had occurred in Russia her armies in Trans-Caucasia had crumbled away and the country had fallen into the hands of the Germans and the Turks. After the armistice was signed British troops were sent to enforce the evacuation of the Turkish army and await the decision of the Peace Conference regarding the future of the country as well as that of Armenia, the Christian country lying to the south and formerly part of the Turkish empire.

On arrival at Batoum the Indian ranks, despite their disappointment at not returning to their homes, responded at once to their beautiful surroundings and were in the highest spirits. While the battalion marched through the town to its billets in the old Russian barracks, the men gave vent to cries of " Ramchandra ki Jai, Hanuman ki Hun," while the local inhabitants—a curious-looking lot—seemed amazed. The Georgian officers in the streets appeared to rejoice in strange kits : enormous astrakhan or white sheepskin caps ; long, flowing, dressing-gown-like robes stuck with knives and daggers and swords ; and maroon or black soft Russian leather, thin-soled boots—very like stage soldiers. Their kit did not look serviceable.

The battalion provided guards in the town and was engaged in training and repair work on the railway which ran alongside the sea to the north. Here the green cliffs coming right down to the water's edge were very pretty, and there was an abundance of wild flowers. The climate was delightful—a trifle relaxing, perhaps ; but the fields looked glorious in green and all the trees in bud and blossom. The rifle range, an old Russian one, was an expanse of green turf, short and crisp, in places carpeted with ordinary English daisies.

On April 24th " D " Company, under Captain J. Crompton and Lieutenant W. M. Andrews, was sent to Gagri, a small port to the north-west of Batoum at the foot of the main range of the Caucasus mountains, where it relieved a detachment of the 26th Middlesex Regiment. Headquarters, with the remainder of the battalion, followed on May 7th, and the British officers were billeted in the house of Prince Oldenberg, while the remainder of the battalion was in various private houses. About an hour's run by car from Gagri the Georgian front line faced the Russians in a condition of suspended hostility, while the small British garrison protected Gagri from Bolshevism pending the decisions of the Peace Conference at Versailles.

Gagri made a deep impression on the regiment as a really beautiful spot. It seemed like a regular Riviera seaside watering-place with its fine hotels and private houses, in some of which the men were billeted. The children of the owners of the houses particularly seemed to take a great interest in the sepoys, regarding the whole show as a sort of game. Actually these once-rich people were in a very parlous state, most of their money gone and very much afraid of the Bolsheviks.*

The battalion was very happy, but there was little to do and all ranks found the life dull. There was little ground available either for training or sport. The men were more or less confined to their own lines, where they engaged in tugs-of-war. Such things impressed the

---

* " GAGRI, 29/6/19. Yesterday we celebrated Kochik's birthday. He is the little three-year-old son of the Count and Countess, our landlords here. He has learnt to say ' Ram Ram ' and ' Salute.' Our cook made him a cake with ' Kochik ' on it. We had luncheon with the Countess, sitting down twenty at table, starting at 2 p.m. and not getting away till 5.30 p.m. The whole show was rather funny. I forget how many Russian princes and princesses were there ; they all belong to the old noblesse, and here they are now, officers without regiments and all with *no place to go*. The Union Jack which floats from the Palace windows, and which is kept there by a handful of Indian troops, is their sure shield. I asked the Countess's mother, did she not think it strange and utterly contrary to all expectations, to see Indian mess servants waiting on us all in the grand dining-room ? She said yes, and how thankful they were to have us with them, and what will it all come to in the end ? Who can tell ?"—*The late Captain Standen, M.C., in a personal letter.*
The fears were justified. An American who visited the country under Bolshevik auspices in 1930 wrote : " Everywhere along the great stretch of natural playground, the palaces of grand dukes and millionaire merchants were being used by workers and peasants. Sallow-skinned factory girls . . . were installed (as was our party of journalists) in a gorgeous chalet brought piecemeal from Switzerland to Gagri's mountain flank by a Russian nobleman."—*Eugene Lyons in " Assignment in Utopia," published 1938.*

local soldiery very much, and they gathered to watch the sepoys wrestling and bayonet fighting.   Officers were able to fish in a trout stream on the Oldenberg estate, but they missed such games as tennis, and as far as riding went, there was, practically speaking, only one road.   Despite rumours of intended attack by the Bolshevik element in the town, all remained quiet, the port constantly being visited by various ships of the Royal Navy.

A collection of gifts from Queen Alexandra which arrived in July delighted the men.   Each packet contained a handkerchief, tobacco, a piece of soap, a candle, a pair of bootlaces and a greeting in Hindi. In some there were steel mirrors.   Much thought went to the wording of the post cards of acknowledgment included with each gift.

On July 16th a company was sent back to Batoum ; five days later the ammunition store of the Georgians in the fort at Gagri blew up, killing eight Georgians and badly injuring seven more, but doing no damage to the guards furnished by the battalion.   Battalion headquarters with two platoons moved to Batoum on July 25th, leaving Gagri under the command of Captain J. D. Standen with whom was Lieutenant M. J. O'Connor.   This detachment was relieved by a company of the 7th Berkshire Regiment on August 17th and embarked the following day on H.M.T. *Tagus*.   The transport picked up battalion headquarters and the remainder of the battalion at Batoum and sailed for Constantinople.   Here some hitch occurred in the arrangements for disembarkation, with the result that the battalion was stuck on board ship for two days, lying out in midstream during coaling operations.

By this time nine months had passed since the Turks had signed the armistice, and there still seemed no early prospect of the Allies coming to an agreement regarding the peace terms.   The Turks were growing exasperated at the delay and the continued occupation of their country, while in May a Greek army had been let loose in Asia Minor without adequate control.   The result was that thousands of Turks flocked to the standard of revolt raised by Mustafa Kemal Pasha, first at Sivas and then at Angora in the heart of Asiatic Turkey.   In order to safeguard Constantinople from these Turkish Nationalists, it was essential to hold the Ismid peninsula, the small bit of land on the Asiatic side of the Bosporus between the Sea of Marmara and the Black Sea.   At first the battalion went into camp twenty-eight kilometres from Constantinople, with one company on detachment at Derindje, later sending another company to Bostanjik, but on October 4th headquarters under the command of Major Atkins moved to the town of Ismid. This is situated on a gulf of the Sea of Marmara near where the peninsula joins the mainland of Anatolia, and here it relieved the 2nd Battalion The Liverpool Regiment.

On the south side of the gulf and opposite Ismid lies the village of

Baggajik, and on October 28th the sound of firing was heard from the direction of this village.   A few days later the battalion received orders to send a piquet of twenty-five other ranks under an Indian officer as a precautionary measure to safeguard the British and American missions there.   On the night of November 12th, while the officers of the destroyer *Tobago* were dining with the officers of the battalion in the palace at Ismid, which served as a mess, a message was received by lamp from Baggajik.   This stated that the platoon had been heavily sniped.   A second message then came in which it was stated one sepoy had been wounded, but that the enemy had been silenced by Lewis-gun fire and all was now quiet.

Accordingly at 6.30 next morning a party of 100 rifles embarked on the destroyer and disembarked on the farther shore at ten o'clock. Major G. W. Atkins, with Commander Dawson of the destroyer, then rode ahead to Baggajik, while the hundred rifles under Captain Standen followed, the village being a stiff four-mile uphill trek from the shore. A neighbouring village which was known to have harboured the malcontents was surrounded and the sheikh arrested.   There was no resistance ; he surrendered at once and was brought away riding on a donkey.   It then began to rain, everyone got soaked to the skin and was glad to get back to the mission at Baggajik soon after five o'clock in the afternoon.   Next morning the party re-embarked on the destroyer and crossed to Ismid, but, owing to the rough sea, was unable to disembark until late in the afternoon.   The sepoy had only a flesh wound, and the incident was regarded as a pleasant break in the monotony.

There followed a period of ceaseless rain and the continuous damp was very bad for the health of the men, who had little or nothing in the way of comforts.   Heavy guard duties also caused them to be run down.   An epidemic of influenza which had swept over the world made a belated, but fortunately not very serious, appearance in the battalion.   A spell of perfect weather in December did much to compensate for the previous rain ; but in February there was heavy snow. At one time there was fifteen inches of it in the camp.   While the snow remained life under canvas was unpleasant, though advantage was taken of it to organize toboggan races, the toboggans being towed by mules.   When the snow began to melt the camp was reduced to a terrible condition.   No sooner was the camp cleaned up than, on the night of February 17th, the battalion and record offices caught fire and were completely destroyed, one sepoy being burnt to death.*

There was a large Turkish dump of ammunition at Ismid and on February 19th H.M.S. *Collier* arrived from Constantinople to remove

---

* The records being destroyed, most of the information contained in this chapter is based on accounts subsequently written, supplemented by extracts from the personal letters of the late Captain Standen, M.C., kindly made available by his sisters.

this.   Working parties from the battalion were detailed as loading parties, but the Turkish troops present objected and took up a defensive position.   They loaded, and in doing so fired two rounds.   Major Atkins walked up to the Turkish line and remonstrated.   The Turks refused to surrender the ammunition and a tense situation resulted. Orders not to proceed with the loading of the ammunition were then received from brigade headquarters and the work was suspended. The following day the situation was eased by the arrival in the harbour of two light cruisers, bringing the divisional commander.   Work on the ammunition was recommenced, the Turks withdrawing their forces on being allowed to have a tallyman at work as the ammunition was shifted.

On March 20th news arrived that a railway bridge, one hundred and eighty-eight kilometres from Constantinople, had been blown up.

1920.   This, presumably, had been done by Turkish Nationalists to cut off a Punjabi battalion which was at Eski Shehr farther along the line.   The 3rd Battalion entrained the following morning and moved to a place called Meheji, where, after posting outposts on the surrounding heights, it remained in the train for the night.   Next day it arrived at the broken bridge and took over some piquet positions from the 2nd Rajputs, who had arrived earlier.   The majority of the men were then employed in helping the Royal Engineers to repair the bridge.

On the 24th a piquet of the Rajputs was fired at during the afternoon, and a sepoy of the 3rd Battalion was hit on the leg by a Turkish bullet while doubling out to his alarm post.   A Turkish ultimatum ordering the British forces to withdraw within twelve hours, and stating they were entirely surrounded by Turkish troops was then received and ignored.

The repair of the bridge was completed next day, and early in the afternoon a train bringing back part of the Punjabis was able to cross.   The night was quiet, although a Turkish cavalry patrol was fired on by a piquet of the Punjabis soon after dark and five saddles emptied ; but the next afternoon the Turks developed a disjointed attack and all piquets were engaged.   Intermittent firing continued the whole afternoon and developed some intensity shortly before midnight, but no casualties occurred among the defenders though the Turks were believed to have suffered considerably.   Before dawn all piquets were withdrawn and the battalion entrained, the withdrawal not being followed up.   By the 28th it was back at Ismid.

There were many rumours of the onward " rush " of the Nationalists Ismid itself was safe ; a destroyer was always present with her guns, and a battleship in addition when any trouble was brewing. H.M.S. *Royal Oak* had come into the harbour quietly after dark on the night

MESOPOTAMIA

Khan Baghdadi
Sahiliya
Hit
Istabulat
Samarra
Adhaim R.
Ramadi
Habbaniyeh Lake
Madhij
Dhibban
Faluja
Mushadie
Euphrates R.
Baquba
Diyala R.
BAGHDAD
Diyala
Ctesiphon
Tigris R.
Hilla
Baghaila
Sannaiyat
Kut-al-Amara
Shaikh Saad
Ali Gharbi
Pusht-i-Kuh Mountains
Amara
Tigris R.
Qala Salih
Ezra's Tomb
Qurna
Old Channel
New Channel
Safi
Shatt-al-Hai
Euphrates R.
Nasiriyah
Kurnat Ali
BASRA
Shaiba
Mohammerah
Karun R.
Fao
Shatt-al-Arab

Scale

Miles 50 40 30 20 10 0   50   100 Miles

By permission of The Controller of H.M. Stationery Office

9th Jat Regt.

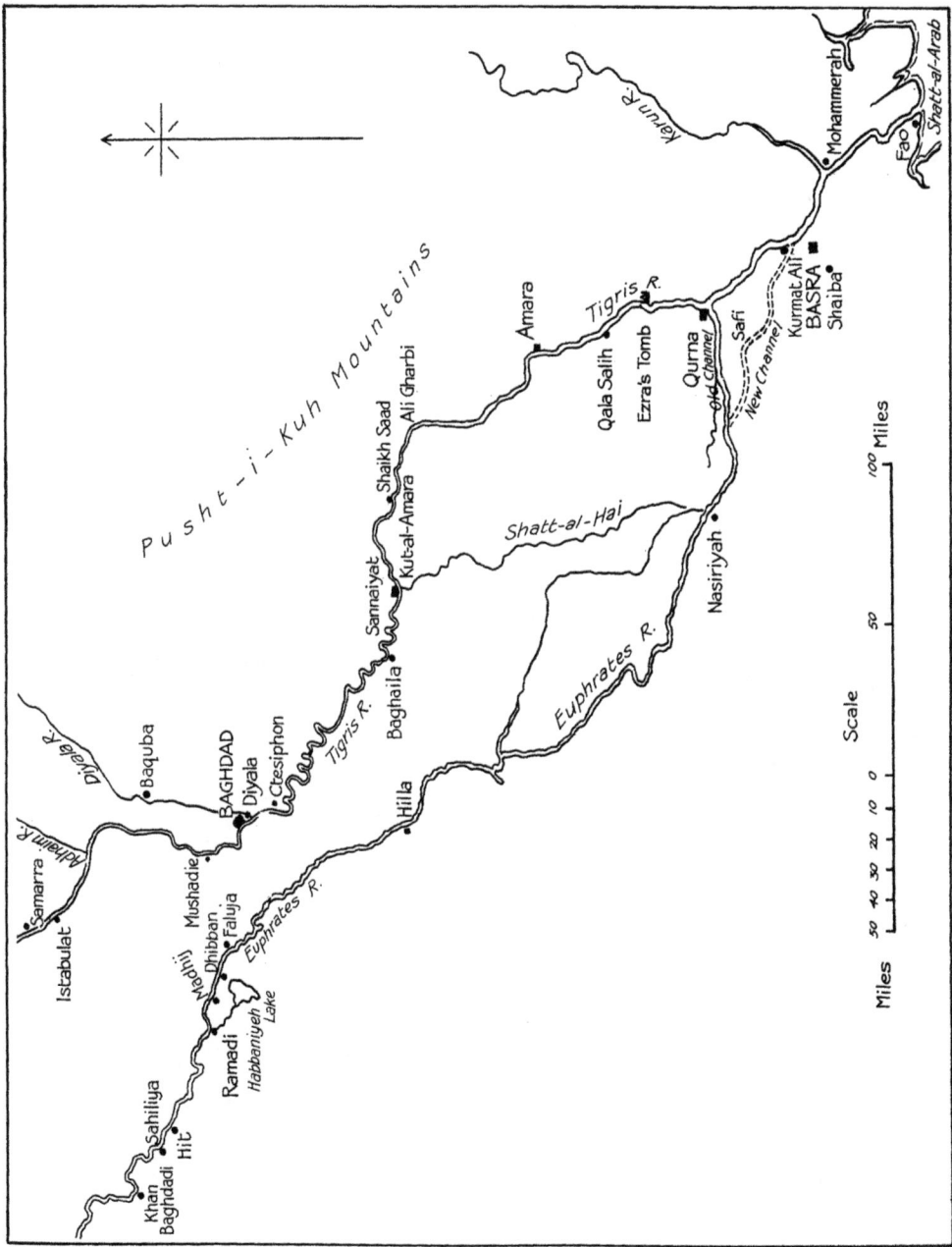

To face page 136

the battalion left.   Inland it was different, but nothing serious developed.   Later it was believed the attack had been made by a subordinate commander without the concurrence of the National High Command, which was anxious to avoid complications with the British. The little expedition had been excellent training for the men—practical hill climbing with a real enemy in the vicinity, marred by more rain than was pleasant.

By July the whole situation had changed and everything seemed peaceful enough again.   Locally this improvement was credited to successes of the Greek army in Asia Minor.   The battalion remained in the Ismid peninsula until November.   On the 9th of that month it embarked at Chanak, and arrived at Jhansi on the 27th.

Chapter XIV

THE THIRD AFGHAN WAR AND WAZIRISTAN

Bibliography—Regimental Records.

THE 1st Royal Battalion returned to India from Mesopotamia in two ships. Of these, the first ship-load arrived at Bombay on April 12th, 1919, and entrained for Jhansi, where it arrived three days later. The depot was absorbed and demobilization and reorganization were started, but men could not be sent off on leave as the trains to the north were not running normally owing to severe riots in the Punjab. While the reorganization was going on the battalion had to remain in a state of readiness to send out parties in aid of civil power should riots break out in the neighbourhood.

1919.
1st Battalion.

The second ship-load arrived at Bombay under the command of Captain A. B. Fletcher, but as riots had broken out in that city the detachment was detained and provided piquets as required in aid of civil power. It was not required to use force, and eventually arrived at Jhansi on May 7th. At the railway station information was received that orders had arrived for the battalion to mobilize again.

The battalion left Jhansi by train before dawn on May 18th. During the journey through the Punjab many signs of the recent riots were evident, especially at Gujranwala, where the gutted remains of the English church and portions of the railway station were seen. It arrived at Peshawar on the evening of the 20th and, leaving there at 4 a.m. on the 22nd, marched eighteen miles to Michni, a small fort on the Mohmand border beyond the Kabul river. Considerable difficulty was experienced in getting the transport across this river which, about two miles short of Michni, was divided in two by a sandy island some five hundred yards broad, the bridges over the two branches of the river not having been completed. All baggage, except such as could be man-handled, had to be ferried across to the island, disembarked, re-embarked on the far side of the island and finally disembarked on the far side of the river. The result was that a portion of the transport could not reach the fort before nightfall and, as a large hostile force was reported to be within striking distance, it was parked for the night on the island, where a perimeter camp was formed and a guard left under the command of Second-Lieutenant B. C. H. Gerty.

At Michni, in addition to the battalion, there was a troop of Indian cavalry with a section of machine guns and a detachment, about eighty strong, of the Mohmand Militia under a British officer. The nearest hostile force was reported to be ten and a half miles away at Ghalanai and to consist of about five hundred Afghan regulars, three to four thousand other Afghans and four to five thousand Bajouri tribesmen, who were expected to attack at dawn. Exaggerated reports are common on the frontier and, though suitable precautions were taken, this one was duly discounted. Very little occurred, and on May 26th the battalion was ordered to return to Peshawar.

The battalion then went into camp on the race-course and was employed in finding station guards and duties and escorts for convoys moving up the Khyber Pass to the troops ahead. The heat was intense, and the small forty-pound tents in which officers lived were the reverse of comfortable. There was firing most nights in the cantonment bazaar, while close to the battalion camp was the Peshawar zoo which, rumour said, was used by Pathan raiders to supply them with the luxury of fresh venison.

On July 30th the battalion was ordered to take over all the piquets in Peshawar city. Peshawar is at all times a turbulent place, and during the Afghan War the duty of enforcing law and order proved too heavy for the police and frontier constabulary. Certain tactical points from which any disturbance could quickly be dealt with, were held by military piquets, and no officer was allowed to leave the piquet he was commanding without an escort of two sepoys. As there were five of these piquets, each of which required a British officer and one or more Indian officers, duties pressed heavily upon the battalion. The city quietened down when peace negotiations were commenced, and the piquets were withdrawn on August 15th, a week after peace had been signed with Afghanistan at Rawalpindi. The battalion remained at Peshawar until September 9th, when it moved into standing camp at Badni Bridge, two miles down the Shabkadr road, and on the 13th entrained for its new peace station, Ferozepore.

Lieutenant-Colonel W. FitzG. Bourne, O.B.E., was mentioned in despatches for distinguished services during these operations, and all ranks received the Indian General Service Medal with the clasp, " Afghanistan, 1919."

At Ferozepore ordinary peace-time routine and training were carried out. The war being over, there was much anxiety among the men as
to when they would be able to leave the service. The
1920.
1st Battalion. battalion was very much over strength and, although
over 280 men were discharged or demobilized from
Ferozepore, the strength still remained excessive. Demobilization was proceeding apace when, on January 30th, 1920, the battalion

received orders to move to Jhansi by train in ten days' time. This came as a great surprise and was especially inconvenient while the demobilization was being carried out. The men had been expecting to stay at Ferozepore for a considerable time, and were disappointed at being moved so far from their homes.

Lieutenant-Colonel Bourne went on eight months' sick leave in March, and at the end of that period was struck off the strength, being succeeded in command by Lieutenant-Colonel P. H. Dundas, D.S.O., O.B.E.

The battalion had been at Jhansi for about eight months when again orders for a move were received. On November 7th it was intimated that the battalion had been selected by the Viceroy as his escort and later to act as escort to His Royal Highness the Duke of Connaught, who was to visit Delhi in the forthcoming winter. Accordingly the battalion left Jhansi on November 18th and moved to Delhi, leaving a depot behind.

His Royal Highness arrived at Delhi on February 7th. He opened the Chamber of Princes, inaugurated the Council of State and the Legislative Assembly, and laid the foundation stone of the **1921.** All India War Memorial, all within a very short space of time after his arrival. On all these occasions the battalion took part in lining the streets, sometimes furnishing guards of honour.

It was on February 10th, at the ceremony of the laying of the foundation stone of the war memorial, that His Royal Highness announced that His Majesty the King had been pleased to confer the title of " Royal " on the battalion. By a happy coincidence, this was the anniversary especially observed as a holiday by the battalion to celebrate the part it had taken in the battle of Sobraon in 1846.

A telegram was received from His Majesty which read as follows :—

> " The King has received with much pleasure your telegram, and appreciates the loyal message which you have addressed to His Majesty on behalf of all ranks on this great occasion in the life of the regiment."

Before his departure from Delhi on February 15th His Royal Highness visited the battalion in camp. It was fortunate that the battalion was at Kingsway to see him depart.

This period spent at Delhi was a time of much ceremonial and many public functions. It was with much regret, at this auspicious time, that the news of the death of Lieutenant-General A. G. Hancock, C.B., the Colonel of the Regiment, was received. He died on February 10th, the date on which the title " Royal " had been conferred.

In April of this year orders were received for the complete reorganization of the whole Indian Army. Under the scheme which was being introduced the battalion was to be one of a group consisting of four active battalions and a training battalion. Each active battalion was to consist of a headquarters and two companies of Jats of the Punjab, one of Musalman Rajputs of the Punjab, and one of cis-Jhelum Punjabi Musalmans. The reorganization was to be effected by transfers arranged mutually between commanding officers. These orders caused a certain amount of consternation among all ranks, coming as they did so soon after the signal honour which the battalion had received for its services in the late war. They would necessitate the demobilization or transfer of two whole companies of Jats from the battalion. The first Mohammedan joined the battalion on April 15th, but it was several months before the reorganization was completed.

In September news was received that Major-General C. F. G. Young, C.B., had been appointed Colonel in place of Lieutenant-General Hancock. The following message was received from Major-General Young :—

" On his appointment to the Colonelcy of the Regiment, Major-General Young wishes to greet all ranks and to express to them the great honour he feels has been conferred on him by this appointment. The fact that his personal connections with the old regiment in which he passed so many happy years have been renewed, and will be maintained as long as he lives, is a source of the greatest possible joy to him. May the years to come bring added honour and happiness to the 6th Royal Jat Light Infantry."

On April 30th the Commanding Officer had received orders that the situation in Waziristan might necessitate the employment of more troops, and the battalion was ordered to hold itself in readiness to move to the frontier at short notice. Men on leave were to be warned but not recalled. With the reorganization just commencing and the depot, with much of the office, still at Jhansi, many difficulties were experienced.

The tribal territory of Waziristan is the mountainous tangle of country to the south of the Kurram valley lying on the British side of the Afghan frontier, but beyond the administered border of British India. Although no attempt had ever been made to administer this territory, certain forts were held by small garrisons of frontier militia, officered by Army officers, but responsible to the civil authorities. During the Third Afghan War these forts had to be evacuated and the whole country became hostile. It was reconquered with the greatest difficulty after the biggest campaign ever fought by the British on the North-West Frontier of India. It was then determined to build a road through the heart of Waziristan, and it was in order to protect the construction of this road that troops were required to dominate the principal villages of the Mahsuds. Other troops were also necessary to keep open the line of communication.

The battalion entrained at Delhi on October 29th, under Colonel P. H. Dundas, and detrained at Darya Khan, whence it marched to Tank, arriving on November 4th. Two companies with two machine guns were then sent to Khirgi.

Tank is situated in the plains, and the cantonment consisted of a number of huts built of unburnt brick scattered over a wide area. The perimeter was enormous and the defences, which consisted of a single apron fence of barbed wire and a number of sandbag piquets separated by long distances, were quite inadequate. The duties were very heavy. Next to the cantonment was a small civil station and, outside the perimeter, the native city, where the sound of rifle fire was so common that no one paid any attention to it. The civil station was normally guarded by frontier constabulary, but when these had to enter the city in force, which was very frequently, the guards in the civil station were taken over by the battalion. The drinking water was very impure and thoroughly dirty in appearance. Daily messages were received reporting the presence of gangs of raiders in the neighbourhood.

The road from Tank into Waziristan proper runs at first along the plains, about nine miles, to Kaur bridge, where there was a strong, well-built fort. At Kaur the road turns back at a sharp angle and climbs up a spur of the hills to Manzai, where brigade headquarters was situated. This spur appeared to be formed throughout of loose sandy earth and round stones. It was treeless and very broken by numerous dry water-courses. From Manzai the road runs across what appears, at first sight, to be a level plateau to Khirgi, but this plateau is actually very broken by nullahs which afforded perfect cover to raiding parties of Mahsuds. Khirgi itself, where half the battalion was now stationed under the command of Captain C. G. Thompson, lies at the foot of the main hills where the Takki Zam river issues from them through the pass known as the Hinnis Tangi. It was a very scattered, unpleasantly dusty camp with a very large perimeter to defend, similar in many respects to that of Tank.

At about 4 a.m. on the morning of November 7th two sepoys, Faquiriya and Kishen Lal, were patrolling the wire between two of the posts on the perimeter at Khirgi when they were suddenly fired on by Mahsuds who were screened behind a wall inside the camp. Faquiriya fell, mortally wounded in the stomach, and about four Mahsuds set on him, stripped him of his equipment, and escaped. Kishen Lal was hit in the hand, but succeeded in making his way to the nearest piquet. A week later another sepoy, Duli Chand, was wounded in the leg by a shot fired from within the camp while patrolling the wire. On this occasion no Mahsuds appeared. A Mahsud was captured at Tank on the 22nd while climbing through the barbed wire.

The detachment at Khirgi moved back to Kaur on December 3rd, and on the 26th the whole battalion moved to Manzai. The following day it marched through Khirgi and the Hinnis Tangi to Jandola, and on the 28th moved forward another seven miles to Kotkai. Kotkai was a well-laid-out and compact camp built on three different *raghzas* or terraces. It was surrounded on three sides by a breastwork and barbed wire, and on the fourth side there was a sheer cliff dropping to the bed of a river, known as the Inzar Algad, which joined the Takki Zam just outside the camp. Here—as everywhere else in Waziristan—the men were very hard worked. One company was always out in the permanent piquets which had been established on the high hills along the banks of the Takki Zam. One company went out daily on road-protection duties to supplement these piquets. One company was absorbed in night piquets round the camp and finding all working parties required during the day. The fourth company was known as the " stand-to " company for the movable column, and that remained in camp ready to move at short notice if required.

The permanent piquets, which were held for ten days at a time by each company in turn, consisted of rock-built walls about eight feet high, with a fire-step, surrounded by a barbed-wire fence.

1922.

The garrisons varied in strength, but were mostly about two sections strong, with two signallers and a Lewis gun. They were all connected to Kotkai by telephone. Each had a tank of water, which had to be refilled every " road open " day. No movement outside the barbed wire could take place except on a road-open day when the road-protection company was in position, and then only along the road. All Mahsuds had to be regarded as friendly until they opened fire or took some other definitely hostile action. Sniping occurred frequently, and a sepoy was wounded in one of the permanent piquets before dawn on January 1st.

The men detailed to take water up to the permanent piquets were not allowed to carry rifles, as these would have been an additional and irresistible temptation to Mahsuds to ambush them—an easy matter, as the mules could only go up the prepared tracks, so that it was impossible to vary the route. On January 15th one of these unarmed watering parties, consisting of three men with two mules, was fired on and a sepoy killed. The mules broke loose, bolted in the direction of the enemy, and were lost.

On January 18th the 48th Pioneers commenced the construction of a new permanent piquet on the right bank of the Inzar Algad, and a company of the 1st Royal Battalion was employed as a working party for collecting the rocks. Another company, together with two companies of the 91st Punjabis, provided the covering party. Sniping started when the withdrawal commenced in the evening, and one sepoy of the 1st Royal Battalion was wounded. The following day the 48th completed the construction of the piquet, a company of the 1st Royal Battalion under Captain C. K. Tester, M.C., covering the construction with three platoons forward and one in support. The piquet was completed by 3 p.m. and the withdrawal commenced, the flank platoons withdrawing first. As soon as the first men of the centre platoon commenced to retire, fire was opened on them. Havildar Hidayat Shah was killed and Sepoy Karim Din wounded. The remainder of the platoon, retiring down the steep hill at their fastest speed, did not see the two men drop. The platoon commander, Subedar Ahmad Khan, did see them and he, together with one sepoy, Ahman-ud-din, stopped under heavy fire to try to carry them in. The subedar, while attempting to lift up the body of Havildar Hidayat Shah, was wounded in the back. Being then unable to carry them he, with the help of the sepoy, took their rifles and equipment and went for help. The withdrawal by this time had been stopped, the forward platoons having passed through the support. A section from the support platoon commenced to advance uphill under covering fire from the remainder of the platoon and of artillery and machine-gun fire from Kotkai camp. By this time the enemy, moving rapidly downhill from rock to rock, had almost reached the wounded sepoy. The section commander, Lance-Naik Badlu,* halted his men and, leaving his rifle with a sepoy for safe custody, went forward alone and brought in the wounded man on his shoulder. The body of Havildar Hidayat Shah was then brought in. Subedar Ahmad Khan, though wounded and weak from loss of blood, resumed command of his platoon and the retirement continued without further hitch. For his gallantry on this occasion Lance-Naik Badlu received the 2nd Class of the Indian Order of Merit and Subedar Ahmad Khan the Indian Distinguished Service Medal.

The number of the enemy who had attacked this company was considerable, and they remained in position during the night to snipe the newly-made piquet. Realizing the likelihood of their doing so, the battalion machine-gun officer had laid two machine guns so as to command a place where they were likely to gather. After dark, when the Mahsuds were engaged in sniping the piquet, these guns opened fire. From political reports which were received later it became known that this fire took the Mahsuds completely by surprise and caused several casualties.

Small parties of the battalion continued to be fired on occasionally, and it was only constant variation in the routes taken and methods

---

* Now Jemadar Badlu Singh, I.O.M.

of approach which prevented any party of the battalion being ambushed while piqueting the road.   On several occasions fire was opened on the permanent piquets and attempts made to enter them at night.

On December 17th two companies of the battalion formed part of a column which moved out a short way from Kotkai to piquet a ridge known as Spinghara, in support of aeroplanes which were bombing Mahsud villages beyond.   A certain amount of sniping took place, but few enemy were seen and the party returned to camp, having only suffered one casualty.   The operation was repeated the next day, and again the companies were fortunate not to suffer more than a few casualties.   At this time the 91st Punjabis, who also took part in the operation, were very short of British officers.   For this reason Lieutenant A. Hancock was lent to them.   He commanded one of their companies which suffered very heavily on the second day.   Lieutenant Hancock received the Military Cross as an immediate reward for his gallantry on this occasion.

On the evening of January 25th, 1923, orders were received that Malikshahi village was to be rounded up by dawn the following day

1923.   and the male inhabitants brought into Kotkai camp as prisoners.   No officer or man had ever been over the ground as it was out of bounds even for training purposes, and any attempt to reconnoitre the routes would have betrayed the intention even had it been possible before dark.   The village was within sight of Kotkai, and after the camp gates were closed for the night each platoon commander was pointed out the position in which he was to be by dawn the following morning.

The battalion, less one and three-quarter companies and two machine guns, left camp at 4.30 a.m.   The night march was a very difficult one across very broken hills, not previously reconnoitred, on a very dark night.   One company found the route up which it first advanced to be impassable and had to return and find a different route. The machine guns had to be man-handled up very steep hills.   Every platoon had to get to a different destination.   Nevertheless, by dawn every platoon was in its correct position and the battalion was in touch with the 91st Punjabis on each flank.   The result was a complete surprise to the Mahsuds, and as soon as it was light the caves, of which the village is composed, were searched.   About sixty Mahsuds were brought back to camp without a single shot being fired at or by the battalion.

Later that month the battalion left Kotkai and moved to Sorarogha, eleven miles further up the Takki Zam.   At this time orders for the evacuation of the additional force in Waziristan were in course of preparation.   Most of the heavy baggage and serviceable tentage had been sent down the line to the base camp at Khirgi.   At Sorarogha,

L

therefore, the battalion was partly in unserviceable tents, which were left there to be burnt when the camp was evacuated, and partly in bivouac. The change of surroundings was very welcome, but Sorarogha was cold and most nights ice formed on all standing water. There was also a considerable amount of rain, with the result that the volume of water in the Takki Zam greatly increased. In such circumstances it was a particularly difficult proposition to send sheep and goats up the line as rations for the forward troops. They had to be man-handled across the streams and their customary slow progress became still more retarded. This was a source of annoyance to the road-protection parties, as it was never a matter of certainty whether the troops would get back to their camp before nightfall. Eventually a method of transporting the sheep and goats was improvised ; each was placed in a gunny-bag, and these were hooked on to the saddles of pack mules. It was a curious sight to see a string of mules moving along the river bed when the only sound which came from them was the bleating and " baa-ing " of sheep and goats.

The battalion left Sorarogha for Tank in April, where it remained throughout the summer of 1923, providing one company as garrison in the fort at Dehra Ismail Khan. At this time Colonel P. H. Dundas, who had been officiating in command of the brigade at Sorarogha, was appointed to the permanent command of the brigade, and command of the battalion devolved upon Major T. de B. Carey, who had been posted to the battalion early in the year. On December 2nd the battalion left Tank for Fyzabad, where it arrived ten days later.

CHAPTER XV

THE POST-WAR PERIOD, 2ND (MOOLTAN) BATTALION

Bibliography—Regimental Records.

THE 2nd Battalion returned to India from its long sojourn in Mesopotamia in 1920 and arrived at Ahmadnagar on May 19th,* when nearly
1920. all the men at once went to their homes on five and a
2nd Battalion. half months' furlough.

The following year proved to be one of great changes. Many of the officers who had accompanied the Battalion overseas in
1921. 1914 now returned, including Majors D'Oyly, Boxwell, Carey and Taylor, and Captain Eccles. In June orders were received from army headquarters for the complete reorganization of the Indian Army.† In the first instance the battalion was selected to be the training battalion of the 6th Regiment (Rajputana Rifles), but, after a long correspondence, it eventually became the 2nd Battalion of the 9th Jat Regiment. The battalion much regretted the severance of its long connection with the 120th and 122nd Infantry, with which it had previously been linked, as both these units became part of the 6th Rajputana Rifles.

Under the new organization scheme the battalion was eventually composed of two companies of Jats of the eastern Punjab, one company of Musalman Rajputs (Ranghars) from the same districts, and one company of Punjabi Musalmans, half of whom were from Poonch State and half from Gujrat district. The reorganization was completed towards the end of 1921 by transfers from other units and by enlistment. After the gallant part played by the Rajputs, Mers, Gujars and Hindustani Musalmans during the war, it was tragic to see these castes either transferred to other units or mustered out.

In December, 1921, the battalion moved from Ahmadnagar to Khirgi in Waziristan, where it was employed on the line of communication.
1922. Throughout the following year, with two companies detached at Jandola, it continued to carry out the monotonous duties of road protection. A severe loss was suffered by the death of Captain Reynolds, who was accidentally killed. Sepoy Amla Ram was awarded the Indian Distinguished Service Medal for gallantry in the field.

* See Chapter XII.　　　　† See Chapter XIV.

In May of the following year the battalion was concentrated at Jandola. During the previous month Lieutenant-Colonel R. T. C. Calvert had vacated command and been succeeded by Lieutenant-Colonel W. S. W. Browne from the 50th Kumaon Rifles. In November it took part in covering the withdrawal of the brigade from Sorarogha.

1923.

December marked the date of a severe loss suffered by the battalion, the regiment and the Indian Army in general. Captain J. D. Standen, M.C., was shot dead while attempting to arrest a Jat sepoy who had run amok at night. The death of Captain Standen was very deeply felt by all ranks. Few officers worked so whole-heartedly in the interests of the battalion generally and of the Jats in particular, and it would appear to have been a cynical turn of fate that Captain Standen should die in this way at the hand of one of the very men for whom he had done so much. Captain Standen had just passed into the staff college at Quetta and was due to go there only a few weeks after the tragedy occurred.

The period of service in Waziristan was extremely unpopular with all ranks and bad for the battalion as a whole. Confined behind barbed wire for most of the time in a notoriously unhealthy climate, with opportunities for training inadequate and difficult to arrange, little opportunity was offered for the battalion to shake down as a compact unit after its reorganization. This was badly needed, for one company alone had received transfers from twenty-three different units.

The battalion moved from Jandola to Manzai in January, 1924, and to Kohat in the following May. There was a general feeling of relief, and it was hoped the battalion would at last be able to settle down, carry out training and complete its musketry course. Difficulties at once arose. On account of the lack of facilities for obtaining furlough or leave from Waziristan, a large proportion of the battalion was absent on one or the other during the course of the year. In addition, shortly after the arrival of the battalion at Kohat two companies were ordered to Thal, sixty miles away, and remained as garrison of Thal Fort until the end of November. The battalion being split up, all duties were doubled ; it was found impossible to carry out any systematic training, and musketry suffered accordingly. However, the battalion became intact again eventually, and all companies were able to carry out company training before the end of the year.

1924.

The following years were devoted to training, with the happy result that the battalion earned the reputation of being the best shooting battalion in the district. In 1927 it was one of the five battalions chosen from the Indian Army to fire and report on a proposed new annual rifle course. This course, with certain modifications based on the reports, was adopted for the army.

1927.

On February 4th, 1927, General Sir Alexander E. Wardrop, K.C.B., C.M.G., D.S.O., was appointed Colonel of the battalion. General Wardrop thus became one of the few officers of the British service appointed to be Colonel of a battalion of the Indian Army. Soon after his appointment, General Wardrop visited the battalion at Kohat, where a ceremonial parade was held in his honour.

In July Lieutenant-Colonel W. S. W. Browne vacated command and was succeeded by Major J. F. Parkin, D.S.O.

In April, 1928, headquarters and two companies moved to the hill station of Parachinar at the head of the Kurram valley, only a few miles **1928.** from the Peiwar Kotal, separating India from Afghanistan. The climate in Parachinar was excellent and there was every opportunity of carrying out good individual training. A detachment remained in Thal throughout the hot weather, and the whole battalion reassembled there in October preparatory to moving to Hangu and Fort Lockhart, which lie approximately midway between Kohat and Thal.

Two companies then went to Fort Lockhart to take over the Samana Ridge, which includes the two forts of Gulistan and Sangar, while headquarters and the remainder of the battalion remained at Hangu.

In April of the following year, headquarters moved to Fort Lockhart, where it remained for the hot weather, leaving a detachment at Hangu. **1929.** Meanwhile the battalion was under orders to go to Jhansi, in the United Provinces, and the advance party, commanded by Major M. Eccles, M.C., left Hangu in September. The remainder of the battalion moved by rail to Jhelum two months later, and from there went by route march to Ludhiana, a distance of two hundred and thirty miles. This march took about four weeks, and several letters were received, including one from General Wardrop, congratulating the battalion on its march discipline and stating how impressed the local inhabitants had been by the general turnout of the men as they marched through the Punjab. The battalion eventually arrived at Jhansi on December 14th, having travelled from Ludhiana by rail.

At Jhansi the battalion formed part of the 9th (Jhansi) Infantry Brigade, commanded by Brigadier D. E. Robertson, D.S.O. January **1930.** was spent in camp at Babina, some seventeen miles away, doing battalion and brigade training. On February 22nd, the ceremony of " Trooping the Colour " was held, General Wardrop being present on the occasion. The four guards were commanded by Major O. Mather, Major M. Eccles, M.C., Major J. H. L. Hindmarsh and Captain J. W. Williams. The whole of Jhansi assembled to view the ceremony, which was most impressive.

In August trouble arose with the Afridis on the North-West Frontier. The Jhansi brigade was ordered to move to Rawalpindi, and the whole brigade had entrained and departed from Jhansi within forty-eight hours of receiving the order. The battalion then found itself back in the Northern Command after an absence of only eight months. It arrived at Rawalpindi on August 16th and stayed there for nearly two months. During this period much training was done in mountain warfare, and the halt enabled all absent personnel to rejoin from leave and furlough.

On October 11th, the Jhansi Brigade moved to Peshawar and thence to Bara, which lies seven miles south-west. The battalion moved with the brigade and was eventually encamped in a perimeter camp at Miri Khel on the Khajuri Plain. Here it remained throughout the remainder of the year, building roads and taking part in several minor engagements with the Afridis.

For distinguished services rendered in the field during these operations Captain G. H. Roberts was subsequently awarded the Military Cross and his name, as well as those of Subedar Qaim Din and Sepoy Harbhaj, was brought to the notice of the Commander-in-Chief in India.

Shortly before the battalion had left Jhansi a machine-gun company had been formed, which was commanded during the operations by Captain J. W. Williams. As a result of this reorganization, class companies ceased to exist and the battalion then consisted of a headquarter wing, commanded by the second-in-command, Major W. R. Warden, three rifle companies and the machine-gun company, the last-named being subsequently known as the support company. The three rifle companies, commanded respectively by Majors Mather, Eccles and Williams, were each composed of two platoons of Jats, one of Punjabi Musalmans and one of Ranghars. The machine-gun company had two platoons, one of which was composed of Jats and the other half Punjabi Musalmans and half Ranghars. Captain E. C. LePatourel, M.C., officiated in command of one of the rifle companies during part of the operations. Captain W. D. Porter was Adjutant, Captain R. H. Lowe Quartermaster and Lieutenant R. H. White Signalling Officer. Lieutenants W. H. Niall and L. S. Spearman also served with the battalion.

The Battalion eventually left Miri Khel on January 17th, 1931, and, having entrained at Peshawar, arrived back at Jhansi on the
1931.   20th. On March 3rd, new Colours were presented to the battalion by the Commander-in-Chief in India,* the Colonel of the battalion, Lieutenant-General Sir A. E. Wardrop, being present.

In July Lieutenant-Colonel J. F. Parkin, D.S.O., vacated command and was succeeded by Brevet Lieutenant-Colonel A. B. McPherson, M.C., who was transferred from the 1st Royal Battalion.
1933.   The following two years were devoted to training and were chiefly remarkable for the long marches carried out ; one company, carrying full equipment and a day's cooked rations on the

---

* See Appendix II.

man, having covered forty-eight miles in well under two days, and the remainder of the battalion nearly as much.

In 1933 Lieutenant-Colonel McPherson went to England in charge of the Indian orderly officers to His Majesty the King-Emperor, one of whom was Subedar Wali Mohamed Khan. His Majesty was graciously pleased to appoint Lieutenant-Colonel McPherson to the Fourth Class of the Royal Victorian Order, and to award the medal of the Order to Subedar Wali Mohamed Khan.

The battalion, being under orders for a transfer to the Khyber for a period of two years, left Jhansi on March 6th, 1934, and arrived at

1934. Landi Kotal on the 9th. Back in the Northern Command once again, the battalion had served for eight years on the North-West Frontier since 1921, followed by four years in Jhansi, which were broken by a further period of six months on the Frontier in 1930. Moreover, though Jhansi is well known as the ideal training station, general opinion in the army gives it the name of " three months' strenuous and continual manœuvres and nine months' hot weather." This was now followed by a further period of nearly two years on the Frontier.

The battalion only remained at Landi Kotal until July, when it moved down the Khyber Pass to Shagai Fort, with a detachment at Ali Masjid, in which places it remained for about seven months.

During most of 1935 the battalion remained in the Khyber, moving from Shagai and Ali Masjid back to Landi Kotal in February. Duties

1935. were very arduous ; a large detachment had to be found at one of the outposts, and training was very difficult to carry out. In May Lieutenant-Colonel A. B. McPherson vacated command, and was succeeded by Major M. Eccles, M.C.

In the normal course of events the battalion was due for relief in the Khyber in March, 1936, and was then to go to Quetta. However, owing to the earthquake which occurred in Quetta in May, the normal procedure was cancelled and the battalion left Landi Kotal by rail on November 4th, for Hyderabad, Sind, where it arrived on the 7th. *En route* one company detrained at Rohri for Bukkur Island, Sukkur, to provide the guards on the Lansdowne Bridge over the Indus river. This detachment was reduced to a platoon shortly before Christmas.

The next two years passed uneventfully. In the year 1936 the Lewis gun was replaced by the Vickers-Berthier light machine gun. During

1937. both 1936 and 1937, the battalion spent a long month of the cold weather in training camp at Hab River, Karachi.

CHAPTER XVI

THE POST-WAR PERIOD, 3RD BATTALION

Bibliography—Regimental Records.

AFTER the return of the 3rd Battalion, under the command of Captain J. J. Waite, from the Black Sea to Jhansi on November 27th, 1920, the next important event was the reorganization of the bat-

1921.
3rd Battalion. talion. By this two companies of Jats were replaced by one of Punjabi Mohammedans and one of Musalman Rajputs. This reorganization was completed by September, 1921.

At this time Waziristan was in a very unsettled state ; certain roads were in course of construction and troops were required to guard these

1923. communications. On January 20th, 1923, the battalion, under the command of Lieutenant-Colonel A. Boxwell, C.I.E., left Delhi, where it had taken a prominent part in the reception of H.R.H. the Prince of Wales, who had presented new Colours to the battalion,* and arrived at Manzai on the 23rd. *En route* it left one company on detachment at Kaur. Of the three companies at Manzai, one was completely absorbed in holding the perimeter piquets, while a second was used up in road-protection duties and in station and regimental guards. The third formed the movable column and was available for training. In addition, men had to be found to man two guns, 10-pounders, which were used for the protection of the post.

On December 6th the battalion, under the command of Major A. N. De V. Scott, marched to join the 9th Brigade which was then concentrating at Chagmalai and Splitoi. Chagmalai is on a tributary of the Takki Zam river, which joins the latter at Jandola after flowing through a very narrow and difficult pass known as the Shahur Tangi. It was in connection with the improvement of the road through the Shahur Tangi that the brigade was being concentrated.

At Chagmalai the duties of the battalion were similar to those at Manzai, involving road protection and the garrisoning of five permanent piquets. The camp was sniped on the nights of the 22nd and 23rd, and on the latter night one of the piquets was attacked by a small party of tribesmen, who were driven off with bombs.

---

* See Appendix II.

Water for the use of the camp was obtained from the river some four hundred yards away. This area was supposed to be protected by friendly tribesmen in the pay of the civil authorities, but as an additional safeguard for persons drawing water a piquet of one non-commissioned officer and six men was sent out daily. On March 16th, while the piquet was going out to take up its positions, it saw some Mahsuds ahead, but believed these to be the friendlies. As the forward party of the piquet reached its position it was suddenly fired on by some thirty or forty men at extremely short range. At the same time another burst of fire was directed at the covering party from a distance of fifty yards, the whole piquet being put out of action, though the Lewis gunner with the covering party succeeded in firing twenty rounds before being killed. Fire was then opened on part of the camp from a position in the hills, presumably to cover the withdrawal of the tribesmen. The whole affair was over in ten minutes, the friendlies taking no action to support the piquet, although they watched the ambush and probably knew it was intended. Troops sent out from camp arrived too late to be of assistance, though the hostiles were fired on from the camp as they made off into the hills. The non-commissioned officer and four sepoys of the piquet were killed or mortally wounded, and the remaining two sepoys were also wounded. Captain and Adjutant R. M. Thompson and one sepoy were killed in camp.

During the remainder of the month rounds were fired on two occasions at piquets of the battalion. On April 10th an attempt to get through the barbed wire surrounding the camp was frustrated by a sentry, who fired two shots and mortally wounded a notorious bad character.

On April 16th Splitoi camp was evacuated, and the battalion co-operated by opening the road as far as Gustankhi and occupying the high ground north of the first part of the pass. Shortly before the battalion was ordered to withdraw fire was opened on " B " Company by a party of tribesmen, estimated at forty strong, from a high hill some thousand yards away. This was replied to by Lewis-gun fire and did no damage. The withdrawal of the battalion was not followed up and camp was reached without further incident.

Chagmalai was evacuated on the 22nd, the battalion marching straight through to Manzai, where it took over the defences from the 2nd (Mooltan) Battalion.* The duties here were considerably less than they had previously been owing to the presence of another half-battalion.

The battalion remained at Manzai until January 23rd, 1925, when it moved to Rawalpindi, arriving there on the 25th. During June of the following year disturbances broke out in Rawalpindi city. From the 15th until the end of the month, the battalion was engaged in quelling these, being complimented on its work

* See Chapter XV.

both by the General Officer Commanding-in-Chief Northern Command and by the Commissioner.

The battalion moved to Santa Cruz in October, 1928, and in 1929 serious disturbances broke out in Bombay city. In the early days these were entirely confined to rioting between the Moham-

1929. medans and Hindus, but later an anti-government feeling developed. Many days were spent in Bombay city quelling riots and rounding up bad characters, the thanks of the local authorities being received.

On October 22nd, 1930, the battalion, under the command of Captain T. G. Lewis, moved to Calcutta and embarked for Hong Kong,

1930. where it arrived on November 10th for a three-year tour of

1931. duty. On September 25th of the following year it was again engaged on riot duty; on this occasion keeping the Chinese and Japanese apart. These riots, which broke out suddenly and, at any rate as far as the battalion was concerned, quite unexpectedly, were speedily quelled.

Lieutenant-Colonel J. G. Lecky completed four years as Commandant of the battalion on February 1st, 1933, and was succeeded by Lieutenant-Colonel W. L. Hailes, M.C.

The battalion embarked at Hong Kong on December 21st, 1933, arriving at Singapore on the 26th, where two days were spent, and at

1934. Penang on the 30th. On January 4th, it arrived at Calcutta, whence it entrained for Jhelum. Throughout the following year a large proportion of the men were absent at their homes on leave and furlough.

In 1935 the battalion was selected to provide the guards over Viceregal Lodge and the Commander-in-Chief's house at Simla. The

1935. detachment was fortunate to be present during the year of the celebration of the Jubilee of His Majesty, King George V.

On February 1st, 1937, Lieutenant-Colonel C. M. Maltby, M.C., succeeded Lieutenant-Colonel Hailes in command. The battalion was represented at the Coronation in London by Major H. V. Bragg, M.C., and Subedar-Major Sudhan, Bahadur.

CHAPTER XVII

1924–37, 1st ROYAL BATTALION (L.I.)

Bibliography—Regimental Records.

THE 1st Royal Battalion arrived at Fyzabad on December 12th, 1923, and had not been there long before it lost the services of one of its ablest and most famous Indian officers—Subedar-Major and Honorary-Lieutenant Dalpat Singh, Sardar Bahadur, I.O.M., who transferred to the pension establishment in November, 1924. On the occasion of his departure the Commandant published the following order :—

1924.
1st Battalion.

" The Commandant wishes to record his appreciation of the services of Subedar-Major and Honorary-Lieutenant Dalpat Singh, Sardar Bahadur, I.O.M., on his retirement. The gallantry of this Indian officer has been displayed frequently on active service, more especially when all other Indian officers of the regiment had become casualties, and he helped the only surviving British Officer to withdraw the remnants of the regiment from the Turkish trenches at Hannah on January 21st, 1916 ; an occasion which caused the publication of a Divisional Order stating the gallantry of the regiment was so great as to be almost phenomenal. His devotion to duty and unusual ability caused his early rise to high rank and affords an excellent example for all ranks of the regiment."

In January, 1925, after manœuvres, the battalion took part in a review held by the Viceroy of India, Lord Reading, at Delhi. After these manœuvres peace-time routine continued at Fyzabad, and on March 10th, 1925, Lieutenant-General Sir George de S. Barrow, K.C.B., K.C.M.G., A.D.C., General Officer Commanding-in-Chief Eastern Command, presented new colours to the battalion.*

1925.

The 1st Royal Battalion remained in Fyzabad for three years. This was its first long spell in a peace station since the Great War had begun. Demobilization and reorganization were things of the past, and the training of the battalion greatly profited in this uninterrupted period ; so much so that it was brought to the favourable notice of His Excellency the Commander-in-Chief in India for its general high standard of efficiency.

---

* See Appendix II.

On July 1st, 1926, Subedar-Major and Honorary-Captain Lakhi Ram,. Bahadur, M.C., I.D.S.M., proceeded on pension after twenty-eight years' **1926.** service. In October, 1926, it moved again to the Frontier. This was an ordinary peace-time relief for a two-year tour of duty in the Khyber. It was stationed at Landi Kotal, Ali Masjid and Jamrud, and was frequently split up into piquets and posts along the pass. Most of the barracks in the Khyber at this time were well-built buildings with tin roofs, and conditions were comfortable. At Ali Masjid, however, there is always in summer a very strong wind which has been remarked upon in records of the campaign there in 1879 ; and once again the battalion experienced the discomfort and heat, which the troops in those days had found so objectionable.

Lieutenant-Colonel R. F. D. Burnett, M.C., was appointed Commandant in succession to Lieutenant-Colonel T. de B. Carey on December **1928.** 25th, 1927. On October 20th, 1928, the 1st Royal Battalion left the Khyber, after having been there almost exactly two years. This time its destination was St. Thomas Mount, a small cantonment about nine miles outside Madras. The special troop train left Jamrud at 9 p.m. on October 20th and arrived at Madras at 12.30 p.m. on October 28th. This long train journey was a great experience for many of the men. It was particularly gratifying both to them and the battalion to have a four-hour halt at Rohtak, where many Jats and Musalman Rajputs of the district had foregathered to welcome the battalion on its way through. Again, at Dholpur, a three-hour halt was made and all ranks were given one pound of sweetmeats and a packet of cigarettes by His Highness the Maharajah of Dholpur, who also entertained the British Officers of the battalion at his palace. So the long journey passed pleasantly, and, traversing as it did a very great part of India, it was not without interest to all.

Soon after the arrival of the battalion in Madras, information was received that Indian infantry battalions would be reorganized on the basis of a headquarter wing and three rifle companies and one machine-gun company. This inception of a machine-gun company was to bring Indian infantry battalions into line with the new organization of the British Army. Accordingly, it was decided that each battalion of the 9th Jat Regiment would be reorganized into six platoons Jats, three platoons Musalman Rajputs, three platoons Punjabi Musalmans ; the machine-gun company being proportionately drawn from all the three classes. " A " Company was composed of four platoons of Jats, " B " Company three platoons Musalman Rajputs and one platoon Punjabi Musalmans ; " C " Company two platoons Jats and two platoons Punjabi Musalmans. In addition, the establishment of battalions was reduced to 726 Indian ranks.

On February 11th, 1929, the battalion trooped the Regimental

Colour at St. Thomas Mount.   It had been the intention to do this on February 10th, which was the anniversary of the battle of Sobraon, but as this day fell on a Sunday, it was not convenient.   The cere-mony was attended by His Excellency the Governor of Madras, Viscount Goschen of Hawkhurst, G.C.I.E., G.B.E., and he took the salute. It was also attended by a great number of the European population of the town ; and after it a large reception was held in the Officers' Mess. This was the first occasion on which the new Colours, which had been presented in Fyzabad in 1925, had been trooped.

1929.

During the year, rifle companies of the battalion were once again reorganized by the inter-company transfers of complete platoons so that each company should consist of two platoons Jats, one platoon Musalman Rajputs and one platoon Punjabi Musalmans.   Another innovation was introduced throughout the army in India in 1930, and this was the protective guards.   Hitherto all guards found by the army were of a strictly ceremonial nature, but owing to general unrest through-out India, the activities of Congress agents, and unsettled conditions in Bengal, it was felt necessary to take special precautions at night.   For this reason all guards posted at night were henceforth to dispense with all ceremony and assume the role of protective piquets.   It no longer was the custom for guards to turn out at night and " present arms " to visiting officers ; instead they fell-in on their alarm posts, and the approach of all strangers was regarded with suspicion and carefully covered.

The 1st Royal Battalion left Madras on November 18th, 1930, and entrained for Delhi.   After having been so far away from their homes for two years, this move was a welcome one for many. The time spent in Madras had been an experience of a strange part of India for all ranks.   On the day when the battalion left, unpre-cedented rain was experienced—2·8 inches fell in forty-five minutes.

1930.

At Delhi the battalion was earmarked for internal-security duties, and one of its chief duties was to provide guards over the Viceroy's house and the Commander-in-Chief's residence.   This entailed a de-tachment of one rifle company being permanently quartered in Body Guard Lines, New Delhi.   Guard mounting over the Viceroy's house was carried out with great ceremony and frequently attended by num-bers of spectators.   The Imperial City of New Delhi, which had been commenced in 1913, was now almost completed, and in February, 1931, His Excellency the Viceroy, Lord Irwin, carried out the inauguratory ceremony.

On October 16th, 1931, Subedar-Major and Honorary-Captain Net Ram, Bahadur, I.D.S.M., proceeded on pension after twenty-eight years' service.   Lieutenant-Colonel A. C. M. Binny was appointed Commandant in succession to Lieutenant-Colonel R. F. D. Burnett, M.C., from December 25th, 1931.

1931.

On March 31st, 1932, a book of remembrance and a panel of honours and awards gained by the men of the 6th Jat Light Infantry in the Great War and in Waziristan, 1919–24, were inaugurated. A parade was held for this purpose, which was attended by a number of pensioned Indian officers and men. The book and panel were presented to the Commanding Officer by Lieutenant-General Sir A. E. Wardrop, K.C.B., C.M.G., Colonel of the 2nd Battalion 9th Jat Regiment. The book and panel in turn were handed over by the Commandant to a guard which marched them to the Quarter Guard, where they have been kept ever since.

1932.

It had been expected that the battalion would remain in Delhi for four years. On August 13th, 1932, however, orders were received that the battalion would move to Mymensingh at the end of October of that year. The terrorist movement in Bengal, which started in the Mymensingh District in 1902, had gradually spread in other districts of Bengal, and in 1931 such was the state of the country that it was found necessary to send troops to Chittagong, where a raid had taken place on an armoury belonging to the Auxiliary Force. The situation showed no signs of improvement and grew steadily worse ; cold-blooded murders of white officials were indulged in, and the power of the civil administration was greatly hampered. For this reason, in August, 1932, the Government of India decided to send two brigades to Bengal to garrison various towns. In September, 1932, the terrorists of Bengal had openly stated that they would loot and murder to such an extent during the forthcoming *poojah* holidays that for ever after those holidays would be known as the " bloody *poojahs*." In order to counteract this, therefore, the Government of India decided that the troops should reach Bengal in secrecy before these events could take place. Accordingly, on September 23rd, the battalion received orders to be ready to move to Bengal at twenty-four hours' notice.

The battalion entrained at New Cantonments, Delhi, on September 26th, and, travelling by broad-gauge railway to Lucknow and thence by metre-gauge railway to Mymensingh, arrived there on September 29th. Mymensingh is a large district situated between the Jamuna and Brahmaputra rivers, the town itself being on the banks of the latter. At this time of year heavy rainfall in these parts was expected, and for this reason orders were given that charpoys would be taken. These charpoys were a source of considerable annoyance during changes on the journey, but were most welcome on arrival at Mymensingh, where the battalion was encamped on the only dry piece of ground, which was the local club's football ground. Indeed, though this ground was carefully drained, frequent showers of rain were so heavy as to flood the whole camp, and it was not an uncommon occurrence for the water in the camp to be knee deep for a short time after rain had fallen. The threatened coup of the terrorists at *poojah* holidays did not take place, and with the arrival of more men and transport at Mymensingh the battalion commenced to " show the Flag." Troops passed through the country marching, or by train where there were no tracks to march on, and everywhere were received with outward signs of welcome and presents of food and vegetables.

The district of Mymensingh remained peaceful however, and nothing untoward occurred during the battalion's stay there ; most of the activities of the terrorists being centred in Chittagong. On **1933.** April 9th, 1933, it was accordingly found necessary to increase the garrison at Chittagong, and one company was sent there from Mymensingh. This company had not been long in Chittagong before one platoon was placed on cordon duty over a house at Gahira. Some of the inmates attempted to escape at night, so fire was opened by the platoon. As a result of this action one absconder and the owner of the house were killed ; one wounded and four absconders captured. These absconders included one Tarakeswar Dastidar, a well-known terrorist, and Kalpana, a girl, both of whom were wanted for their numerous past activities. This was a very successful capture and the participants in the action received many congratulations. The Chief of the General Staff, Army Headquarters, wrote as follows: " I am directed by His Excellency the Commander-in-Chief to request you to be good enough to convey to the troops concerned His Excellency's heartiest congratulations on the success which attended their efforts on the night of May 18-19th." And the Government of India expressed their appreciation in the following terms : " I am also to convey the high appreciation of the Government of India of the efficiency with which the operation was carried out." For his conduct and gallantry on this occasion, Jemadar Mohammed Hussain received the second class of the Indian Order of Merit, and two sepoys were awarded the Indian Distinguished Service Medal.

Lieutenant-Colonel A. C. M. Binny, having proceeded on leave ex India in April, died as the result of an operation in London, and Lieutenant-Colonel C. A. Raynor, D.S.O., M.C., was appointed Commandant on May 6th, 1933.

In October, 1933, it was found necessary to reinforce the garrison at Chittagong and two companies of the battalion were sent there under Major Keene. At Chittagong on January 7th, 1934, a number of the British population, including officers, had collected after a cricket match. Suddenly two youths armed with bombs attacked the Superintendent of Police as he was leaving the cricket ground in his car. Two other youths also attacked the remaining Europeans with a bomb, which failed to explode, and one of them fired a revolver at the crowd. This man was immediately tackled by Major Brett, M.C., who brought him down. There was fortunately no casualty amongst the Europeans, and of the four terrorists concerned in the attack, one was killed, two wounded and one captured. For his gallantry and personal disregard of danger on this occasion, Major Brett was awarded the Empire Gallantry Medal. The situation in Chittagong was not improving and on March 11th, 1934, the remainder of the battalion joined from Mymensingh. In spite of the numerous garrison at this place, the duties and work there were very heavy. The battalion was spread over a large area of the country, mostly in platoon posts, and throughout this time activity against the terrorists was maintained. This took the form of ambushes, searches and cordoning houses and villages with the assistance of the police. The battalion was accommodated in tents, schools and matting huts as available. Information about the terrorists was scarce, and though no spectacular results were obtained against them, there was no doubt that their activity was severely restricted. In June the battalion, less " A " Company, left Chittagong for Mymensingh, where it remained until October.

Throughout its stay in Bengal the work done by the battalion received great praise both from the civil authorities and the higher military commanders. His Excellency the Commander-in-Chief in India wrote : " I greatly appreciate the services of this battalion during its two years in Bengal. That under such conditions it should have maintained such a high all round standard of efficiency reflects the greatest credit on all ranks."

Subedar-Major and Honorary-Lieutenant Hem Raj, Sardar Bahadur, I.D.S.M., proceeded to England in 1934 as Orderly Officer to His
1934.   Majesty the King-Emperor. He was forced to return prior to the expiry of his duty owing to reasons of health, and went on pension after twenty-nine and a half years' service on September 26th, 1934.

On October 7th, 1934, the battalion, having been relieved by the 2/8th Punjab Regiment, proceeded to its new station, Lucknow, where it arrived three days later. On January 20th, 1935, the battalion proceeded to take part in Eastern Command manœuvres at Gurgaon, near Delhi ; they were followed by a review on January 31st.

The rest of the time spent at Lucknow, where the 1st Royal Battalion is still stationed was, on the whole, uneventful.

In May, 1935, the Commandant and twenty-three Indian Ranks were awarded Jubilee Medals. On January 1st, 1936, Subedar-Major
1935.   Sardara, I.D.S.M., was awarded the Order of British India, second class, with the title of Bahadur, and nine months later he was granted the rank of Honorary Lieutenant.

On June 18th, 1936, the battalion motor-bus was involved in a bad accident in Lucknow, and it is regretted that Lieutenant R. J. B. Kelly

Scale of Miles

0   50   100   200

AFGHANISTAN

KASHMIR

HIMALAYA MTS.

UNITED PROV.

PUNJAB

RAJPUTANA

BALUCHISTAN

SIND

BOMBAY

Istalif
Kabul
Ghazni
Kandahar
Jalalabad
Khyber P.
Ali Masjid
Peshawar
Nowshera
Attock
Abbottabad
Murree
Rawalpindi
Sialkot
Gujrat
Ramnagar
Chillianwala
R. Chenab
R. Jhelum
R. Indus
R. Gomal
Quetta
Dadur
Dera Ghazi Khan
Jacobabad
Shikarpur
Sukkur
Rohri
Subzilkote
Meeanee
Hyderabad
Karachi
R. Indus
Multan
Bahawalpur
R. Sutlej
R. Ravi
Lahore
Amritsar
Sobraon
Ferozeshah
Ferozepore
Aliwal
Mudki
Jullundur
Ludhiana
Subathu
Bagshai
Simla
Ambala
Roorkee
Karnal
Panipat
Delhi
Meerut
Rampur
Bareilly
Kutra
Aligarh
Muttra
Deig
Bharatpur
Agra
Laswari
Fatehgarh
Etawah
Cawnpore
Karrah
Lahar
Gohud
Gwalior
Maharajpore
Punniar
Jhansi
R. Betwa
R. Jumna
Bikaner
Jodhpur

9th Jat Regt.

and Sepoy Maman both died in hospital as a result of the injuries they received. On August 1st, 1936, and August 20th, 1937, respectively, the battalion lost the services of two of its oldest British officers when Major R. L. O'Connor proceeded on leave pending his retirement, and Major W. V. McCalmont, M.C., was appointed Commandant of the Training Battalion.

1936.

In January, 1937, Major E. R. S. Dods, M.C., arrived on transfer from the 2/4th (King Edward VII's Own) Bombay Grenadiers, and was appointed Commandant *vice* Lieutenant-Colonel C. A. Raynor, D.S.O., M.C., who went on two months' leave from March 5th pending retirement.

1937.

A fitting conclusion to this chapter is to remark that the 1st Royal Battalion was worthily represented at the Coronation of their Majesties King George VI and Queen Elizabeth in London by Subedar-Major and Honorary-Lieutenant Sardara, Bahadur, I.D.S.M., whilst in India the Commandant and eighteen Indian ranks were presented with Coronation Medals.

M

CHAPTER XVIII

WAZIRISTAN, 1937

Bibliography—Regimental Records.

IN 1936, owing to various religious reasons fomented by a firebrand styling himself the " Fakir of Ipi," the Tori Khel sections of the Wazirs, aided by Mahsud recalcitrants and large numbers of tribesmen from the Afghan side of the border, made attacks on a British column moving into the lower Khaisora valley. A small punitive expedition was sent and a new road was constructed from the Khajuri plain into the valley. The tribes appeared to become pacified. The preaching of the Fakir of Ipi again unsettled the tribes, resulting in the murder of British officers. Early in March, 1937, the Indian Government was forced to send a further expedition into the country.

The tasks of this expedition were, firstly, to restore the safety of the communications to the advanced cantonments of Razmak and Wana and outlying scout posts, and, secondly, to bring the tribes to reason. In addition to the troops permanently stationed in Waziristan, infantry amounting to nearly two divisions were sent to the country. The 3rd Battalion received orders to move at a strength of five hundred rifles on March 6th and under the command of Lieutenant-Colonel C. M. Maltby, M.C., was concentrated at Mir Ali as part of the 3rd Jhelum Infantry Brigade by the 12th. Here one of its early duties was to round up some villages on the Sharatala plain in conjunction with some of the Tochi Scouts and light tanks.

As far as the battalion was concerned, the operations then divided themselves into three phases, each interspersed with a great deal of road-protection work.

The first phase was the advance of 1st Divisional Headquarters with the 2nd and 3rd Brigades into the Khaisora valley, with the 1st Brigade co-operating from Damdil. At this time Lieutenant-Colonel Maltby assumed officiating command of the 3rd Brigade *vice* the permanent brigadier, who had gone sick on April 22nd. Except for April 27th and 28th and from June 10th to 17th, he remained in command of the brigade until July 25th, when, after ten days' casual leave, he rejoined the battalion.

162

The troops involved in the first phase concentrated at Mir Ali, and the advance commenced on April 23rd. The 3rd Battalion, under the command of Major T. G. Lewis, led the advance, starting in the dark and making good the south bank of the Tochi river, with mounted infantry of the Tochi Scouts co-operating on their right flank. The remaining troops then passed through, coming under fire from high ground west of the line of advance immediately after passing through the battalion, and sustaining some casualties.

Camp was formed about three miles beyond the river at a point which became known as Tochi camp, but for the time being the 3rd Battalion was given as its task the protection of communications from Mir Ali to the river, and was based on Mir Ali. The mounted infantry of the Tochi Scouts and a mechanized section of 4·5-inch howitzers were placed under the command of the battalion. On the second day "A" Company under Lieutenant H. E. Syer and a platoon of machine guns under Jemadar Samandar Singh crossed the river and helped in the defence of Tochi camp, replacing units which moved farther forward. The ground held by the battalion was terraced and covered with crops and trees, making observation difficult, but the presence of mounted troops was probably a great deterrent to hostile action.

The operation during this phase was very successful, enemy casualties outnumbering ours by at least three to one, while a few villages were destroyed and the follow-up during the withdrawal was very half-hearted.

Lieutenant Syer with his detachment rejoined the battalion the day before the division recrossed the river on its return journey. For this operation the 3rd Battalion formed the covering force from the near bank and then acted as rearguard during the rest of the march to Idak. Only a few shots were fired at the battalion from long range just before the positions were evacuated. These were replied to by gun fire and by the movement of light tanks to patrol the area.

From Idak the 3rd Brigade moved to Damdil, where Major Lewis was injured by his horse, and command of the battalion devolved on Major W. M. Morgan, M.C., A.M. The brigade then moved to Dosalli. In that area the 3rd and 1st Brigades and troops of the Wazir division, Bannu and Razmak columns, were concentrated for the second phase. This was a march across the Sham plain to Arsal Kot, the headquarters of the Fakir of Ipi, with a view to the destruction of the caves there.

The initial preparations involved a great deal of road protection while stores were being collected. The actual advance was commenced on the night of May 11th-12th, when the 1st Brigade and the Bannu Brigade advanced on to the Sham plain and, subsequently, to the caves of Arsal Kot. Here they joined hands with the 2nd Brigade, which had marched from Mir Ali to the Khaisora and then across country to the

Shaktu. The caves and some towers were destroyed and the forces withdrew to the Sham plain. Here preparations were made for the third phase, the building of roads and some flag marches.

During this period the battalion moved from Dosalli to Coronation camp and was attached to the 2nd Brigade for a week. The 1st and 2nd Brigades were engaged in supporting the Bannu Brigade in the earlier stages of a flag march which it carried out through the Mahsud country from Ghariom through Janata and Sorarogha to Razmak. The battalion was employed in camp-protection duties at Coronation camp and road-protection duties on the Sham plain between Coronation and Ghariom camps. When it became apparent that the Mahsuds had no intention of opposing the march through their country the battalion was relieved of these duties and returned to Dosalli.

On June 14th, the whole of the 3rd Brigade moved to Ghariom camp, which was situated at the southern end of the Sham plain. Here the battalion remained until July 8th, carrying out road-protection duties and providing working parties for the new road being constructed to Madamir Kilai.

While at Ghariom the battalion took part in two operations. On June 15th, when the first brigade advanced to Shawali Algad to disperse a mixed *lashkar* in that area, the battalion gave them " a leg forward," covering their right flank in the initial stages towards Waladin and drawing the first fire from the enemy, which, however, proved ineffective.

Again, on June 23rd, the battalion was attached to the 1st Brigade, which was carrying out a surprise round-up of the area of Baramand and the village of Gul Zamir Kot. This is on the south bank of the Shaktu, near Arsal, and it was hoped the elusive fakir was hiding there. Marching from Ghariom camp at a quarter to five in the morning the battalion was in position on the high ground north-west of the village by eight o'clock. On its right was a Gurkha battalion of the 1st Brigade. The village was then searched by parties of the South Waziristan and Tochi Scouts. The surprise was completely successful, twelve prisoners and four rifles being captured ; one hostile killed and two Hindus rescued. Camp piquets were then put out and camp formed at Pasal by two o'clock in the afternoon.

In the withdrawal, next day, the battalion was employed partly as piqueting troops, partly as brigade reserve and partly as rear-guard. The column passed through the 3rd Brigade, which was covering the last part of the withdrawal, and reached Ghariom camp before midday. Here the battalion reverted to the 3rd Brigade.

After this diversion the battalion moved on July 8th with the rest of the 3rd Brigade, to Bahadur camp, which was made and occupied that day. After the attacks on camp piquets and sniping, which invariably attend the occupation of a new camp, had subsided, the battalion settled down to a reasonably peaceful time. It was employed on road construction and protecting road construction, occasionally providing escorts to the army commander, the divisional commander and engineer officers reconnoitring the alignment of the road. On July 10th, while covering one of the reconnaissances beyond Bahadur camp, a piquet, under Jemadar Munshi Khan, was sniped from a dominating position just beyond the piquet position. The piquet was ordered to go forward and occupy this feature. As the men reached their objective they came under fire from about ten enemy in position four hundred yards beyond. No. 8150 Naik Habib Khan was slightly wounded in the foot above the heel. The piquet fired thirty-six rounds, and the light machine gun covering the piquet was able to bring fire to bear from a flank on the foremost enemy. One burst resulted in two enemy being rolled over on the skyline. Later two enemy attempted to remove the casualties, but were fired on and driven back. Eventually they managed to get the casualties away by creeping up behind the crest line. The enemy were in two parties, one four hundred and the other eight hundred yards away.

On July 28th Pimple piquet, one of the permanent camp piquets garrisoned by the battalion, was heavily sniped during the night and No. 11929 Sepoy Lakhi Ram, one of the sentries, was severely wounded in the hand. About this time the piquets round Bahadur camp had the somewhat frequent attention of snipers. It appeared to be the work of disgruntled Kikarai Mahsuds who considered they had been unjustly treated over road contracts, and did little damage.

On August 6th, Lieutenant-Colonel Maltby resumed command of the battalion from Major Morgan.

At 7.35 p.m. on August 19th shots were fired into Last piquet, about two and a half miles from the camp and garrisoned by the battalion. Subedar Mahboob Khan was severely wounded in the shoulder and No. 9011 Sepoy Farid Khan slightly wounded in the arm. The garrison replied with light machine-gun fire, and a party of enemy was seen to withdraw over the crest of a hill. It was not known whether any of them were hit. A rifle company and machine-gun platoon of the battalion, with an artillery forward observation officer, a medical officer and stretcher-bearers, under the command of Major J. W. Williams, left camp before 8 p.m. to evacuate the wounded. The subedar's condition proved to be not so serious as was at first believed. After the wounds had been dressed the withdrawal started at 8.55 p.m., and all were back in camp, without incident, by 9.50 p.m. The whole operation was carried out—over really difficult country, after dark, but fortunately aided by a moon—most expeditiously.

On August 21st, another operation was carried out by the brigade to

Madamir Kilai to cover the construction of a camp for Tochi Scouts. This passed off without incident.

After this the battalion had a dull period of road work and road protection. The normal routine was three days' construction followed by one day of protection. The road towards the Kam Sham and Biche Kashkai was being made by road-construction battalions under the protection of Tochi Scouts. On August 28th the brigade moved out to construct a new camp for the Scouts just short of the Kam Sham. This was known as Forward camp. The battalion constructed two of the camp piquets and assisted in the construction of the perimeter wall and the wiring. No incidents took place. The road was opened to traffic to Madamir Kilai on Thursday, September 30th.

The following day the battalion marched to Dosalli, and three days later Bahadur camp was closed down, the 3rd Brigade relieving the 2nd Brigade at Shawali.

The battalion had been warned that it was to destroy the tower of a certain hostile in Dosalli village on October 2nd, he having been concerned in cutting the pipe-line to Dosalli. This did not take place as the villagers themselves volunteered to destroy the tower.

On October 3rd, the battalion marched to Damdil camp, where it was to come under the orders of the 9th Brigade for operations in that area. Certain buildings were to be destroyed in Asad Khel and Musakki villages. On the evening of the 3rd news was received that the hostile in Musakki had given himself up, so that village was left in peace; on the 4th the brigade with its attached troops moved out to destroy the building in Asad Khel. The battalion, with a section of light tanks and a section of the 7th Field Battery, protected the right flank, crossed the Khaisora river and piqueted the high ground to the south. The withdrawal was completed without incident. The brigadier of the 9th Brigade complimented the men on their speed on the hills.

On October 5th the battalion moved by mechanical transport to Bannu, the men being well pleased, as was shown by their cheers, and entrained there on the 9th, arriving at Jhelum on the morning of the 10th in order to reorganize for a move to the Khyber Pass.

Before leaving Waziristan all ranks were thanked by the brigade commander for their excellent work throughout, for the cheerful and energetic manner in which they answered every call made on them, and for the excellent relations which they always maintained with the staff and other units. The divisional commander expressed his high regard for their fighting qualities, exemplary conduct and high standard of efficiency. The commander-in-chief expressed himself as being very sorry the battalion was leaving the force, and thanked everyone for the fighting qualities displayed and the real hard work put into the somewhat monotonous task of road construction.

The names of the undermentioned were brought to notice by His Excellency the Commander-in-Chief for services rendered during the operations :—

> Lieutenant-Colonel C. M. Maltby, M.C.
> Major W. M. Morgan, M.C., A.M.
> Captain H. E. Syer.
> Subedar Lall Khan.
> Jemadar Munshi Khan.

The Army Commander also issued certificates to the following to intimate that their services had been brought to his notice for devotion to duty :—

> Subedar Kutab Khan.
> No. 8150 Naik Habib Khan.
> Subedar Manphul.
> Jemadar Abbas Ali.
> No. 8666 Naik Des Ram.

During the various phases of the operations the following officers were present with or joined the Battalion :—

1ST PHASE, 9TH MARCH–8TH MAY, 1937.

> Lieutenant-Colonel C. M. Maltby, M.C.
> Major T. G. Lewis.
> Major W. M. Morgan, M.C., A.M.
> Lieutenant H. E. Syer.
> Lieutenant R. N. Heale.
> Second-Lieutenant H. A. Lambert.

Attached Officers.

> Captain G. C. Welply, I.M.S.
> Lieutenant Bhola Nath, Dubey, Kashmir State Forces.
> Lieutenant Dina Nath, Thakur, Kashmir State Forces.
> Lieutenant Parkash Chand, Kashmir State Forces.

2ND PHASE, 9TH MAY–5TH JUNE, 1937.

> Lieutenant-Colonel C. M. Maltby, M.C.
> Major W. M. Morgan, M.C., A.M.
> Lieutenant H. E. Syer.
> Lieutenant R. N. Heale.
> Second-Lieutenant J. D. Rawlins.
> Second-Lieutenant H. A. Lambert.

Attached Officers.

Captain G. C. Welply, I.M.S.
Lieutenant Bhola Nath, Dubey.
Lieutenant Dina Nath, Thakur.
Lieutenant Parkash Chand.

3RD PHASE, 6TH JUNE–5TH OCTOBER, 1937.

Lieutenant-Colonel C. M. Maltby, M.C.
Major W. M. Morgan, M.C., A.M.
Captain J. W. Hay.
Lieutenant H. E. Syer.
Second-Lieutenant J. D. Rawlins.
Second-Lieutenant H. A. Lambert.

Attached Officers.

Major J. W. Williams, 2nd (Mooltan) Battn., 9th Jat Regiment.
Major H. L. C. Youngman, M.C., 1/4th Bombay Grenadiers.
Captain S. J. Parker, 1st Royal Battn., 9th Jat Regiment, L.I.
Lieutenant Parkash Chand.

THE TRAINING BATTALION

The 10th Battalion, 9th Jat Regiment, was raised at Agra on November 20th, 1917, by Major G. E. Hardie, as the 2nd Battalion, 6th Jat Light Infantry.

On February 12th, 1920, it left Agra to embark for Mesopotamia, where it took part in the suppression of the Arab rebellion. The most **1920.** important action in which it took part was fought on May 14th. At this time battalion headquarters was stationed at Ana on the Euphrates, with detachments as far up the river as Abu Kamal. A convoy, which had marched at 1 a.m., was suddenly attacked at a quarter to four by a party of about five hundred Arabs who had dug trenches across the road, while two hundred more were on the opposite bank of the river, endeavouring to cross in boats. The escort consisted of two companies of the battalion, " B " and " C." A large number of camels, mules and donkeys were killed. The enemy were driven off, but continued to follow up the convoy until 11.30, so that the fight was continued for nearly eight hours. During this fight, which commenced at the Wadi Hauran between Hit and Ana, the battalion lost four killed and fourteen wounded, while eighty-six enemy dead were counted, most of whom were killed by Lewis-gun fire. For gallantry on this occasion Lieutenant Arnold received the Military Cross, Subedars Sultan and Ram Kala* were admitted to the Indian Order of Merit, Second Class, and Bugle-Major Sarup Lal and Lance-Naik Simbhu and Sepoy Ram Sarup received the Indian Distinguished Service Medal.

On July 8th " D " Company was stationed in a fort between Ana and Abu Kamal. While the men were on parade outside the fort they were suddenly attacked at about midday. A signaller, with great difficulty, succeeded in fixing a helio on the roof and getting a message through, as all the telephone wires had been cut, but was killed immediately afterwards. A column consisting of " A " Company of the battalion, a battery and two squadrons of cavalry immediately started to the rescue, and the artillery trotted five miles. On their arrival the enemy fled, suffering heavy casualties. The casualties in " D " Company were two killed and two wounded. The relieving

---

* The *London Gazette* stated that Lieutenant Arnold displayed absolute fearlessness throughout this action, while Subedar Ram Kala, who was largely responsible for checking the rapid advance of the enemy during the rearguard action, displayed bravery " beyond all description."

column remained for a couple of days and then moved out to attack the villages which were known to have been implicated. Several villages were burnt and considerable opposition was encountered ; when night came on the column withdrew. The fort was then evacuated and the whole column withdrew to Ana ; during the withdrawal it was fired on, but no casualties occurred.

Shortly after this one of the piquets at Ana was attacked at night ; the attackers were driven off with heavy casualties, the battalion losing one follower killed. The Arabs then attacked the main camp, but suffered severely from machine-gun fire and withdrew without doing any damage.

On November 16th two companies moved out with a battery and two squadrons of cavalry and burnt eight villages near Ramadi as a punishment for an attack made upon some boats. Three men of the battalion were wounded.

These were the principal events which occurred while the battalion was in Mesopotamia, and when the rising was finally suppressed it returned to Agra.*

On February 10th, 1921, His Royal Highness the Duke of Connaught announced that His Majesty the King-Emperor had been pleased to confer the title of "Royal" on the regiment, and the battalion became the 2nd Battalion, 6th Royal Jat Light Infantry.

1921.

When the reorganization of the Indian Army took place the battalion was one of the very few second battalions retained in the service, and moved to Bareilly to become training battalion to the 9th Group.

On January 1st, 1922, the battalion became the 10th Battalion, 9th Jat Regiment, and its first recorded report stated that it was "second to none among the training battalions of the Eastern Command."

1922.

On August 24th, 1923, orders were issued for the disbandment of the 4th Battalion, and A.H.Q. letter No. A/21171/1 (A.G.2) laid down that, in order to ensure that the identity of the late 18th Infantry was preserved in the regular army, it would in future be identified with the 10th Battalion, 9th Jat Regiment, and that the name of the 2nd Battalion, 6th Royal Jat Light Infantry, would disappear from the Army List. No men were transferred at the time to the battalion.

1923.

The 4th Battalion was originally raised by Captain Henry De Castro as a corps of militia in 1795 for duty in Calcutta, and was recruited almost entirely in the province of Bihar. Having remained

---

* Accounts of actions fought by the 2nd/6th in Mesopotamia are taken from the personal statements of Indian ranks present in Bareilly in February, 1931, and believed to be reliable. The Digest of Services for the period is blank.

untainted throughout the Mutiny, it was, in 1859, placed on the footing of a corps of the line and designated " The Alipore Regiment."

The battalion was renamed the 22nd Regiment of Bengal Native Infantry in 1861 and, later in the same year, the 18th Regiment of Bengal Native Infantry.

It saw its first active service in 1880 when the right wing joined the Naga Hills Field Force, but did not take part in any fighting.

In 1864 its name was changed to the 18th (The Alipore) Regiment of Bengal Native Infantry, and in 1885 to the 18th Regiment of Bengal Infantry.

In 1885 the battalion volunteered *en masse* for active service in Burma and sailed from Calcutta on January 23rd, 1886, under the command of Lieutenant-Colonel A. C. Toker (later Major-General Sir Alliston C. Toker, K.C.B., Colonel of the 10th Battalion).

Mandalay was captured during the cold weather before the arrival of the battalion, but the country was left very disturbed, and during the next two years it took part in a great deal of fighting, and very greatly distinguished itself, while the country was reduced to order and the internal troubles quashed. The battalion returned to India on July 25th, 1887.

In 1891 the battalion took part in the Manipur campaign, in the Silchar column. Although, so far as casualties from enemy's fire go, the campaign of the Silchar column may be described as a " bloodless " one, viewing it from the point of view of a hazardous march, undertaken at the most unhealthy time of the year, through a pestilential wilderness, without tents, without shelter or even proper clearances of jungle to halt at, on a very small scale of baggage, it may be called a " deadly " one. In the following year 300 men of the battalion took part in an expedition to the North Lushai Hills and greatly distinguished themselves.

In 1902, while stationed in Mauritius, the battalion was renamed the 18th Musalman Rajput Infantry, and the following year became the 18th Infantry.

New Colours were presented to the battalion at Delhi on December 11th, 1911, by His Imperial Majesty the King-Emperor.

On January 11th, 1914, the battalion took over various outposts in Waziristan, where a number of skirmishes occurred ; and on January 31st it was relieved and ordered to China. It remained in China until June, 1920, and was thus prevented from taking an active part in the Great War.

In 1922 it became the 4th Battalion, 9th Jat Regiment.

In 1925 the Kumaon Rifles, who had been affiliated to the 9th Jat Regiment since 1922, were transferred to the 19th Hyderabad Regiment.

Lieutenant-Colonel G. S. Douglas, C.I.E., took over command of the battalion in November, 1926, from Lieutenant-Colonel A. Boxwell, C.I.E., who had commanded since March, 1924.

The rebuilding of the barracks was completed in 1927, the last word in luxury as compared with the previous edifices erected some sixty years before.

The 3rd and 4th Battalions of the Bombay Grenadiers having been disbanded, it was decided to amalgamate the 10th/4th and 10th/9th Training Battalions at Bareilly.

Work was started on the building of new barracks to accommodate the affiliated companies of the 1st/4th and 2nd/4th (K.E.O.) Bombay **1930.** Grenadiers, and on April 1st, 1930, Lieutenant-Colonel A. MacKrell, commandant, 10th Battalion, 4th Bombay Grenadiers, at Ajmer, was transferred in that capacity in relief of Lieutenant-Colonel G. S. Douglas, C.I.E., whose tenure was completed.

The 10th Battalion, 4th Bombay Grenadiers, was amalgamated on October 1st, 1930, and two companies of Grenadiers arrived from Ajmer on that date. It was decided that the combined Training Battalion be designated the 10th Battalion, 4th/9th Regiments, from October 1st.

Major W. R. Warden arrived from the 2nd (Mooltan) Battalion to take over command from Lieutenant-Colonel A. MacKrell, appointed **1931.** Recruiting Officer, Poona, on completion of his tenure of command, on January 1st, 1931.

On February 12th a representative party of 2 Indian officers and 10 other ranks attended the unveiling of the All India War Memorial at Delhi.

Captain R. A. Johnson, 3rd Battalion, Adjutant of the Training **1932.** Battalion, died in the British Military Hospital, Bareilly, on April 23rd, 1932.

On the night of June 21st-22nd, a serious fire broke out in the city. Two companies were sent down to assist. A highly laudatory letter of appreciation was received from the Chief Secretary to the United Provinces Government, who had it in command from His Excellency the Governor.

On August 26th the Battalion dairy was started, the buildings being constructed by a contractor assisted by working parties from the Battalion. Twenty buffaloes and four cows were purchased.

On January 18th, 1933, Lieutenant-Colonel W. R. Warden went on twelve months' leave pending retirement, and was succeeded by **1933.** Lieutenant-Colonel S. G. G. Fraser, M.C., Hazara Pioneers, on April 13th, Major W. V. McCalmont, M.C., officiating in the interim.

The regimental funds of the Grenadiers and Jats, which had hitherto been kept separately, were amalgamated with effect from

October 1st, and a stipulation was made that in the event of the two regiments separating, the amalgamated funds would be divided in the proportion of two-fifths to the Grenadiers and three-fifths to the Jats.

The first recruits' training programme common to all companies was printed and issued in 1935. In 1922 Colonel G. E. Hardie started **1935.** the Training Battalion with each company having its own programme; this lasted until 1927, when Colonel G. S. Douglas, C.I.E., organized the Battalion into pooled recruit divisions under pooled instructors, working to a common programme.

In 1930, the arrival of the Grenadiers from Ajmer made this system rather unwieldy, so Lieutenant-Colonel W. R. Warden, in 1931, reinstituted company training under two programmes, the Ajmer programme for the Grenadier companies, and the existing programme for the Jat companies.

This latter system prevailed, with minor modifications, until January of this year, when a common programme was issued for training on a company basis.

In January, 1936, Subedar-Major and Honorary-Lieutenant Nur Din Khan left on retirement. He left, as a permanent reminder of his **1936.** connection with the Training Battalion, the nucleus of a well-stocked vegetable and fruit garden. He was granted the rank of Honorary Captain on retirement.

On March 14th Lieutenant-Colonel S. G. G. Fraser, M.C., was succeeded in command by Lieutenant-Colonel C. M. Maltby, M.C.

On April 13th the Colonel of the Training Battalion, Major-General Sir Alliston Toker, K.C.B., died. He joined the Bengal Army in 1860 and served for thirty-seven years on the Active List. His campaigns included the Bhutan Expedition of 1864–65, the Egyptian Campaign of 1882 and the Burmese War of 1886–87. After retirement, and at the age of seventy-two, he served with the Indian Expeditionary Force in France in 1916. He was a noted linguist and held high honours in many oriental languages.

On February 1st Lieutenant-Colonel C. M. Maltby, M.C., was succeeded as commandant by Lieutenant-Colonel W. V. McCalmont, **1937.** M.C., the former being transferred as commandant of the 3rd Battalion.

On April 6th the Training Battalion quota of the Coronation contingent left for Poona *en route* to England. Subedar-Major Taj Mohamed represented the Training Battalion.

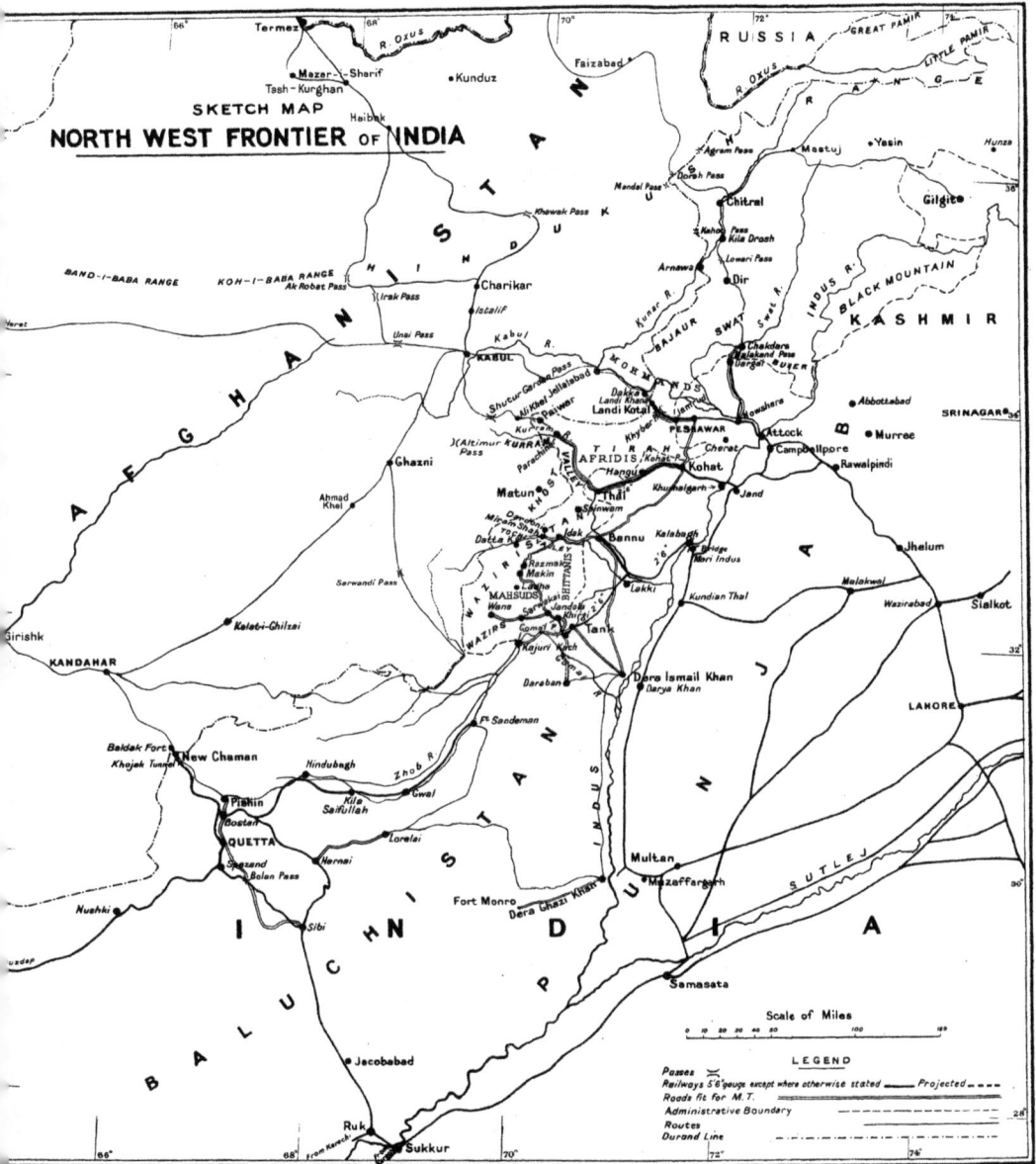

SKETCH MAP
NORTH WEST FRONTIER OF INDIA

RUSSIA

AFGHANISTAN

KASHMIR

BALUCHISTAN

INDIA

PUNJAB

BAND-I-BABA RANGE   KOH-I-BABA RANGE
Ak Robat Pass

Termez
Mazar-i-Sharif
Tash-Kurghan
Haibak
Kunduz
Faizabad
GREAT PAMIR
LITTLE PAMIR
Yasin
Hunza
Mastuj
Agram Pass
Mandal Pass
Dorah Pass
Gilgit
Chitral
Nahar Pass
Kila Drosh
Lowari Pass
Arnawai
Dir
Chakdara
Malakand Pass
Dargai
BUNER
SWAT
BAJAUR
Khawak Pass
Irak Pass
Istalif
Charikar
Kabul R.
Unai Pass
KABUL
Shutur Gardan Pass
Ali Khel Jellalabad
Peiwar
Dakka
Landi Khana
Landi Kotal
Khyber
PESHAWAR
Kurram
Parachinar
Altimur Pass
KURRAM
Ghazni
Ahmad Khel
AFRIDIS
Kohat Pass
Cherat
Kohat
Hangu
Thal
Matun
Shinwam
Khushalgarh
Jand
Mari Indus
Bannu
Kalabagh
Idak
Datta Khel
Razmak
Makin
Ladha
MAHSUDS
Wana
Kaniguram
Jandola
Kirti
Tank
Sarwandi Pass
Kalat-i-Ghilzai
Abbottabad
Murree
SRINAGAR
Attock
Campbellpore
Rawalpindi
Jhelum
Jhelum
Wazirabad
Sialkot
Malakwal
Kundian Thal
Lakki
Daraban
Dera Ismail Khan
Darya Khan
LAHORE
Rajuri Kotch
Fort Sandeman
KANDAHAR
Girishk
Baldak Fort
New Chaman
Khojak Tunnel
Hindubagh
Gwal
Kila Saifullah
Pishin
Bostan
QUETTA
Spezand
Bolan Pass
Harnai
Lorelai
Zhob R.
Fort Monro
Dera Ghazi Khan
Multan
Muzaffargarh
SUTLEJ
Nushki
Sibi
Samasata
Jacobabad
Ruk
Sukkur
From Quetta

Scale of Miles

LEGEND

Passes
Railways 5'6" gauge except where otherwise stated   Projected
Roads fit for M.T.
Administrative Boundary
Routes
Durand Line

Reprinted from "Imperial Military Geography" by Major D.H.Cole,
by permission of Messrs Sifton Praed & Co. Ltd.

APPENDICES

APPENDIX I

HONOURS AND AWARDS

(*Subsequent to* 1914)

NOTE.—It has been found impracticable to prepare a complete list of all honours and awards since the regiment was first raised.

1st ROYAL BATTALION.

GAZETTE.			PLACE.
		C.B.	
313 of	2/4/15	Lieutenant-Colonel H. J. Roche	France.
		C.M.G.	
485 of	13/3/20	Major C. J. M. Thornhill, D.S.O.	Russia.
		D.S.O.	
313 of	2/4/15	Major P. H. Dundas	France.
187 of	18/2/16	Captain R. C. Ross	,,
536 of	16/3/18	Major C. J. M. Thornhill	Russia.
		Bar to D.S.O.	
894 of	8/6/17	Captain R. C. Ross	Mesopotamia.
465 of	1/3/19	Major C. J. M. Thornhill	Russia.
		O.B.E.	
263 of	1/2/19	Captain J. de la Hay Gordon, M.C.	Mesopotamia.
2413 of	11/7/19	Lieutenant-Colonel W. F. G. Bourne	,,
2413 of	11/7/19	Major P. H. Dundas, D.S.O.	,,
		M.C.	
111 of	29/1/15	Lieutenant C. J. Cockburn	France.
187 of	18/2/16	Captain J. de la Hay Gordon	,,
187 of	18/2/16	Captain A. B. McPherson	,,
1556 of	30/12/16	Captain G. Ives, I.A.R.O.	Mesopotamia.
1556 of	30/12/16	Captain D. H. Rai	,,
1556 of	30/12/16	Captain F. W. A. Wells	,,
2934 of	14/12/18	Captain W. L. Hailes	,,
2934 of	14/12/18	Lieutenant T. C. McCarthy	,,
	18/12/22	Captain A. Hancock	Waziristan.
465 of	1/3/19	Lieutenant C. K. Tester	Mesopotamia.
		M.C.	
111 of	29/1/15	Jemadar Inchha Ram	France.
313 of	2/4/15	Jemadar Lakhi Ram	,,
		O.B.I., 1st Class.	
3 of	1/1/15	Subedar-Major Gugan, Bahadur	France.

GAZETTE.			PLACE.
	O.B.I., 2nd Class.		
725 of 4/8/15 ...	Subedar Shib Lal		France.
725 of 4/8/15 ...	Subedar Inchha Ram		,,
1629 of 19/7/18 ...	Subedar-Major Dalpat Singh, I.O.M. ...		Mesopotamia.
2086 of 3/6/19 ...	Subedar Rup Chand		,,
826 of 25/6/26 ...	Subedar-Major Lakhi Ram, M.C., I.D.S.M.		Waziristan.
	I.O.M.		
356 of 16/4/15 ...	1821 Havildar Jai Lal		France.
356 of 16/4/15 ...	1230 S.A.S. Pargan Singh, 2nd Class	...	,,
187 of 18/2/16 ...	1230 S.A.S. Pargan Singh, 1st Class	...	Mesopotamia.
524 of 12/5/16 ...	Subedar-Major Dalpat Singh ...	...	,,
524 of 12/5/16 ...	1906 Hadildar Jug Lal	...	,,
524 of 12/5/16 ...	2798 Havildar Chandgi	...	,,
524 of 12/5/16 ...	3171 Lance-Naik Matu	...	,,
524 of 12/5/16 ...	2822 Naik Harduwari...	...	,,
524 of 12/5/16 ...	3375 Sepoy Harnam	...	,,
1385 of 17/11/16 ...	2472 Sepoy Shadi	...	,,
756 of 28/4/22 ...	1698 Sepoy Badlu	...	Waziristan.
	I.D.S.M.		
313 of 2/4/15 ...	Jemadar Lakhi Ram	...	France.
313 of 2/4/15 ...	Jemadar Badlu Singh ...	...	,,
313 of 2/4/15 ...	3426 Sepoy Risal	...	,,
313 of 2/4/15 ...	1698 Havildar Harphul	...	,,
313 of 2/4/15 ...	2685 Lance-Naik Maru	...	,,
313 of 2/4/15 ...	1004 Sepoy Bagmal	...	,,
313 of 2/4/15 ...	1574 Havildar Mula	...	,,
563 of 11/6/15 ...	2960 Sepoy Ram Bhagat	...	,,
187 of 18/2/16 ...	Subedar Ratna	...	,,
187 of 18/2/16 ...	1767 Havildar Har Lal	...	,,
187 of 18/2/16 ...	2822 Naik Harduwari...	...	,,
187 of 18/2/16 ...	3108 Bugler Bhup Singh	...	,,
187 of 18/2/16 ...	3415 Sepoy Larhi	...	,,
563 of 11/6/15 ...	Subedar Parshadi Singh ...	...	,,
525 of 12/5/16 ...	3852 Sepoy Naubat		Mesopotamia.
525 of 12/5/16 ...	Subedar Sheo Lal	...	,,
525 of 12/5/16 ...	Subedar Jai Chand	...	,,
1386 of 17/11/16 ...	4301 Lance-Naik Mangli	...	,,
1388 of 17/11/16 ...	3619 Naik Sukh Ram	...	,,
1388 of 17/11/16 ...	3574 Sepoy Kanahiya	...	,,
1388 of 17/11/16 ...	3751 Sepoy Des Ram	...	,,
1388 of 17/11/16 ...	4075 Sepoy Ram Singh	...	,,
1178 of 3/6/18 ...	3934 Sepoy Girdhala	...	,,
89 of 11/1/19 ...	5063 Sepoy Lakhi Ram	...	,,
89 of 11/1/19 ...	4038 Sepoy Udmi	...	,,
1388 of 17/11/16 ...	1105 S.A.S. Karta Ram, I.M.D. ...	...	,,
534 of 8/3/19 ...	Jemadar Sardara 11	...	,,
2086 of 3/6/19 ...	Subedar Net Ram	...	,,
19/1/22 ...	Subedar Hem Raj	...	Waziristan.
756 of 28/4/22 ...	Subedar Ahmed Khan	...	,,
	I.M.S.M.		
1361 of 17/8/17 ...	3569 Sepoy Harphul, I.D.S.M. ...	...	Mesopotamia.
1361 of 17/8/17 ...	2597 Havildar Lajje Ram	...	,,
1361 of 17/8/17 ...	1388 Sepoy Ramji Lal	...	,,
1361 of 17/8/17 ...	1870 Sepoy Sukhde Lal	...	,,
2537 of 25/10/18 ...	2892 Havildar Ratan Singh	...	France.
Immediate Award 1918	6024 Lance-Naik Sohan	...	Mesopotamia.
534 of 8/3/19 ...	3335 Havildar Ami Lal	...	,,
2086 of 3/6/19 ...	5215 Havildar Sukhde	...	,,
534 of 8/3/19 ...	5082 Havildar Jhunda	...	,,

FOREIGN DECORATIONS.

GAZETTE.			PLACE.

Gold Medal (Serbia).

534 of	13/4/17	...	3108 Bugler Bhup Singh ... ...
534 of	13/4/17	...	3375 Sepoy Harnam, I.O.M. ... ...

Silver Medal.

534 of	13/4/17	...	2893 Sepoy Sis Ram ... ...

Cross of Karageorge, 1st Class with Swords (Serbia).

534 of	13/4/17	...	2688 Havildar Ujala ... ...

Cross of St. George, 2nd Class (Russia).

1065 of	6/7/17	...	1105 S.A.S. Karta Ram, I.M.D. ... ...

Cross of St. George, 3rd Class (Russia).

1065 of	6/7/17	...	3302 Havildar Sardara ... ...
1065 of	6/7/17	...	4201 Havildar Gulab Ram ... ...

Cross of St. George, 4th Class (Russia).

1065 of	6/7/17	...	2693 Sepoy Debi Sahai ... ...

Medal of St. George, 2nd Class (Russia).

1065 of	6/7/17	...	2822 Naik Harduwari, I.O.M. ... ...

Medal of St. George, 3rd Class (Russia).

1065 of	6/7/17	...	3851 Sepoy Sheo Ram ... ...
1065 of	6/7/17	...	3495 Lance-Naik Siri Chand ... ...

Order of the White Eagle, 4th Class (Russia).

2365 of 27/11/20	...	Lieutenant-Colonel C. J. M. Thornhill, C.M.G. D.S.O. ... ...

Croix de Chevalier (France).

3057 of 24/12/18	...	Brevet Lieutenant-Colonel C. J. M. Thornhill, D.S.O. ... ...

Order of the Rising Sun (Japan).

420 of	11/3/22	...	Lieutenant-Colonel C. J. M. Thornhill, C.M.G., D.S.O. ... ...

OTHER AWARDS.

Royal Victorian Medal.

24/7/25	...	Subedar-Major and Honorary-Lieutenant Lakhi Ram, M.C., O.B.I., I.D.S.M. ...	

O.B.I., 2nd Class (Bahadur).

3/6/32	...	Subedar-Major Hem Raj, I.D.S.M.	Delhi.

I.O.M., 2nd Class.

17/7/33	...	Jemadar Mohd Hussain	Chittagong.

I.D.S.M.

17/7/33	...	10435 Sepoy Alam Beg	,,
17/7/33	...	2133 Sepoy Amir Ali	,,

O.B.I., 1st Class (Sardar Bahadur).

947 of	2/6/22	...	Subedar-Major Dalpat Singh, Bahadur, I.O.M.	
	6/10/32	...	Subedar-Major Hem Raj, Bahadur, I.D.S.M.	Mymensingh.

N

GAZETTE.					PLACE.

O.B.I., 2nd Class (Bahadur).

4/6/35 ... Subedar-Major Sardara, I.D.S.M. ... ... Lucknow.

Empire Gallantry Medal.

5/6/34 ... Major D. A. Brett, M.C. ... ... Chittagong.

2ND (MOOLTAN) BATTALION.

C.I.E.

24/4/18 ... Major J. R. Darley ... ... Mesopotamia.

Captain A. Boxwell ... ... ,,

D.S.O.

18/8/16 ... Major J. R. Darley ... ... ,,
(also six times mentioned in despatches).

O.B.E.

3/6/19 ... Captain G. H. Knowland ... ... ,,
(I.A.R.O., attached).

M.C.

14/4/15 ... Captain J. J. Harper Nelson ... ... ,,
(I.M.S., attached).

29/10/15 ... Lieutenant M. Eccles ... ... ,,

2/2/16 ... Lieutenant (Temporary Captain) G. H.
Chambers ... ... ,,
(Notts and Derby Regiment, attached).

19/10/16 ... Captain F. I. O. Brickman ... ... ,,

19/10/16 ... 2nd-Lieutenant E. C. LePatourel ... ... ,,
(I.A.R.O., attached).

15/10/18 ... Lieutenant E. H. Keeling ... ... ,,
(I.A.R.O., attached).

21/4/16 ... Lieutenant J. P. Wood ... ... ,,
(I.A.R.O., attached).

Brevet of Colonel.

29/10/15 ... Lieutenant-Colonel W. W. Chitty ... ... ,,

M.B.E.

3/6/19 ... Lieutenant (acting Captain) H. O. Crowther ,,
(I.A.R.O., attached).

O.B.I., 2nd Class.

725 of 4/8/15 ... Subedar Uma Rawat ... ... Prisoner of War.

I.O.M., 1st Class.

692 of 16/4/20 ... Subedar Unad Singh, I.O.M. ... ... Mesopotamia.

I.O.M., 2nd Class.

727 of 4/8/15 ... 3887 Naik Natha Singh ... ... ,,

727 of 4/8/15 ... 3639 Havildar Uma Rawat ... ... ,,

727 of 4/8/15 ... 3486 Sepoy Ramlal Singh ... ... ,,

1244 of 10/12/15 ... Subedar Unad Singh ... ... ,,

1244 of 10/12/15 ... Subedar Sarfraz Khan ... ... ,,

1244 of 10/12/15 ... Havildar Gul Mahamed ... ... ,,

692 of 16/4/20 ... Havildar Chaman Singh ... ... ,,

GAZETTE.				PLACE.

I.D.S.M.

GAZETTE.		Name	PLACE.
728 of	4/8/15 ...	4025 Sepoy Dewa Rawat	Mesopotamia.
728 of	4/8/15 ...	4166 Sepoy Gokal	,,
728 of	4/8/15 ...	4112 Sepoy Dhanna Rawat	,,
728 of	4/8/15 ...	4229 Lance-Naik Makna Rawat	,,
728 of	4/8/15 ...	2939 Sepoy Nabi Baksh	,,
		3606 Havildar Mahomed Safi Khan ...	,,
		Subedar Hira	,,
1357 of	17/8/17 ...	3318 Sepoy Hukma	,,
1357 of	17/8/17 ...	4526 Sepoy Baloo Singh	,,
1357 of	17/8/17 ...	4036 Sepoy Rudmal Singh	,,
1360 of	17/8/17 ...	Jemadar Gulla Ram	,,
534 of	8/3/19 ...	Subedar (Temporary Subedar-Major) Shikari	,,
534 of	8/3/19 ...	Jemadar Khushal Singh	,,
2086 of	3/6/19 ...	4309 Naik Imtiaz Khan	,,
692 of	16/4/20 ...	3985 Naik Teja Rawat	,,
692 of	16/4/20 ...	4398 Sepoy Gina Rawat	,,
692 of	16/4/20 ...	Havildar Usman Gani Khan	,,
692 of	16/4/20 ...	4330 Sepoy Abdul Gafur Khan	,,
692 of	16/4/20 ...	3728 Naik Sardar Singh	,,
692 of	16/4/20 ...	4070 Lance-Naik Ram Narain	,,
692 of	16/4/20 ...	3318 Naik Hukma	,,
692 of	16/4/20 ...	Bhisty Nanda	,,

I.M.S.M.

GAZETTE.		Name	PLACE.
692 of	16/4/20 ...	4194 Lance-Naik Bachan Singh	,,
692 of	16/4/20 ...	3940 Havildar Kasim Khan	,,
755 of	23/4/20 ...	1451 Naik Dharm Singh	,,
755 of	23/4/20 ...	2900 Sepoy Dada Rawat	,,
1364 of	9/7/20 ...	3936 Havildar Jabba Ahmad Khan ...	,,
1364 of	9/7/20 ...	5038 Sepoy Bhamboo	,,
1364 of	9/7/20 ...	4434 Sepoy Ram Lal	,,

FOREIGN DECORATIONS.

Order of the White Eagle, 4th Class with Swords (Serbia).

534 of	13/4/17 ...	Captain (Temporary Major) T. de B. Carey	,,

Order of Karageorge, 4th Class with Swords (Serbia).

534 of	13/4/17 ...	Major P. M. Heath ... ... (110th Mahrattas, attached).	,,

Order of the Crown of Roumania (Chevalier).

	20/9/19 ...	Captain G. H. Knowland, I.A.R.O. (attached)	

Gold Medal of Serbia.

534 of	13/4/17 ...	1620 Sepoy Kan Singh ... ... (120th Infantry, attached).	,,

Silver Medal of Serbia.

534 of	13/4/17 ...	5309 Sepoy Intiaz Khan	,,

OTHER AWARDS.

Royal Victorian Order (4th Class).

	1933 ...	Lieutenant-Colonel A. B. McPherson, M.C. ...	

Royal Victorian Medal.

	1933 ...	Subedar Wali Mohamed Khan	

3RD BATTALION.

GAZETTE.			PLACE.
	D.S.O.		
17/2/17	...	Captain (Brevet Major) E. K. Twiss	France.
	M.C.		
16/8/20	...	Lieutenant H. V. Bragg	Mesopotamia.
27/9/20	...	Lieutenant W. V. McCalmont	,,
18/2/21	...	Captain J. D. Standen	Black Sea.
	O.B.E.		
12/12/19	...	Captain J. Crompton	N.W.F.
	M.B.E.		
13/3/25	...	Lieutenant T. M. Layng, M.C.*	India.
	Brevet of Colonel.		
29/10/15	...	Lieutenant-Colonel H. E. Lowis ...	N.W.F.
	Brevet of Major.		
3/6/16	...	Captain E. K. Twiss	France.
	O.B.I., 1st Class.		
5/2/21	...	Subedar-Major Raje Ram, Bahadur	India.
6/10/32	...	Subedar-Major Shahzaman Khan, Bahadur	Hong Kong.
5/6/35	...	Subedar-Major Sudhan, Bahadur	India.
	O.B.I., 2nd Class.		
	Subedar-Major Nand Ram		India.
3/6/19	...	Subedar Rupchand	Black Sea.
	Subedar Umrao Singh		India.
8/3/19	...	Subedar-Major Raje Ram	Black Sea.
27/3/31	...	Subedar-Major Shahzaman Khan	India.
1/1/35	...	Subedar-Major Sudhan	,,
	I.O.M.		
1385 of 17/11/16	...	2495 Sepoy Kalu Ram	Mesopotamia.
	I.D.S.M.		
529 of 3/6/15	...	2399 Sepoy Pirdan	N.W.F.
1388 of 17/11/16	...	3363 Sepoy Bhola	Mesopotamia.
89 of 11/1/19	...	3701 Sepoy Dodh Ram	,,
	I.M.S.M.		
1361 of 17/8/17	...	2079 Sepoy Khema	,,
1361 of 17/8/17	...	1772 Havildar Sobhat	,,
6 of 1/1/20	...	2872 Naik Khem Chand	Black Sea.
6 of 1/1/20	...	1650 Sepoy Jhanda	,, ,,
6 of 1/1/20	...	3369 Sepoy Jage Ram	,, ,,
801 of 30/4/20	...	2764 Havildar Bahorang Lal	India.
6 of 1/1/20	...	2949 Havildar Manphul	Black Sea.
6 of 1/1/20	...	2678 Naik Mamraj	,, ,,

FOREIGN DECORATION.

Medal of St. George, 3rd Class (Russia).

1065 of 6/7/17	...	3363 Sepoy Bhola	Mesopotamia.

OTHER AWARD.

Rai Sahib.

26/8/32	...	Pundit Jugeshwar Misra	Hong Kong.

* This Military Cross was earned before Lieutenant Layng was posted to the regiment

TRAINING BATTALION.

GAZETTE.			PLACE.

M.C.

L.G. of 28/10/20	...	Lieutenant V. D. Arnold	Arab Rebellion.

I.O.M., 2nd Class.

| 683 of 19/5/23 | ... | Subedar Ram Kala ... ... | ,, ,, |
| 683 of 19/5/23 | ... | Subedar Sultan ... ... | ,, ,, |

I.D.S.M.

2322 of 26/11/20	...	1729 Bugle-Major Sarup Lal	,, ,,
2322 of 26/11/20	...	1050 Bugler Arjun	,, ,,
2322 of 26/11/20	...	814 Sepoy Rup Chand	,, ,,
1972 of 7/10/21	...	292 Sepoy Udmi	,, ,,
683 of 19/5/23	...	1381 Lance-Naik Simbhu	,, ,,
683 of 19/5/23	...	1162 Sepoy Ram Sarup	,, ,,

I.M.S.M.

| 801 of 30/4/20 | ... | 28 Havildar-Major Chandgi Ram ... | Mesopotamia. |
| 801 of 30/4/20 | ... | 25 Havildar Jot Ram ... ... | ,, |

OTHER AWARDS.

O.B.I., 2nd Class (Bahadur).

4/6/35	...	Subedar-Major Nur Din Khan	Bareilly.

I.M.S.M.

1925	...	17 Havildar Ram Narain Lal	,,
1926	...	3223 Havildar Lal Khan	,,
1931	...	682 Bugle-Major Mir Zaman Khan ...	,,
1935	...	3228 Havildar Nazar Ali	,,
1936	...	1941 Bugle-Major Nizam Uddin Khan ...	,,

APPENDIX II

THE COLOURS

1st ROYAL BATTALION.

It is not known when the first set of Colours was presented, but it is presumed it was presented soon after the raising of the battalion.

The first set of which any record exists was presented on November 13th, 1844, by the Honourable Lieutenant-Governor of the North-West Province, Mr. Thomson, at Fatehgarh. "Affghanistan," "Candahar," "Ghaznee," "Cabool" and "Maharajpore" were emblazoned on them.

Colours were next presented on November 25th, 1869, by Brigadier-General G. Bourchier, Commanding Eastern Frontier District, at Jalpaiguri.

The original facings worn by the battalion were pea-green, and green Colours had always been carried. When the title "Light Infantry" was bestowed on the battalion, as a recognition of its march from Kandahar to Kabul, green Colours became indissolubly bound up with its traditions. After the reorganization of the Indian Army in 1901 the battalion was ordered to wear white facings. Subsequently, whenever an offer of new Colours was made to the battalion, the offer was accepted with the stipulation that they should be green. This request was repeatedly refused and the battalion continued to carry the old Colours long after they were worn out. In 1921 it was with much gratification that the news was received that His Majesty had sanctioned the carrying of green Colours by the battalion in perpetuity.

New Colours were then asked for, but owing to the operations in Waziristan, it was not until March 10th, 1925, the anniversary of Sobraon and the conferment of the title "Royal" on the battalion, that these could be presented. Many pensioned Indian officers and other ranks were present, among them one who had been present fifty-six years previously when the old Colours were presented. Lieutenant-General Sir George de S. Barrow, K.C.B., K.C.M.G., A.D.C., General Officer Commanding-in-Chief, Eastern Command, who made the presentation, addressed the battalion as follows :—

> "Colonel Carey, Officers, Non-commissioned Officers and men of the 1st Royal Battalion, 9th Jat Regiment (Light Infantry),—Since your battalion was first raised, more than 120 years ago, you have marched steadily along the road to honour and reputation. You have taken part in many fights at the call of your King-Emperor and your country, in India, on the borders of India and beyond. Three times you have entered Afghanistan and your activities have extended as far as China ; and in the Great War you fought in France and Mesopotamia with a gallantry and determination which has been the admiration of all soldiers. The King-Emperor, in order to show his appreciation of your distinguished services, singled you out, together with seven other units of the Indian Army, in order to confer on you the proud distinction of being a Royal battalion. I present you with these Colours in the full assurance that you will never fail to provide the strong hands and brave hearts to hold them high and keep them untarnished emblems of your loyalty to the King-Emperor ; your resolution to fight as you have done before when necessity calls in defence of your country and in support of the British Raj and for the maintenance of your own high honour."

2ND (MOOLTAN) BATTALION.

The first set of Colours was presented by Colonel Kennedy at Dapoli on March 4th, 1819. The next set was presented on September 14th, 1829.

The third set, bearing the honours " Ghazni " and " Afghanistan," was presented at Bombay on January 9th, 1843, by Lady McMahon, in the presence of His Excellency Sir Thomas McMahon, the Commander-in-Chief, and of His Excellency Sir George Arthur, Bart., the Governor of Bombay.

The fourth set was presented on December 15th, 1858, by Major-General Michel, C.B., commanding the Malwa Division, and bore the additional honours " Punjab," " Mooltan " and " Gujrat."

The fifth set, bearing the additional honours " Kandahar 1880," " Afghanistan 1878 to 1880," was presented by His Excellency Sir James Ferguson, K.C.M.G., Governor of Bombay, at Malegaon on January 7th, 1883.

On March 3rd, 1931, new Colours were presented by His Excellency General Sir Philip W. Chetwode, Bart., G.C.B., K.C.M.G., D.S.O., A.D.C., Commander-in-Chief in India. The Colonel of the battalion, Lieutenant-General Sir A. E. Wardrop, K.C.B., C.M.G., was present.

The guards were commanded by Captain R. H. Lowe, Captain J. W. Williams and Lieutenant W. H. Niall, while the Colours were carried by Subedars Vishram Gangaram and Jalaluddin Khan.

3RD BATTALION.

The original Colours bear the title " 65th Bengal Native Infantry," and so were presumably presented in the year 1824, or soon after.

These were replaced by Colours bearing the title " 10th Jat Regiment" on December 27th, 1899. These were presented by Lieutenant-General Sir George Luck, K.C.B., commanding the forces in Bengal.

On February 19th, 1922, Colours bearing the title " 10th Jats " were presented at Rawalpindi by His Royal Highness the Prince of Wales.

TRAINING BATTALION.

The Training Battalion carried no Colours until it took over the identity of the former 18th Infantry in 1923. From that date it carried Colours presented by His Imperial Majesty King George V at Delhi on December 11th, 1911, the Regimental Colour bearing the title " XVIII Infantry," and the single battle honour, " Burma, 1885-87."

New Colours, bearing the battle honours of the 9th Jat Regiment, were presented by His Excellency the Commander-in-Chief, General Sir Philip Chetwode, Bart., G.C.B., K.C.M.G., D.S.O., A.D.C., at Jhansi, on March 3rd, 1931, at the same time that Colours were presented to the 2nd (Mooltan) Battalion. A detachment was sent from Bareilly which included Lieutenant-Colonel W. R. Warden, Captain R. S. Tonkin and Captain A. G. Porter.

The old Colours were laid up at the Viceroy's House at Delhi on November 24th, 1931.

www.ingramcontent.com/pod-product-compliance
Lightning Source LLC
Chambersburg PA
CBHW070408100426
42812CB00005B/1669